Cambridge English

OFFICIAL

T0373863

FUN for Flyers

4th edition

TEACHER'S BOOK

Anne Robinson
Karen Saxby

Cambridge University Press
www.cambridge.org/elt

Cambridge Assessment English
www.cambridgeenglish.org

Information on this title: www.cambridge.org/9781316617601

© Cambridge University Press & Assessment 2016

First published 2006
Second edition 2010
Third edition 2015
Fourth edition 2016

20 19 18 17 16 15 14

Printed in Poland by Opolgraf

A catalogue record for this publication is available from the British Library

ISBN 978-1-316-61758-8 Student's Book with online activities with audio and Home Fun booklet
ISBN 978-1-316-63200-0 Student's Book with online activities with audio
ISBN 978-1-316-61760-1 Teacher's Book with downloadable audio
ISBN 978-1-108-72814-0 Presentation Plus

Contents

Introduction

Welcome to *Fun for Flyers Fourth edition*

Fun for Flyers Fourth edition is the third in a series of three books written for learners aged between 7 and 13 years old. *Fun for Starters Fourth edition* is the first book in the series and *Fun for Movers Fourth edition* is the second.

Who is *Fun for Flyers Fourth edition* for?

Fun for Flyers is suitable for:

o   learners who need comprehensive preparation for the *Cambridge English: Flyers* test, in addition to their general English course

o   mixed classes where some of the learners are preparing to take the *Cambridge English: Flyers (YLE Flyers)*, and who need motivating and fun English lessons

o   small and large groups of learners

o   monolingual and multilingual classes

Fun for Flyers supports the development of good learning habits and language practice in meaningful, fun, creative and interactive ways. It is ideal for learners who have been studying English for between two and four years, and who need to consolidate their language and skills.

The key features include:

o   complete coverage of the vocabulary and grammar on the *Cambridge English: Flyers* syllabus

o   thorough preparation for all parts of the *Cambridge English: Flyers* test

o   a focus on all four skills, with an emphasis on those areas most likely to cause problems for young learners at this level

o   recycling of language and topics

o   fun activities that practise English in a meaningful way

o   opportunities for learners to personalise the language and make the tasks relevant to them

Cambridge English: Young Learners

For more information on *Cambridge English: Young Learners*, please visit https://www.cambridgeenglish.org/exams-and-tests/. From here, you can download the handbook for teachers, which includes information about each level of the Young Learners exams. You can also find information for candidates and their parents, including links to videos of the Speaking test at each level. There are also sample test papers, as well as games, and links to the Teaching Support website.

Course components
Student's Book with downloadable class audio and online activities

The Student's Book has been updated to include:

o   words and phrases from the most up-to-date *Cambridge English: Flyers* vocabulary list

o   even more opportunities for test practice. In most units, there will be at least one authentic test-style task. The instructions for these tasks are shown in blue, while instructions for tasks which provide more general test practice are shown in black.

o   new illustrations, designed to stimulate learner engagement

o   a variety of fun activities, such as games, puzzles, drawing and colouring, to ensure your learners are involved in, and enjoy, their English lessons

o   recordings for the listening tasks, which are available via the access code at the front of the book, so that learners can practise at home.

o   online activities, available via the access code at the front of the book, which provide further practice of the grammar and vocabulary featured in the Student's Book as well as exam preparation activities

o   projects that encourage learners to explore topics in more depth and produce work more independently

Teacher's Book with downloadable class audio

In the Fourth edition of the Teacher's Book, you can find:

o   clear signalling of *Cambridge English: Flyers* test practice tasks and authentic test-style tasks that appear in each unit. These are listed in the information boxes at the start of each unit, under **Flyers practice** or **Flyers test**. In the unit notes, an icon like this Listening **2** indicates the part of *Cambridge English: Flyers* that an authentic test-style task replicates.

o   useful tips to guide and support learners in their preparation for each part of the test.

o   materials and equipment needed to teach each unit. This means less preparation is needed, as you can see at a glance the audio resources or numbers of photocopies you need for each lesson.

o   suggested wording of classroom language at the learners' level of English

o   support for teaching pronunciation activities in a fun and motivating way for learners of this age

o   ideas for maximising the involvement of learners in their learning process

o   ideas for extending activities into simple, fun projects that give learners the chance to explore topics more independently and consolidate their English in creative ways

o   additional resources, visuals and lesson ideas for teachers, and interactive games and activities to accompany *Fun for Flyers*.

Online audio

The audio is available to download by following the instructions and using the access code at the front of the Student's Book.

Presentation plus

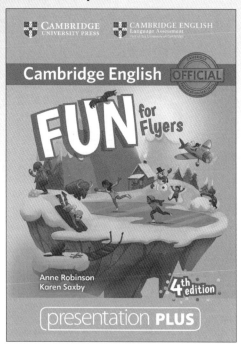

Presentation plus contains a digital version of the Student's Book and all the audio to complete the listening tasks. The integrated tools enable you to make notes, highlight activities and turn the Student's Book into an interactive experience for your learners. The Presentation plus includes:

○ all the Student's Book pages
○ all the audio for the Student's Book
○ pdfs of the Teacher's Book, including a complete practice test with the Listening audio
○ unit tests – one per unit, testing the key language covered in each unit

An app for mobile phones and tablets

For further practice of the vocabulary for the *Cambridge English: Flyers* tests, download our new app and encourage your learners to practise their vocabulary while having fun

Online activities

The online activities provide students with extra practice in grammar, vocabulary and exam tasks. All of the students' online work can be tracked and reviewed by the teacher. It has also been fully updated to reflect task types and new words in the word list.

For access to Fun for Flyers online content, contact your local Cambridge representative.

How is the Student's Book organised?

Contents
This lists the Student's Book unit numbers and titles.

56 units
Each unit is topic-based and designed to provide between 75 and 90 minutes of class time. Language is presented and practised throughout the unit and the final activity usually provides freer, fun practice of the unit's key content language. In most units, at least one task will provide *Cambridge English: Flyers* test practice. The title instructions for these tasks are shown in a (blue lozenge). The title instructions for all other tasks are shown in black lettering.

Ideas for project work on topic are included in many units and signalled by a icon, as are fun activities to practise specific phonemes or other key aspects of pronunciation.

Pairwork activities
Learners will use these in specific unit tasks.

Unit wordlist
This is a list of the key words which appear in each unit (organised by topic or word class).

Listings are not repeated if they have already featured in a previous unit.

List of irregular verbs
This includes all the irregular verbs in the *Cambridge English: Flyers* test. Space is provided for learners to write translations.

How is the Teacher's Book organised?

Contents
This shows where to find each section of the Teacher's Book.

Introduction
This will help you use *Fun for Flyers Fourth edition*. It includes:

○ a **quick guide** to how units in the Teacher's books are organised (page 6)
○ suggestions for **games and activities** (page 6)
○ suggestions for how to use **pictures in the Student's Book** (page 7)
○ suggestions for **using dictation** (pages 7–8)

Checklist for Cambridge English: Flyers *Test preparation* (page 9)

○ a quick guide to what learners have to do in each part of the Flyers test and units where each part is covered in the Student's Book. 'Test' indicates those activities that reflect the format of the Flyers Listening, Reading and Writing or Speaking test. 'Practice' indicates activities that prepare for a particular part of Flyers, but do not reflect the identical format of the test.

Map of the Student's Book (pages 10–13)

○ an overview of the content and organisation of all the units in the Student's Book.

Topics and grammar indexes (pages 14–15)

Unit guides / Teacher's notes
The teacher's notes for each of the 56 units. See below for a detailed guide to these.

Photocopiable activities (pages 128–146)

○ these relate to specific units as indicated in the teacher's notes.

Photocopiable practice test pages 147–169

○ a complete Flyers practice test (Listening, Reading and Writing, Speaking) to photocopy and use with learners. Audioscripts, a sample Examiner's script for the Speaking and a key are also provided.

How is each unit organised?

Topics, and non Flyers words
This is a list of all the topics, areas of grammar and pronunciation covered in the unit. Any words that appear in the unit but not in the Flyers wordlist are also listed here.

Equipment needed
This lists any equipment, for example: audio resources and/or material needed for the unit, including the number of photocopies needed for any activities. Pages to be photocopied are found at the back of the Teacher's Book.

Instructions
These are usually labelled A, B, C, etc. and correspond to the different activities which appear in the Student's Book. There are some activities that appear only in the teacher's notes and are not labelled A, B, C, etc.

Audioscripts
The audioscripts for each Listening are at the end of the activity where they are used.

Project work
There are a number of suggestions for projects. The instructions for these generally appear at the ends of units.

Listening tasks
In the Listening tasks with a icon, the lengths of the pauses in the audio are the same as in the test the first time they are played.

When the audio is heard the second time in the test, the pauses are slightly shorter, allowing time to add any missing answers and/or to check answers.

For all other Listening tasks in this book, the lengths of pauses are approximate. You may want to re-start or stop the audio to allow your learners less or more time in which to complete tasks.

Fun and games
The following games and activities can be done in class to practise or revise a wide range of vocabulary or grammar.

Bingo
Learners make a grid of six or nine squares, in two or three rows of three. They write a word in each square. Read out words, one by one. If learners have the word, they cross it out or cover it with a small piece of paper.
The first learner to cross out or cover all their words is the winner. Check that learners have heard the right words by asking them to say the words and comparing them with your list of words.

Seven lives ('Hangman')
Draw (or stick) seven body outlines on the board.

𝕏𝕏𝕏𝕏𝕏𝕏𝕏

Choose a word. Draw one line on the board for each letter in the word, for example: __ __ __ __ __ __. (shorts) Learners put up their hands to say letters. If the letter is in the word, you write it on the line. If the letter is not in the word, you remove one of the bodies from the board. The game finishes when the learners complete the word or they lose all seven lives. Learners then play in groups, drawing lines for their own words.

The long sentence
Choose a simple sentence which can grow if words are added to the end of it.
For example:
Teacher: *In my bedroom, there's a bed.*
Learner 1: *In my bedroom, there's a bed and a table.*
Continue round the class, with each learner repeating the sentence and all the words which have been added, before then adding another word or phrase. The winner is the person who remembers all the words in the correct order when everyone else has been eliminated.

Change places
Learners sit in a circle. Say sentences starting with the words: *Change places if …* For example: *Change places if you got up at 8 o'clock today.* All the learners who got up at 8 o'clock have to stand up and move to sit in a different place.

Group or order the words
Take any group of words (related or not) and ask learners to group or order them:

- **from longest to shortest**
  Learners either write the words in order according to the number of letters they have, or they write the words in order according to the number of vowels they have.
- **from smallest to biggest**
  Learners write the words starting with the smallest thing /animal / food item etc.
- **in alphabetical order**
  Learners write the words in alphabetical order.
- **in colour groups**
  Learners write words in groups according to their colour.
- **in sound groups**
  Learners write words in groups according to pronunciation similarities (stress patterns, vowel sounds etc).

Backs to the board

○ Make teams of 4–8 learners, depending on the size of the class.

○ Put one chair for each team at the front of the class. A learner from each team comes and sits on their chair, with their back to the board.

○ Write a word on the board (for example: 'page'). One team gives clues to the learners on the chairs so that they can guess the word.

○ The first learner who thinks they know the word stands up and gives their answer. If they are right, their team gets one point. If they are wrong, they have to sit down again, their team doesn't get the point and more clues are given until the word is correctly guessed. Different learners from each team then come to the front of the class, sit down and the game is repeated.

Fun with pictures

You can use the pictures in the Student's Book in many different ways to revise and practise language. Here are some suggestions.

Which picture?

In pairs or small groups, one learner chooses a picture from any page. The other learner(s) have to ask questions to discover which picture. For example: *Are there any people? Is it inside? Are there any other pictures on the page?* Once the other learner(s) have found the picture, they choose a picture and are asked questions.

Differences

Tell learners to look at two different pictures in the Student's Book, for example: page 30, Unit 13 and page 70, Unit 33. In pairs, they find similarities and differences between the two pictures. (For example: *In both pictures, we can see people. In the first picture, some children are playing, but in the second picture, no one is playing.*)

Yes or no?

In small groups, learners write sentences about a picture in the Student's Book. Some sentences should be true for the picture and some should be false. They either pass their sentences on to another group or they say the sentences to the other group. The other group has to say or write *yes* for the true sentences and *no* for the false ones.

Listen and draw

Learners work in pairs or small groups. One learner looks at one of the pictures in the Student's Book. This person describes the picture to the other learner(s), who listen and try to draw the picture.

Where's the treasure?

Tell learners to imagine that there is some treasure hidden somewhere in the picture. Learners have to find it by asking questions. For example: page 62, Unit 29: *Is it on the balcony?* (No) *Is it in the snowman?* (Yes!)

Say something more!

○ Divide the class into groups of 6–8 and ask them to sit in circles. All learners look at the same picture in the Student's Book (for example: page 93, Unit 44). One learner starts and says a sentence about the picture. For example: *The people are in the living room.* The learner's neighbour on the left says another sentence about the picture. For example: *A boy is lying on the sofa.*

○ Continue round the circle. If a learner repeats a sentence that someone else has said, they are eliminated (or lose a point).

Variation: Each learner has to repeat the previous sentences and then add a new one.

What can't you see?

Learners work in groups to imagine and talk about details of the picture that aren't shown. For example: page 6, Unit 1: *How many children go to this school? What games do they play in this playground? What are the classrooms like? What time do lessons start/end? How do most of the children travel to this school? What's behind/next to/opposite the school?* etc.

Tell me more about these people.

Learners work in pairs to imagine and talk or write about the people in the picture. For example: page 8, Unit 2: *Who is this girl? What's her name? Where is she going to go? What does she like doing? What's in her top pocket and rucksack?*

What are they saying?

Pairs decide what different animals or people could be saying to each other in the picture. For example: page 19, Unit 7: *What's the farmer saying to the dog? What's the dog saying to the sheep? What are the sheep saying to each other?*

What was happening before? What will happen next?

Pairs look at a picture and decide what was happening just before this picture and what will happen next. For example: page 50, Unit 23. *Who was in the street? / What was the weather like? / What could you see in the office windows an hour before / an hour later?*

How many words?

Teams look at a picture and write as many different words as they can for things they can see. For example: page 31, D, Unit 13: *Clouds, rain, trees, umbrella, skirt, trousers, sunglasses* etc. The winners are the team with the most number of correctly spelt words.

Fun with dictations

Dictations don't have to be boring! They are great for practising spelling, word order and prediction. Here are some different ways you can use dictation in class.

Word dictations

o   Spell a word, letter by letter. Learners listen and write the letters. When a learner thinks they know the word you are spelling, they shout *Stop!* and say the word and the remaining letters. If the learner is correct, give them a point for every remaining letter they guessed.

o   Dictate the letters of a word, but not in the right order. Learners have to write the letters, then un-jumble them and write the word, correctly spelt, as quickly as possible.

o   Dictate all the consonants from a word (indicating the gaps for vowels). Learners have to complete the word with *a-e-i-o-u*.

Sentence dictations

o   Dictate the key words from a sentence which has appeared in the unit or text. Learners have to write the full sentence so that it is similar (or identical) to the original sentence.

o   Dictate a sentence a word at a time. (For example: a definition sentence like those which appear in Flyers Reading and Writing Part 1.) Learners write the words and shout *Stop!* when they think they can complete the sentence (or say what is being defined).

o   Dictate only the start of sentences. Learners complete the sentences with their own words. For example:
    Teacher: *This morning I put on …*
    Learner (writes): *my clothes.*

o   Learners listen to a sentence. They only write the longest word (with the most letters) in the sentence.

o   Learners listen to a sentence. They say how many words were in the sentence. For example: I don't know him very well but he's quite nice. (12). Don't forget to agree at the beginning if contractions will count as one or two words!

Text dictations

Choose a text from a unit (for example: page 15, Unit 5,C). Read the text aloud, at normal speed. Learners listen and write down the important words. Read the text again at normal speed. Learners add more words to their notes. In pairs, or groups of three, learners rewrite the text using their notes. When they have finished, they compare their text with the original text. They may find that the sentences they have written are correct, but not identical to the original text.

Checklist for Cambridge English: Flyers preparation

Paper	Part	Task	Unit
Listening Approx. 25 minutes	1	Draw lines between names outside a picture to figures inside.	*Practice:* 4, 15, 33, 38 *Test:* 2, 13, 15, 29, 42, 44, 49, 56
	2	Write words or numbers.	*Practice:* 4, 15, 25, 51, 56 *Test:* 1, 8, 10, 34, 48, 50
	3	Match pictures by writing a letter in the box.	*Practice:* 42, 51 *Test:* 6, 17, 24, 32, 39. 46, 47
	4	Multiple choice. Tick the correct picture.	*Practice:* 14 *Test:* 9, 18, 28, 45, 53
	5	Colour objects and write.	*Practice:* 12, 16, 19, 28, 40, 52 *Test:* 3, 11, 26, 35, 41, 54
Reading and Writing 40 minutes	1	Match words to definitions by copying the word.	*Practice:* 2, 5, 6, 8, 9, 11, 12, 14, 16, 17, 21, 24, 29, 32, 33, 35, 52, 55, 56 *Test:* 10, 23, 39, 53
	2	Read the dialogue and choose the best answer.	*Practice:* 1, 33, 36, 43, 46, 50 *Test:* 8, 11, 26, 31, 44, 54
	3	Gap fill. Write one word in each gap. Choose the best name for the story.	*Practice:* 12, 20, 36, 37, 38, 41, 50 *Test:* 7, 18, 19, 27, 39, 48, 55
	4	Complete the text by selecting the correct word and copying it into the gap.	*Practice:* 23, 26, 35, 40 *Test:* 5, 12, 15, 22, 32, 43, 45
	5	Write answers (maximum four words) to complete the sentences about the story.	*Practice:* 5, 7, 38, 42, 48 *Test:* 16, 25, 30, 34, 40, 46, 52
	6	Write one word in each of the five gaps.	*Practice:* 5, 7, 14, 23, 26, 30, 36, 40, 49, 51, 54 *Test:* 4, 8, 21, 28, 34, 38, 42, 44
	7	Write a story about three pictures.	*Practice:* 1, 3, 20, 21, 26, 30, 54, 55 *Test:* 23, 31, 40, 43, 49
Speaking 7–9 minutes	1 Find the difference	Identify and describe differences between pictures by responding to the Examiner's statements about his/her picture.	*Practice:* 1, 3, 13, 15, 24, 26, 31, 55 *Test:* 12, 21, 29, 31, 36, 42, 49
	2 Information exchange	Answer and ask questions about two people, objects or situations.	*Practice:* 5, 6, 9, 12, 15, 16, 20, 24, 33, 37, 44, 50 *Test:* 25, 35, 48, 51
	3 Picture story	Describe the pictures.	*Practice:* 7, 10, 13, 16, 19, 27, 41, 55 *Test:* 17, 26, 30, 38, 50, 56
	4 Personal questions	Answer personal questions.	*Practice:* 2, 4, 5, 6, 7, 8, 9, 10, 11, 14, 19, 20, 21, 22, 23, 24, 26, 27, 28, 29, 32, 38, 39, 40, 43, 45, 46, 47, 48, 49, 52, 54, 56 *Test:* 15, 41, 53

Map of the Student's Book

Unit	Topic	Grammar	Exam practice
1 Hello again	colours, clothes, sports and leisure	present simple, present continuous, questions	Reading and Writing Part 2 Test: Listening Part 2, Speaking Part 1
2 Wearing and carrying	clothes, colours, body and face	present continuous, present simple, *when* clauses	Reading and Writing Part 1, Speaking Part 4 Test: Listening Part 1
3 Spots and stripes	clothes, leisure, colours	prepositions of place, relative clauses, present continuous	Speaking Part 1 Test: Listening Part 5, Reading and Writing Part 2
4 My friends and my pets	names, family and friends, animals	present continuous, present simple, superlative adjectives	Speaking Part 4 Test: Listening Part 1, Reading and Writing Part 7
5 About animals	animals, body and face, the world around us	prepositions, comparative adjectives, pronouns	Reading and Writing Parts 1, 5 and 7, Speaking Parts 2 and 4 Test: Reading and Writing Part 4
6 My things	animals, clothes, family and friends	conjunctions (*and, because, so*), questions, past simple	Reading and Writing Part 1, Speaking Parts 2 and 4 Test: Listening Part 3
7 Moving and speaking	body and face, the world around us	questions, present continuous, past simple	Reading and Writing Parts 5 and 7, Speaking Parts 3 and 4 Test: Reading and Writing Part 3
8 School subjects	school, places	*if* + present simple, *want* + infinitive	Reading and Writing Part 1, Speaking Part 4 Test: Listening Part 2, Reading and Writing Parts 2 and 6
9 In my classroom	school	infinitive of purpose, questions	Reading and Writing Part 1, Speaking Parts 2 and 4 Test: Listening Part 4
10 Clothes, animals and school	clothes, animals, school	present and past simple, questions	Speaking Parts 3 and 4 Test: Listening Part 2, Reading and Writing Part 1
11 Visiting different places	the world around us, sports and leisure	questions, prepositions	Reading and Writing Part 1, Speaking Part 4 Test: Listening Part 5, Reading and Writing Part 2
12 A journey into space	the world around us, names	prepositions of place, *would like* + infinitive, question words	Listening Part 5, Reading and Writing Parts 1 and 4, Speaking Part 2 Test: Reading and Writing Part 4, Speaking Part 1
13 What horrible weather!	weather, names	*How / What about* + *ing, could* and *shall* for suggestions	Speaking Parts 1 and 3 Test: Listening Part 1
14 Are you hungry? Thirsty?	food and drink	adverbs of frequency, *How often?*	Listening Part 4, Reading and Writing Parts 1 and 7, Speaking Part 4

Unit	Topic	Grammar	Exam practice
15 What's for dinner?	food and drink, animals, time	prepositions of place and time, comparative and superlative adjectives	Listening Part 1, Reading and Writing Part 2, Speaking Parts 1 and 2 Test: Reading and Writing Part 4, Speaking Part 4
16 Let's have a picnic!	food and drink, the home, materials	*such/so*, *shall* and *let's* for suggestions, past simple, past continuous	Listening Part 5, Reading and Writing Part 1, Speaking Parts 2 and 3 Test: Reading and Writing Part 5
17 A day's work	work, places	present simple, *like* + infinitive, questions	Reading and Writing Part 1 Test: Listening Part 3, Speaking Part 3
18 Time and work	time, work	prepositions of time (*at*, *until*), questions	Test : Listening Part 4, Reading and Writing Part 3
19 Answer my questions	the world around us, time, family	questions in present simple, present continuous, present perfect, past simple	Listening Part 5, Reading and Writing Part 2, Speaking Part 4 Test: Reading and Writing Part 3
20 Calling and sending	time, numbers, the home	past simple, prepositions of time, questions	Reading and Writing Part 4, Speaking Part 4, Speaking Part 2
21 The time of the year	the world around us, weather, time	present simple, past simple, *ing* forms as nouns	Reading and Writing Part 1, Speaking Part 4 Test: Reading and Writing Part 6, Speaking Part 1
22 Important numbers	time, numbers, family and friends	questions, superlative adjectives, past simple	Speaking Part 4 Test: Reading and Writing Part 4
23 World, weather, work	the world around us, weather, work	*might*, adverbs of time, contractions	Reading and Writing Part 6, Speaking Part 4 Test: Reading and Writing Parts 1 and 7
24 Leaving and arriving	transport, places	questions, past simple, prepositions (*by*, *on*)	Reading and Writing Part 1, Speaking Parts 1, 2 and 4 Test: Listening Part 3
25 What shall we do next?	sports and leisure	questions, *be going to*	Listening Part 2, Reading and Writing Part 2 Test: Reading and Writing Part 5, Speaking Part 2
26 Where can we go on holiday?	sports and leisure	prepositions of place and time, *be going to*, *Have you ever?*	Reading and Writing Parts 6 and 7, Speaking Parts 1 and 4 Test: Listening Part 5, Reading and Writing Part 2, Speaking Part 3
27 It's the holidays! Bye!	transport, the world around us	prepositions of time, *be going to*	Speaking Parts 3 and 4 Test: Reading and Writing Part 3

Unit	Topic	Grammar	Exam practice
28 I want to win!	sports and leisure	past simple and continuous	Listening Part 5, Speaking Part 4, Reading and Writing Part 7 Test: Listening Part 4, Reading and Writing Part 6
29 Doing sport! Having fun!	sports and leisure, body and face	present continuous and simple, prepositions of place	Reading and Writing Part 1, Speaking Part 4 Test: Listening Part 1, Speaking Part 1
30 Summer and winter sports	sports and leisure, transport	conjunctions (*because, so*), infinitive of purpose, present and past continuous	Reading and Writing Part 7 Test: Reading and Writing Part 5, Speaking Part 3
31 Here and there	the home, weather	prepositions of place, pronouns, determiners, conjunctions	Listening Part 1 Test: Reading and Writing Parts 2 and 7, Speaking Part 1
32 Where?	places, the home	conjunctions, relative clauses, prepositions of place	Reading and Writing Part 1, Speaking Part 4 Test: Listening Part 3, Reading and Writing Part 4
33 At the hospital	health, body and face	present simple and continuous	Reading and Writing Parts 1, 2 and 3, Speaking Part 2
34 Oliver goes to hospital	health, sports and leisure, time	past continuous and simple, adverbs of manner	Test: Listening Part 2, Reading and Writing Parts 5 and 6
35 What's it made of?	materials, the home, the world around us	*be made of / from / with*, past simple and continuous, adverbs of time	Reading and Writing Parts 1 and 6 Test: Listening Part 5, Speaking Part 2
36 Silver, plastic, glass, gold	materials, the home	present perfect, imperatives, prepositions	Reading and Writing Parts 2, 3, 4 and 7 Test: Speaking Part 1
37 Exciting days!	work, clothes	present simple and continuous, prepositions of time	Reading and Writing Parts 4 and 7, Speaking Part 2
38 Famous people	work, sports and leisure	present and past simple and continuous, *would like +* infinitive, *will*	Listening Part 1, Reading and Writing Parts 4 and 5, Speaking Part 4 Test: Reading and Writing Part 6, Speaking Part 3
39 In villages and towns	places, sports and leisure	questions, *when* clauses, compound nouns (eg *computer mouse*)	Speaking Part 4 Test: Listening Part 3, Reading and Writing Parts 1 and 3
40 What a strange planet!	animals, body and face, the world around us	comparatives and superlatives, present perfect with *ever*, past continuous	Listening Part 5, Reading and Writing Part 6, Speaking Parts 4 Test: Reading and Writing Parts 5 and 7
41 Meet the pirate actors	family, the world around us, clothes	present simple and continuous, past simple and continuous, prepositions of place, relative clauses	Reading and Writing Part 4, Speaking Part 3 Test: Listening Part 5, Speaking Part 4
42 Holiday news	sports and leisure, places	present perfect with *already* and *yet, will, be going to,* relative clauses	Listening Part 3, Reading and Writing Part 5 Test: Listening Part 1, Reading and Writing Part 6, Speaking Part 1

Unit	Topic	Grammar	Exam practice
43 Have you ever … ?	sports and leisure	present perfect (*Have you ever … ?*) and short answers (*Yes, I have. No, I haven't.*), adding -*er* to verbs to make nouns, quantifiers	Reading and Writing Part 2, Speaking Part 4 Test: Reading and Writing Part 4
44 What has just happened?	friends, leisure, the home	present perfect with *just*, pronouns	Speaking Part 2 Test: Listening Part 1, Reading and Writing Part 6
45 Talking about the time	time, numbers	*be going to*, *will*, ordinal numbers (*1st – 31st*), prepositions of time	Speaking Part 4 Test: Listening Part 4, Reading and Writing Part 4
46 We're all at home today	the home, sports and leisure	short answers and auxiliary verbs, past continuous	Reading and Writing Part 3, Speaking Part 4 Test: Listening Part 3, Reading and Writing Part 5
47 I will or perhaps I won't	work, family and friends	*will*, predictions (*will*, *may*, *might*, *won't*), short answers	Speaking Part 4 Test: Listening Part 3
48 Doing different things	family and friends, work, sports and leisure	*ing* forms as nouns, *will*, *look like*	Reading and Writing Part 5, Speaking Part 4 Test: Listening Part 2, Reading and Writing Part 3, Speaking Part 2
49 Busy families	family and friends, the home, weather	*too* and *enough*, *make* and *do*	Speaking Part 4 Test: Reading and Writing Part 7, Listening Part 1, Speaking Part 1
50 On TV	work, places	present simple and continuous, past simple and continuous	Reading and Writing Parts 3 and 4, Speaking Part 2 Test: Listening Part 2, Reading and Writing Part 2, Speaking Part 3
51 Here's my news	school, sports and leisure, time	relative clauses, conjunctions	Listening Parts 2 and 3, Reading and Writing Part 7 Test: Speaking Part 2
52 What a lot of questions!	the world around us, sports and leisure	questions	Listening Part 5, Reading and Writing Part 1, Speaking Part 4 Test: Reading and Writing Part 5
53 Finding your way	places and directions	prepositions of place, adverbs of time, past continuous, tag questions	Test: Listening Part 4, Reading and Writing Part 1, Speaking Part 4
54 Let's have some fun!	sports and leisure, places	suggestions (*We could, How about? What about? Would you like to? Shall we? Why don't we? Let's …*)	Reading and Writing Part 7, Speaking Part 4 Test: Listening Part 5, Reading and Writing Part 2
55 If I feel bored	family and friends, health	conjunctions, *if* clauses, past simple	Reading and Writing Part 1, Speaking Parts 1 and 3 Test: Reading and Writing Part 3
56 Fun and games	family and friends, sports and leisure	revision of tenses, imperatives	Listening Part 2, Reading and Writing Part 1, Speaking Part 4 Test: Listening Part 1, Speaking Part 3

Fun for Flyers topic index

Topics	Units	
Clothes and colours	1 Hello again! 2 Wearing and carrying 3 Spots and stripes	
Animals, body and face, family and friends	4 My friends and my pets 5 About animals 6 My things 7 Moving and speaking	
School	8 School subjects 9 In my classroom 10 Clothes, animals and school	
The world and weather	11 Visiting different places 12 A journey into space 13 What horrible weather!	
Food and drink, the home	14 Are you hungry? Thirsty? 15 What's for dinner? 16 Let's have a picnic!	
Work, time and numbers	17 A day's work 18 Time and work 19 Answer my questions 20 Calling and sending	21 The time of the year 22 Important numbers 23 World, weather, work
Transport	24 Leaving and arriving 25 What shall we do next? 26 Where can we go on holiday?	
Sports and leisure	27 It's the holidays! Bye! 28 I want to win! 29 Doing sport! Having fun! 30 Summer and winter sports	
The home and other places	31 Here and there 32 Where?	
Health	33 At the hospital 34 Oliver goes to hospital	
Materials	35 What's it made of? 36 Silver, plastic, glass, gold	
Work and places	37 Exciting days! 38 Famous people 39 In villages and towns 40 What a strange planet! 41 Meet the pirate actors	
Leisure time – past and future	42 Holiday news 43 Have you ever…? 44 What has just happened? 45 Talking about the time 46 We're all at home today	
People's lives and work	47 I will or perhaps I won't 48 Doing different things 49 Busy families 50 On TV 51 Here's my news 52 What a lot of questions!	
Directions	53 Finding your way	
Fun!	54 Let's have some fun! 55 If I feel bored 56 Fun and games	

Fun for Flyers grammar index

Grammar	Grammar	Units
adjectives	comparatives and superlatives	4, 5, 15, 22, 40
adverbs		14, 23, 34, 35, 49, 53
clauses		2, 3, 8, 32, 39, 41, 42, 51 53, 55
conjunctions		6, 30, 31, 32, 51, 55
determiners		31
prepositions	place	3, 5, 11, 12, 15, 24, 26, 29, 31, 31, 36, 41, 53
	time	15, 18, 20, 26, 27, 37, 45
pronouns		5, 44
questions		1, 6, 7, 9, 10, 11, 12, 17, 18, 20, 22, 25, 39, 52
	short answers	43, 46, 47
	tag questions	53
verb tenses	present simple	1, 2, 4, 10, 17, 19, 21, 29, 33, 37, 38, 41, 50
	present continuous	1, 2, 4, 7, 19, 29, 30, 33, 37, 38, 41, 50
	past simple	6, 7, 10, 16, 19, 20, 21, 22, 24, 28, 34, 35, 38, 41, 50, 55
	past continuous	16, 28, 30, 34, 35, 38, 40, 41, 46, 50, 53
	present perfect	19, 26, 36, 40, 42, 43, 44
	be going to	25, 26, 27, 42, 46
	will + infinitive	38, 45, 47, 48
modal verbs		13, 23, 47, 54
other verb forms	*shall*	13, 16, 54
	to + infinitive of purpose	9, 30
	verb + infinitive	8, 12, 17, 38, 54
	verb + *ing*	54
	ing forms as nouns	21, 48

1 Hello again

Topics colours, clothes, sports and leisure

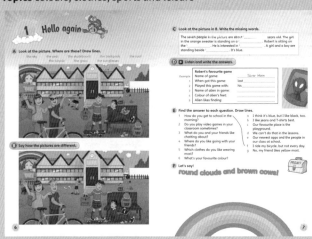

Equipment needed

○ Flyers audio 1D.
○ A glass / water / paper / CD (sec F).
○ Photocopies of page 128 (one for each learner / pair of learners. See Project.

A Look at the picture. Where are these? Draw lines.

○ Ask learners for different ways they can say 'Hello!' (Hi! Good morning / afternoon / evening.) Say: What about when you leave someone, what do you say then? (Bye, Goodbye, See you later/ tomorrow.)

○ Learners look at the picture. Ask questions:
How many children are there in the playground? (6)
What's the building that's behind the children? (the school)
How many grown-ups can you see? (1)
Do you think she's a teacher? (yes)

○ Teach/revise the eight words in **A**. Ask: What other words can you use for bicycle (bike), seat (chair) and backpack (rucksack)? Point to the backpack in the picture and ask: Why do you think this is called a backpack? (because you carry it on your back) Teach/revise 'shoulders', too.

○ Learners draw lines from the words to the parts of the picture where they can see these things. Check answers in open class.

B Say how the pictures are different. Speaking Part 1

> **Flyers tip**
> In Speaking Part 1, the 'Find the difference' pictures will have about ten differences but, after talking about the example, candidates will only be asked about six more differences.

○ Say: Look at the two pictures in A and B. The first picture is nearly the same as the second picture, but some things are different. For example, in the first picture, two children are waving, but in the second picture, only one child is waving. OK?

○ Point to the first picture. Say: This is my picture. Point to the second picture. Say: This is your picture. In my picture, the teacher is running.
Encourage different learners to say how their picture is different. For example: In my picture, she's walking.

○ Do the same to talk about other differences:
Say: In my picture:
1 the skateboard is purple and grey. (The skateboard's/It's pink and **yellow**.)
2 the boy is sitting on the seat. (The boy is/He's sitting on the **grass**.)
3 there's an alien on the screen. (There's **a moon** on the screen.)
4 there are two birds on the roof. (There are **no birds** on the roof.)
5 there's a backpack in front of the seat. (There's a backpack **on** the seat.)
6 the girl with the pink bag is wearing a sweater. (The girl with the pink bag is wearing a **T-shirt**.)

○ Learners could talk about the other differences in pairs or write sentences about them for homework.
Make sure they know the key words: square, o'clock.
Suggestions
Two children are waving. **One girl is** waving.
The boy with the bicycle is wearing sunglasses. The boy with the bicycle is wearing **glasses**.
The orange bag is round. The orange bag is **square**.
It's nine o'clock. It's **eleven** o'clock.

C Look at the picture in B. Write the missing words.

○ Point to the rucksack with the name 'Robert' in the picture in **B** and ask learners to decide who this belongs to (the boy sitting on the grass).

○ Point to the lorry in the picture in **B** and ask: What's this? (a lorry/ truck) What do think is inside this lorry/truck? Food? Clothes? Learners say what they think is inside the lorry.
Point to the clock and ask: What time is it? (11 o'clock) Why do you think these children are in the playground at 11 o'clock? Learners say why they think the children are in the playground. (For example: Because it's their school break.)
Note: Encourage learners to use their imagination. Accept any reasonable answers.

○ The text in this task is a model for the kind of writing tasks students are asked to do in later units. Ask the students the questions below to lead into the task.
1 How old are these children?
2 What is Robert interested in?
3 Find the girl in the orange sweater. What's inside her school bag?
4 One boy has a bicycle. What's his name?
5 What do you think the girl in the purple jeans is thinking?
Point to the text in **C** and say: Now, in pairs, read this text and write answers in your notebook. Remember, there can be lots of different ways to fill the gaps! Pairs of learners read the text and write their answers in their notebooks.
Pairs of learners compare their answers.
Ask a learner to read out the first sentence. Different learners say their answer. Their answers will probably be similar.
Ask one learner to read out the second sentence and their answer. The other learners suggest different answers. Do the same with other learners. Repeat this with 3-5.
Optional extension
Learners could write a short text about the school. Or, they could write or say sentences about how the school building in B is different from their school.

○ In pairs, learners then decide what the friends might be saying to each other. Learners then write mini dialogues including the names in the conversations. Accept any appropriate ideas.

D ▶ **Listen and write the answers.** Listening ^{Part} **2**

○ Tell learners they are going to hear a girl asking a boy about a game.
Ask: *Whose game is it?* (Robert's) *What's the name of this game?* (Silver Moon)

○ Learners practise asking these questions:
What's the name of your game?
When did you get your game?
Who do you like playing your game with?
Write these questions on the board and leave them there.

○ Point at the three questions on the board and say: *The girl might ask these questions but she might ask them a different way. Listen carefully.*

○ Play the audio once. Learners write any answers they are sure of. Play the audio a second time. Learners complete their answers, then check their answers in pairs. If necessary play the audio a third time.

> **Check answers:**
> **1** Friday **2** brother **3** Zappy **4** orange **5** (red) socks

○ Say: *Now ask and answer questions about your favourite games.* In pairs, learners ask and answer three questions about games using the questions on the board.

Audioscript

Listen and look at the picture. There is one example.
Girl: Is that your new game, Robert?
Boy: Yes, but it's quite difficult to play.
Girl: But you're really good at computer games …
Boy: Not always! Shall I teach you how to play it?
Girl: OK, yes! What's it called?
Boy: Silver Moon.

Can you see the answer? Now you listen and write.
Girl: So, it's a new game. When did you get it?
Boy: It was my birthday last Friday. My grandparents gave it to me when they came to see me that day. I really love it!
Girl: Let me see … Can you play it with another person?
Boy: Yes. My brother and I played it a lot yesterday. We had lots of fun with it, but he always wants to win!
Girl: Ha! So, who's that alien? The one on the screen?
Boy: It's called Zappy. You spell that Z-A-double P-Y. There's a website too where you can choose other aliens to add to the game.
Girl: Wow! Its face is a funny colour green. Is its body green, too?
Boy: Yes. But its feet are orange. Look!
Girl: OK. So what happens in the game?
Boy: The alien hops from one place to another and you've got to give it food because it gets tired. It collects socks from different places.
Girl: What do you mean?
Boy: It loves socks. It takes them from washing lines in people's gardens and puts them in its backpack. It likes socks that are any colour, but red ones are its favourite!
Girl: Mmm … I don't think I want to play it, Robert. Skateboarding is MUCH more exciting.

E **Find the answer to each question. Draw lines.**

○ Learners read question 1. Ask: *How many more questions are there?* (5) *How many more answers are there?* (6) Say: *So there is one answer that you don't need to use.* In pairs, learners find the answers and draw lines.

> **Check answers:**
> **2** d **3** e **4** c **5** b **6** a

○ Ask: *Which answer didn't you need?* (g) Learners suggest questions for that answer, e.g. *Is your friend's favourite colour pink?*

F **Let's say!**

Round clouds and brown cows.

○ Say: *Look at the picture in A again.* Ask: *Can you see something that's round?* (the orange backpack, the school clock) *Can you see something that's brown?* (the cow, the seat)

○ Divide the class into A and B groups. Turn to group A and say: *Listen to your sentence. 'Wow, look at the round clouds!' Can you say that?* (Learners in group A repeat the sentence.) Turn to group B and say: *Listen to your sentence. 'And look at the brown cow, now!' Can you say that?* (Learners in group B repeat their sentence.)

○ Check the correct pronunciation of /aʊ/ in 'wow', 'round', 'clouds', 'brown', 'cow', 'now'. Groups then take turns to repeat their sentences. Direct them so they repeat their sentences faster and faster!

Note: you may also like to practise 'house', 'town' and 'ground' here.

🧳 **Making rainbows!**

○ Ask: *Where's the rainbow in the picture in A?* (above the house) *How many colours are there in a rainbow?* (7) *Which colours can you see in a rainbow?*
Suggestions: red, yellow, pink, blue, orange, purple, green.

○ Using either method or both methods below, tell learners these ways they can make rainbows. You might like to dictate the instructions then check them.
   1 Find a CD. Make sure it's clean. Put the CD on a table, silver side up, under a light or in front of a sunny window. Look at the CD and see the rainbow on it.
   2 Fill a glass with water. Put the glass in front of a sunny window. Put a sheet of white paper on the floor. Wet the window with warm water. Move the glass and the paper until you see a rainbow.

Explain to learners they will only see a rainbow outside if the sun is behind them and wet weather is in front of them.

○ In smaller classes, divide learners into groups of 3–4 and let learners make their own rainbows.

○ Give each learner or pair of learners a copy of the 'Rainbow Story' on page 128. Learners choose how to complete their stories by writing one word on each line. Ask 3–4 learners to read out parts or all of their stories.

Optional extension:

If possible, learners research rainbows on the internet to learn more about them and how they are formed. They might also research how rain is formed.

Learners glue their 'Rainbow Story' onto a piece of larger paper or card and add to it:
   any rainbow photos they have found
   a rainbow picture they have drawn
   a rainbow fact file.

Learners add their completed 'Rainbow Story' page to their project file. Alternatively, display learners' work on the classroom wall if possible.

2 Wearing and carrying

Topics clothes, colours, body and face

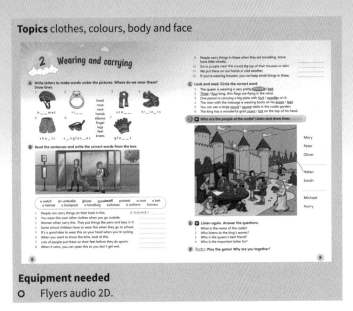

Equipment needed
- Flyers audio 2D.

A Write letters to make words under the pictures. Where do we wear these? Draw lines.

- Say to different learners: *Tell me a sentence about one thing that I'm wearing.* Encourage them to say the colour too. (For example: *You're wearing a white shirt / black shoes / a red sweater.*)

  Say to other learners: *Tell me one thing that you're wearing today.* (For example: *I'm wearing black shorts / a blue T-shirt / green socks.*)

- Say: *Look at the pictures.* Point to each picture in turn and ask: *What is this/these?* Teach/revise: *trainers, ring, scarf, shorts, sunglasses, helmet, gloves.* Ask: *Are you wearing a ring / gloves (etc) today?* Learners nod and point to their ring/gloves (etc) or shake their heads if they are not wearing them.

- Learners complete the words under the pictures by writing in the missing letters.

  > **Check answers:**
  > 1 helmet 2 ring 3 scarf 4 trainers 5 shorts 6 sunglasses
  > 7 gloves

- Point to the body words in the middle of the pictures. Point to each part of your body. Learners read out the word for each part of your body. (*head, nose, neck, hands, elbow, finger, legs, feet, knees*)

- Learners draw lines between the pictures in **A** and the body words to show where people wear these things.

  > **Check answers:**
  > 1 helmet – head 2 ring – finger 3 scarf – neck 4 trainers – feet
  > 5 shorts – legs 6 sunglasses – nose 7 gloves – hands

- Write on the board: *Some people wear … when they ….* Ask learners to complete the sentence about 'a ring'.

  Suggested answer: Some people wear a ring when they dress up.

  In pairs, learners write sentences about the other clothes. Ask different pairs to tell you one of their sentences.

  Suggested answers: Some people wear a helmet when they cycle. Some people wear a scarf when they are cold. Some people wear trainers when they do sport. Some people wear sunglasses when they go to the beach. Some people wear shorts when they do sport. Some people wear gloves when they go skiing.

- Point to the word 'nose' in **A** and ask: *What do you wear on your nose? I know! Something to help you see better! What do you wear on your nose?* (glasses)

  Point to the word 'elbows' and say: *Your elbow is part of your …* (arm). *Is it at the end of your arm?* (no) *Which part of your arm is your elbow?* (the middle)

Point to your elbow then your knee and say: *My elbow is in the middle of my arm and my … (knee) is in the (middle) of my (leg).* Say the whole sentence again. Learners say it too and point to their elbow and their knee.

- Explain that 'elbow' and 'knee' are difficult words to spell because they both have silent letters. To help learners remember their spellings, they can remember sentences with words for each letter. Write on the board: *Emma loves butterflies or whales!* Underline the first letter of each word. *What do the letters spell?* (elbow) *And what do the first letters of 'Katy never eats eggs' spell?* (knee) Learners could make up their own sentences to remember these or other difficult words to spell.

B Read the sentences and write the correct words from the box.

- Point to the picture of the boy and say: *This is Dan. What's he wearing?* (a white T-shirt, green shorts and black shoes, green sunglasses) *What's on his T-shirt?* (a lion's head)

  Ask: *What's he carrying?* (a blue rucksack) *How many pockets of the rucksack can you see?* (3) *What's in the biggest pocket?* (a torch)

  Say: *Dan's going camping with his school this weekend.*

- Point to the girl and say: *And this is Sally. Which words in the box can we use to describe Sally?* (a uniform, an umbrella, suitcase, a coat)

  Say: *Sally's staying with a friend after school today.*

- Read out sentence 1: *People can carry things on their back in this.* Point to the words 'a rucksack' on the line at the end of this sentence. Ask: *Can you find another word for rucksack in the box?* (a backpack)

  Say: *This is another word we use for this kind of bag. American people don't usually say 'rucksack' they say (backpack).* Learners write 'a backpack' on the second line.

- Say: *Draw a circle round the words in the box for the 'things we wear'.* (*a belt, a coat, a helmet, gloves, a uniform, watch, trainers*)

- Learners read sentences 2–12 and write words on the lines.

  > **Check answers:**
  > 1 a backpack 2 a coat 3 a handbag 4 a uniform 5 a helmet
  > 6 a watch 7 trainers 8 an umbrella 9 suitcases 10 a belt
  > 11 gloves 12 pockets

- Point to the words in the box under the picture in **B** and ask: *Which of these things do people wear?* (a coat, helmet, watch, belt, gloves, a uniform, trainers) *What do you do with a backpack? You don't wear it, you …* (carry it). *Which of the other things in B do you carry?* (an umbrella, a handbag, suitcases)

- Write on opposite sides of the board: *suitcase* *shorts*

  Say both these words, then say: /s/, *suitcase*; /ʃ/ *shorts*. Say other words starting with these sounds. Learners point to 'suitcase' if they start with /s/ and 'shorts' if they start with /ʃ/.

  Words to say: *socks, shoes, sunglasses, scarf, shirt, silver, sugar, sure*

  Say the words again. Different learners write each word under *suitcase* or *shorts*.

  Note: 'su' at the beginning of some words (for example: 'sugar' and 'sure') is pronounced /ʃ/. Other words that start with the letters 'su' start with /s/: Sue, supermarket, Sunday.

- Say: *Listen and write this sentence: Sarah's son, Sam, wore a spotted shirt and striped shorts and shoes with sheep on them!*

C Look and read. Circle the correct word.

o Learners look at the castle picture in **D**. Ask:
Are most of these people outside the castle? (yes)
Is one person running? (yes)

o Read out sentence 1: *The queen is wearing a very pretty necklace/belt.* Point to the circle round *necklace*, then point to the queen in the picture. Say: *The queen's wearing a necklace, not a belt.*

o In pairs, learners read sentences 2–6 and circle the correct word.

> **Check answers:**
> **2** three **3** fruit **4** feet **5** round **6** crown

D ▶ Who are the people at the castle? Listen and draw lines.
Listening Part **1**

o Ask: *How many people are there in the picture?* (ten)
How many names are there? (seven)
What are the king and queen doing? (sitting, laughing)
What are the other people doing? (waving, carrying, playing music, smiling, reading, running, standing, sitting)
Which animal can you see? (a dog)

o Play the audio twice. Learners listen to the example and look at the line from Helen to the queen. Check learners know what to do. Learners then listen to questions 1–5 and draw lines from the names to the people in the picture. Play the audio a second time if necessary.

> **Flyers tip**
> In Listening Part 1, a person in the picture might be identified by the colour of something they are wearing, for example: *The woman who's wearing a pink coat is called Grace.* Make sure learners are familiar with all the clothes items and colours on the YLE vocabulary lists.

> **Check answers:**
> Lines should be drawn between:
> *Harry* and king
> *Michael* and man with the string instrument
> *Mary* and girl playing with puppy
> *Sarah* and woman carrying fruit
> *Peter* and man running with piece of paper

E ▶ Listen again. Answer the questions.

o Learners answer the questions. You may need to play the audio again for learners to answer. Ask:
1 *What is the name of the castle?* (Sky Castle)
2 *Who listens to the king's secrets?* (Michael)
3 *Who is the queen's best friend?* (Sarah)
4 *Who is the important letter for?* (the king)

o Ask: *Which name didn't we hear? Can you remember?* (Oliver)
Which people have not got a line to a name? (the boy reading, the man playing the drums, the girl at the top of the castle, the boy with the water)

o The whole class decides which person is Oliver and learners draw a line from this name to the chosen boy/man in the picture. Learners suggest names for the other three people. Write some of these on the board. The class chooses three names from the list. Learners write these names on the three lines in their books and draw lines from the names to the other two people.

o Point to the drum and ask: *Does anyone know the word for this?* (If not, tell one learner to look in a dictionary and find the word.) Ask them to spell it for the class. Write it on the board.
Ask: *What other words do you know for things that make music?* (piano, guitar, violin etc) Ask different learners how to spell these words and then write them on the board, too. Ask: *Can anyone play the piano, guitar, violin, drums?* Learners answer.

Audioscript

Listen and look. There is one example.
Girl: This is my favourite picture in my storybook about 'Sky Castle', Uncle Jack.
Man: It looks great. Who are all these people?
Girl: Well, the queen, the woman in the long silver dress who's sitting in the smaller chair, is called Helen.
Man: I see.
Can you see the line? This is an example.
Now you listen and draw lines.

Man: And who's that person? Is he the king?
Girl: Yes. I love his blue jacket and curly black hair.
Man: He looks very important. What's his name?
Girl: He's called Harry in the story.

Girl: And there's Michael. He's very clever. The king tells him all his secrets.
Man: Which one's he?
Girl: The man on the path who's playing that instrument. It's not a guitar.
Man: Yes. It's not a guitar, but it looks like one, doesn't it?
Girl: Yes, it does. But it's much older, I think.

Girl: And there's the queen's daughter.
Man: The girl who's waving on the castle wall?
Girl: No, not her. I mean the girl with the long blonde hair.
Man: Oh, you mean the one who's sitting on the grass.
Girl: That's right. She's called Mary.

Man: And what about the woman who's carrying the fruit?
Girl: That's Sarah. She's the queen's best friend, but she works in the castle kitchen.
Man: Is she a cook?
Girl: Yes. I love her green belt. I think it's fantastic. The queen gave it to her.

Man: Why is that person hurrying?
Girl: You mean the man with the piece of paper in his hand?
Man: Yes.
Girl: He's got an important letter for the king. His name's Peter.
Man: Oh!
Girl: I'm going to read the next part of this amazing story now!
Man: Great!

F Play the game! Why are you together?

o Choose a particular feature (see suggestions below), which a number of learners in the class have in common.

o Ask groups of different learners to move to certain parts of the room. Do not say which feature (for example, black hair) they share.
For example, say: *Marta, Maria, Juan. Go and stand beside the door.*

o Learners guess why each group is standing together. They put up their hands to answer. For example: *They all have black hair.* Learners can also guess why their own group is standing together. For example: *We're all girls.*

Note: Large classes could play this in teams, with teams trying to guess the reason and winning a point.

Suggested features: boys or girls / what learners are wearing / the colour of learners' clothes / the length or kind of hair they have / the colour of their eyes / their height / the first letter of their names / their interests if known / their ages if known.

3   Spots and stripes

Topics clothes, leisure, colours

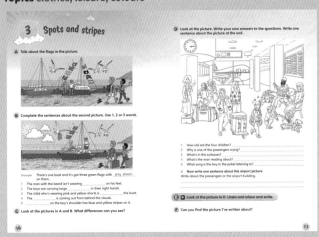

Equipment needed
o   Flyers audio 3E.
o   Colouring pens or pencils.
o   Pictures of different flags. See A.
o   Magazines with pictures of people (one for each group of three learners). See F.

Ⓐ Talk about the flags in the picture.
o   Ask: *Can you tell me ten things that you can see in the picture in A?*
    Suggestions: boats, flags, rucksacks, birds, T-shirts, shorts, jeans, towel, boys, girl, man, etc.
o   Ask: *How many flags can you see?* (8)
    Which flag is blue and has a rainbow on it? (learners point to that flag)
    Ask: *What can you see on the different flags?* (a square, stripes, spots, a crown, a moon, a lion, a cross)
o   In pairs, learners choose two flags and write a sentence about each in their notebooks. They say what colour the flag is and the colour of the object on the flag. For example: *There's a black flag with a white crown on it.*
    Ask one pair to read out one of the sentences. The other learners listen and say which flags they are.
o   Ask learners to describe flags for different countries they know (including their own country's flag). You could take in pictures of different flags.

    Optional extension:
    Make sure learners have colouring pencils. Learners work in pairs. Each learner chooses one flag (either from this picture, or another country flag) and describes it. Their partner listens and draws and colours the flag.
    Note: You could also ask learners to design their own flag and then describe it to their partner to draw.

Ⓑ Complete the sentences about the second picture. Use 1, 2 or 3 words.
o   Say: *Read the first sentence. Can you find the boat, the green flags and the sharks?*
o   Learners complete sentences 1–5. Remind them that they can use only one, two or three words.

Check answers:
1 (any) shoes   **2** square/heavy suitcases   **3** cleaning/washing
4 (hot) sun   **5** The (nice/new/long) towel

Ⓒ Look at the pictures in A and B. What differences can you see?
o   Point to the two pictures in **A** and **B** and say:
    Here are two pictures. They're nearly the same, but some things are different. For example, in this picture (point to the picture in **A**) *there are two boats, but in this picture* (point to the picture in **B**) *there's one.*
    In pairs, learners discuss what the differences are and how they can describe them.
o   Point to the picture in **A** and say:
    In my picture, the two boys are carrying rucksacks.
    Learners tell you how the picture in **B** is different. (*In this picture, the two boys are carrying* **suitcases**.)
o   Do the same for these sentences and differences:
    In my picture:
    The man and the girl are trying to catch some fish. (The man and **boy** are washing/cleaning the boat.)
    The birds have got black stripes on their wings. (They **don't have** / have**n't** got black stripes on their wings.)
    Eight flags are flying in the wind. (**Three** flags are flying in the wind.)
    A girl is wearing pink and yellow shorts. (A **boy** is wearing pink and yellow shorts.)
    You can't see any clouds in the sky. (There are **three** clouds in the sky.)
o   *In my picture, the girl on the boat has long, straight fair hair.* (The **boy** has **short**, **curly** fair hair.)

Ⓓ Look at the picture. Write your own answers to the questions. Write one sentence about the picture at the end.
o   Say: *Look at the picture in D.* Ask:
    How many people are there? (10)
    Where are they? (At the airport)
    How many planes can you see? (three – one big plane and two toy planes.)
    Note: Point out that stripes and spots can be described in two ways. Write on the board:
    A bear **with spots** *on it. A* **spotted** *bear.*
    A jacket **with stripes** *on it. A* **striped** *jacket*
    Ask learners to point to the bear with spots and the striped jacket in the picture.
o   Say: *Look at the picture again. Choose one person in the picture. Ready? Now, listen to my questions and think about your answers for the person you chose.* Read out the questions below, allowing time for learners to look at the person and to think about their answers.
    How old is this person? What's this person wearing? Some of the people in this picture have flowers or stripes on their clothes. Does your person have either of these? What's this person doing? Is the person sitting or standing? Are they carrying or holding anything? How does this person feel? Happy or unhappy? Bored or interested?
    Learners work in pairs or small groups. Ask each question again. Each learner talks about the person that they chose.
    Say: *Now look at the questions in D. Look at the first question: How old are the four children? Which people in the picture are children?* (the boy and girl who are sitting on the ground and the two boys with the mother and the suitcases) *Did anyone choose one of these people to answer my questions?* Ask different learners who chose one of the four children: *How old is this boy/girl?* Learners answer.
    Write on the board:
    The children are …..

A learner comes to the board and completes the sentence about the children's ages. Everyone then copies the sentence onto the line next to the first question in **D**.

Read out the second question: *Why is one of the passengers crying?* Ask: *Which passenger is crying?* (the woman sitting on the seat on the left) *Why is she crying?* Different learners suggest reasons. Accept any reasonable answer.

Suggestions

She lost her bag/ticket. She missed her plane. Her plane is late.

Learners write a sentence on the line next to this question.

Learners read the last three questions and write answers on the lines in **D**.

Check answers by asking different learners to say what is inside the suitcases (probably clothes and combs, toothbrushes, etc), what the man is reading about (perhaps the sports news) and what song the boy is listening to.

E ▶ **Look at the picture in D.**   Listening **5**^Part
Listen and colour and write.

o   Say: *Look at the picture again*. Play the example on the audio. Ask: *What two things did you hear about this man?* (He's sitting down, reading a newspaper and he has a brown beard.)

o   Play the rest of the audio twice, pausing the audio the first time to give learners 15 seconds to colour or write.

Check answers:

1 Colour taller boy's trainers – purple
2 Write 'Times' on noticeboard
3 Colour skirt of woman drinking coffee – blue
4 Write 'sport' on bag next to girl on the phone
5 Colour flower on small girl's dress – orange

Flyers tip

In Listening Part 5, candidates need to colour three things that are in the picture, for example: a pair of gloves, a plant and a clock. There are usually <u>two</u> of each of these things so they need to listen carefully to make sure they have understood which gloves, plant and clock to colour.

Audioscript

Listen and look at the picture. There is one example.

Girl: I like this picture. It's great!
Man: Can you see the man who's sitting down?
Girl: Yes, I can. He's reading a newspaper!
Man: That's right. Colour his beard brown.
Girl: OK. I'm doing that now.

Can you see the man with the brown beard? Now you listen and colour and write.

1   Man: Now find the boy who's walking with his mother.
      Girl: I can see him. He's taller than his brother.
      Man: Yes, he is. Colour his trainers purple, please.
      Girl: OK, I can do that!

2   Man: Would you like to do some writing now?
      Girl: Yes please! I like writing.
      Man: Good! Look at the board that's on the wall. The large one.
      Girl: OK.
      Man;   Write: TIMES on the top of that. The people need to know when the planes are arriving and leaving.
      Girl: Yes! That's really important!

3   Man: Now, can you see the woman who's drinking some hot coffee?
      Girl: The one whose feet you can't see?
      Man: That's right. Colour her skirt.
      Girl: OK. Can I colour it green?
      Man: I'd like you to make it blue, actually.
      Girl: Right. I'll do that, now.

4   Man: And now write something else in the picture.
      Girl: Fine! What shall I write?
      Man: Well, can you see the bag?
      Girl: The one that's in front of the girl in shorts?
      Man: Yes. That one. Can you write 'sport' on it, please?
      Girl: OK. That's easy!

5   Girl: And what else can I colour?
      Man: I know. Can you see the two children who are playing with the model planes?
      Girl: Yes. Shall I colour one of those?
      Man: No. Colour the flower on the little girl's dress. Make it orange.
      Girl: I love that colour. It's my favourite! There!
      Man: Brilliant! Thank you.

Complete the sentences about the picture.

o   On the board, write the beginning of sentences about where the person is or what they are doing or wearing in the picture in **D** (see below). Learners put their hands up and suggest ways of completing them.

1 *The woman who's drinking coffee* … (is under the clock.)
2 *The man with the beard* … (is sitting down / is reading a newspaper.)
3 *The children who are sitting on the floor* … (are playing with toy planes.)
4 *The girl who's crying* … (has got curly hair / is wearing a long skirt and T-shirt.)
5 *The woman with the suitcases* … (has got two sons)

o   Write on the board: *newspaper*. Ask: *Can you find the two words that make this word?* (news, paper)

o   Write on the board: *armchair* and ask: *Which two words make this word?* (arm, chair) Point to the first syllable in each of these words as you say them. Say: *With words that we make from two words, the first word is usually louder and longer: NEWSpaper, ARMchair.* Learners say the words.

o   Ask: *Do you know any words that start with 'grand'?* (grandma, grandmother, grandpa, grandfather, granddaughter, grandson) Make sure that learners stress the first syllable ('grand') in each.

o   Write on the board: ………… board. Ask: *Do you know any words that end with 'board'?* Learners say words. Make sure they stress the first part of these words.
Suggestions: blackboard, keyboard, skateboard, snowboard
Note: If your learners' first language has rules for stressing syllables, you could compare their rules with the above.

o   Learners practise saying other words made up of more than one word.
Suggestions: SUNglasses, FOOTball, TIMEtable.

F **Can you find the picture I've written about?**

o   Give one magazine to each group of three learners. They choose a picture of at least one person and write a detailed description (what they are wearing and doing, how they are feeling, what they are thinking, etc), without saying the page number (or the product if the picture is part of an advert).

o   Groups pass on their magazine and description to another group, who read the description, find the picture and show it to the first group to check it is the right picture.

Optional extension:

Cut out pictures of people from magazines and give four or five to each group. Learners choose one and write a description.

4   My friends and my pets

Topics names, family and friends, animals

Not in YLE wordlists: *the same … as*

Equipment needed

O   Flyers audio 4B, 4E.

(A) Let's talk about your friends and family.

O   Different learners ask you questions 1 and 2 in **A**. Answer their questions.

O   Learners read questions 1–5 and think about their answers. Then ask different learners the questions and ask further questions about each one:

   1 *Who's the youngest person in your house?*

   2 *What's your surname?*

   3 *What's your teacher called?*

   4 *Where do you go?*

   5 *How old is she/he? Is she/he tall? What colour hair has she/he got?*

O   In groups of 3–4, learners ask and answer the questions.

> **Flyers tip**
>
> In Speaking Part 4, candidates are asked three open questions on the <u>same</u> topic, for example, 'your friends'. They might be asked:
>
> *What do you and your friends like doing?*
>
> *How often do you phone or text your friends?*
>
> *Where do you and your friends like going?*
>
> They are then asked a 'Tell me about' question, for example:
>
> *Tell me about your best friend.*

(B) ▶ What does Holly say about her friends? Listen, write names, then draw lines.

O   Point to the girl in the purple dress who's dancing and say:

   This is Holly and this is a picture of Holly's birthday party. You are going to listen to Holly talking about the eight people who came to her birthday party. For example, her best friend Jane came.

   Play the audio. Learners listen and write the seven other names. (They do not draw lines to the letters yet.)

   Check answers by asking different learners to spell the names.

> **Check answers:**
>
> **2** Daisy   **3** Harry   **4** Pat   **5** Nick   **6** Lucy   **7** Bill   **8** Helen

O   Point to the line from 1 *Jane* to *d*. *Jane is Holly's best friend.*

   Play the audio again. Learners listen and draw lines between each person and what Holly says about them.

> **Check answers:**
>
> **2** Daisy e   **3** Harry f   **4** Pat h   **5** Nick g   **6** Lucy b   **7** Bill c
>
> **8** Helen a

> **Flyers tip**
>
> In Listening Part 2, candidates sometimes have to write a name. Candidates need to know how to spell all the names on the YLE vocabulary lists, how they are pronounced, which are girls' or boys' names (and which can be either). This will help them link names with different people in Listening Part 1.

O   Point to the picture and ask: *How many people can you see in the picture?* (7) *How many people did Holly talk about* (8) Explain: *Not everyone who came to the party is in the picture!*

O   Read out the sentence about Pat: *Pat is a loud singer.* Point to the picture again and ask: *Which boy is Pat? What's he wearing?* (The boy in the orange striped T-shirt and blue trousers.) *What tune is he singing? Is it rock music or pop music?* Accept any reasonable answer.

O   Ask: *Holly says that her cousin Bill is boring. Which boy in the picture might be Bill?* (The boy sitting down.) *Who likes dancing and the same music as Holly?* (Daisy) *Which girl do you think is Daisy?* (The girl in the green top and shorts.)

O   Ask: *Who do you think the girl standing at the table is? What other girls' names do we have in B?* (Jane, Lucy, Helen) *Do you think this is Holly's best friend, the girl that she has guitar lessons with, or the girl in her class?*

O   Ask: *Who do you think the other two boys are? Who is pointing? Harry or Nick? Harry is Pat the singer's brother. Which boy looks like Pat?* (Maybe the boy in the black T-shirt because he has the same brown hair too?)

Audioscript

> *Who came to Holly's birthday party? Listen and write names.*
>
> My party was excellent! My best friend Jane came, of course, and Daisy too. Daisy and I like the same kind of music. We also love dancing. And I invited the two boys who live in the house that's next to ours. Harry's the older one. He always makes me laugh on the school bus. His younger brother is Pat. I didn't know him, but I do now! He didn't stop singing all afternoon and was very loud! I often go sailing with Nick so I invited him. We both go to the sailing club on Wednesday evenings. Oh, and Lucy came too. She's in my class. We often do our homework together. Who else? Let me think … Oh yes, Bill and Helen were there. Helen and I are learning to play the guitar together. She's great. Bill is boring, but I had to invite him because he's my cousin!

(C) Now write the names of people you know.

O   Ask: *How many students are in this class? Has anybody here got more than one first name?* (Students who have put up their hands tell the rest of the class their other first name and spell it.)

O   Teach/revise 'surname'. Ask: *How many letters are there in your surname? Who has got a surname with more than eight letters in it?* Learners put up their hands. Ask each learner: *Tell us how many letters are in your surname.* Ask the rest of the class: *Who has the most letters?* (eg Rodriguez!) Ask that person to spell their surname: (eg Fernando), *spell your surname for us, please! Thanks!)*

O   Learners read the sentences and write names of their friends or family on the lines to complete them.

O   Ask different learners about the people they wrote about.

   Suggested questions: 1 *What kind of music do you and your friend like? What's your favourite band?* 2 *Why does this person make you laugh?* 3 *What songs does this person like singing?* 4 *What's this person's favourite sport?*

D Read the email and write the missing words. Write one word on each line.

Reading & Writing Part 6

o Point to the photo by the email and say: *This is Sally. Her family are living in a new house. She's emailing her friend Hugo to tell him about her new house and her new pet.*

o Learners read the email (no writing yet). Ask:
When does Sally want Hugo to visit her? (on Monday)
Who must catch a bus? (Hugo)
Who's got a new pet? (Sally)
What can the friends watch? (the football match)

o Look at the example with learners. Explain that in front of a superlative adjective like 'best', we use 'the'. Point to the sentences in **C** and ask: *Can you find another example of this?* (**2** .... is the funniest person in this class.)

o Learners write the missing words (one word only) in each gap.

> **Check answers:**
> **1** by **2** than **3** of **4** If **5** What/Which

o Ask different learners: *What's your favourite football/basketball team?* (Choose the sport that is popular in the country where you teach.)

E ▶ Listen and write the names.

o Say: *Now, you're going to hear Sally talking to Hugo on the phone. Sally said that her new pet is green and red, really sweet and … (naughty!) What is Sally's pet?* (a parrot) *Let's find out! Listen and write the names.* Play the audio twice.

o Learners take it in turns to spell the answers. Ask: *How do you spell:*
  1 *Sally's surname?*
  2 *the name of the street where the bus stops?*
  3 *the name of Sally's road?*
  4 *the name of Sally's house?*
  5 *Sally's dog's name?*
  6 *Sally's parrot's name?*

> **Check answers:**
> **1** (Sally) Powis **2** Derby **3** Jacinto **4** Bulrush **5** Fangs
> **6** Chirpy

Audioscript

> *Listen and write the names. There is one example.*
>
> Boy: How do you spell your name, Sally?
> Girl: It's S-A-L-L-Y!
> Boy: Sorry! Yes, of course!
> *Can you see the name Sally? Now you listen and write the names.*
> Boy: And what's your surname, Sally? I can't remember!
> Girl: It's Powis. P-O-W-I-S.
> Boy: Oh yes. I saw it on your school book.
> Girl: Would you like to come to my house this afternoon?
> Boy: Yes!
> Girl: Great. You can come by bus.
> Boy: OK. Where must I get off?
> Girl: You should get off the bus in Derby Street.
> Boy: How do you spell that?
> Girl: It's D-E-R-B-Y.
> Boy: And is your house in Derby Street?
> Girl: No, but it's very near. We live in Jacinto Road. It's easy to see.
> Boy: OK. Do you spell that J-A-K-I-N-T-O?
> Girl: No. You spell it J-A-C-I-N-T-O. It's a kind of flower.
> Boy: And what number do you live at?
> Girl: My house doesn't have a number. It has a name.
> Boy: Does it? That's funny! What's its name, then?
> Girl: Bulrush. B-U-L-R-U-S-H.
> Boy: All right. And have you still got that big dog?
> Girl: Yes. But he's not dangerous!
> Boy: That's good! What was his name?

> Girl: Fangs.
> Boy: F-A-N-S?
> Girl: No. You spell his name F-A-N-G-S. And I have another pet now.
> Boy: Have you? Is it another dog?
> Girl: No. My uncle gave me a parrot for my birthday.
> Boy: Wow! And what's your parrot called?
> Girl: Chirpy. C-H-I-R-P-Y.

F Where are the 'h's?

o Point to the word 'house' in **A**. Say: *H-O-U-S-E. The first letter in this word is 'h'. Can you find seven more words in this unit that start with the letter 'h'? Let's see who's the quickest.* In pairs, learners look for seven more words starting with 'h' in Unit 4 and write them in their notebooks. The first pair to find and write seven words shouts 'stop!'. Check that the words are all in the unit and are correctly spelt: *Harry, has, he, Helen, her, here, Hi, his, hobbies, Holly, Hugo*

o Say: *Listen and count! How many words in this sentence start with 'h'? Harry has lots of history homework.* (4) *And in this sentence? Poor Holly! Her hand hurts and she has a headache too!* (6)

o Say: *The 'h' at the start of words is a quiet sound, but it's very important!* Write on the board and say the word: *and.* Add the letter 'h' to this word. Ask: *Now how do we say this word?* (hand) *Point to your left hand!*

o Explain: *There are other pairs of words like this.* Write and say: *All.* *Add 'h' to the start and you get a room in a house.* (hall) Write and say: *hair. You can comb your* (hair). Cross off the 'h' and say: *We need air to live!*

o Say: *Listen and write the word you hear.* Say the following words pausing between words to allow learners time to write.
1 ear 2 I 3 hill 4 ill 5 high 6 at 7 hat 8 our 9 hour

o Check answers by asking different pairs to come to the board. One learner spells the word and the other writes it. Ask the class if they agree with the spelling.
For 8 and 9, explain: The word 'hour' is special. It's different because it doesn't have the /h/ sound at the start. So, it sounds the same as 'our'. Our train leaves in one hour!

5   About animals

Topics animals, body and face, the world around us

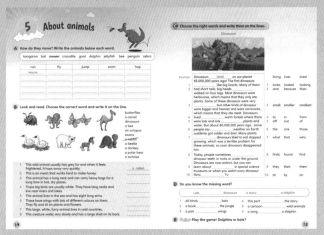

Not in YLE wordlists: *bone*

Equipment needed

o   Photocopies (one for each group of 3–4 learners) of the pictures and sentences on page 129. See E.

o   Scissors – one pair for each group of 3–4 learners. See E.

Animal alphabet

o   Learners take it in turns to say each letter of the alphabet. Write the letters on the board as they say them.

o   Learners work in teams of 3–4. Say: *You have five minutes to write an animal starting with every letter of the alphabet.* Say: *If you can't think of an animal for one of the letters, you can write another word before it.*

For example: **a** angry lion, **n** nine monkeys, **r** red fish, **z** zoo animals.

o   **Suggested answers** (using words which appear in the wordlists for all three YLE levels and a few other animals that learners might know):

a angry lion   **b** bat, bear, bee, beetle, bird, butterfly   **c** camel, cat, chicken, cow   **d** dog, dolphin, donkey, duck   **e** elephant, eagle **f** fish, fly, frog   **g** giraffe, goat   **h** hippo, horse   **i** insect **j** jellyfish   **k** kangaroo   **l** lion, lizard   **m** monkey, mouse **n** naughty monkey   **o** octopus   **p** pet, panda, penguin, parrot, polar bear   **q** quiet tiger   **r** rabbit   **s** shark, sheep, snail, snake, spider, swan   **t** tiger   **u** ugly spider   **v** very big hippo   **w** whale **y** yellow lizard   **z** zebra, zoo animals

Ⓐ How do they move? Write the animals below each word.

o   Check learners know the meaning of verbs: run, fly, jump, swim and hop. Say one of the verbs and ask learners to do the action. Point to the kangaroo to teach 'hop'.

o   Learners write each of the ten animal words from the box in the columns below according to how they move. Point to the example (*run – mouse*).

Suggested answers: *run* – goat, crocodile, penguin, zebra; *fly* – bat, bee; *jump* – dolphin, goat, kangaroo, penguin; *swim* – crocodile, dolphin, jellyfish, penguin; *hop* – kangaroo, penguin

o   Learners try to fill the columns with as many other animals as possible.

Suggested answers (accept any reasonable answers): *run* – tiger, cat, kitten, dog, puppy, lion; *fly* – duck, eagle, parrot, swan, insect, butterfly, fly; *jump* – frog, cat, dog, sheep, monkey, horse; *swim* – hippo, crocodile, shark, whale, octopus, dog; *hop* – rabbit, parrot, insect

Ⓑ Look and read. Choose the correct word and write it on the line.

o   Ask 4–5 different learners: *What colour is your favourite animal? What can it do?* (For example: brown, hop)

Other learners try to guess what the favourite animal is (*kangaroo*).

o   Learners look at the example in the list to the right of the pictures (a rabbit). Ask different learners to tell you about rabbits. Say: *A rabbit is …* (For example: *grey. A rabbit can hop. A rabbit eats carrots.*)

o   Learners read the example (1). They underline the key words that describe a rabbit (wild, animal, grey, fur, hops).

o   In pairs, learners read 2–8, decide which animals are being described and write the words for the animals on the lines. (Ask them to underline the key words in each description.)

> **Flyers tip**
>
> In Reading and Writing Part 1, candidates have to write each answer using exactly the same word or words in the possible answers. For example in this task: an octopus, swans. Remind them to check the spelling and whether the words are singular or plural.

> **Check answers:**
>
> **2** a bee (*insect, make honey*)
> **3** a camel (*long neck, carry, hot, dry places*)
> **4** swans (*big birds, long necks, near rivers and lakes*)
> **5** an octopus (*sea, eight long arms*)
> **6** butterflies (*wings, different colours, fly, sit on plants, flowers*)
> **7** a polar bear (*large, white, furry animal, lives in cold countries*)
> **8** a tortoise (*creature that walks very slowly, large shell on its back*)

o   Write on the board: *This animal lives … It eats … It's … It's got …* Ask: *Which animal in B did you not read about?* (a donkey, dinosaurs, a beetle) *What kind of animal is a beetle?* (an insect) Point to the sentences on the board and say: *Let's complete these sentences about a beetle. Where does it live?* (This animal lives in many different places). *What does it eat? Plants? Meat? It eats plants and fruit. What does it look like? Is it big or small? What colour is it?* (Beetles can be many different colours.) *Does it have spots or stripes? Wings? How does it move?* (Some beetles have stripes or spots. Some beetles have wings. Some beetles fly. Other beetles only crawl.)

Say: *Now, think of an animal.*

Where does it live? In water? On land? In hot or cold places?

What does it eat? Plants? Meat?

What does it look like? Is your animal big or small? What colour is it? Does it have spots or stripes? Does it have legs? Wings? How does it move?

o   Pairs write sentences about their animals, using the sentence starts on the board. If you have access to the internet, they could look for more information about their chosen animal and produce a poster or a blog entry about it.

Dinosaurs!

o Tell learners to close their eyes and imagine a dinosaur. Ask: *Is your dinosaur big or small? What colour is it? How many feet does it stand on? Can it run? Does it have a long tail? How many teeth does it have? Is it noisy?* Learners do not speak or write words.

Say: *Open your eyes now and draw your dinosaur!* Learners draw their dinosaur in their notebooks.

o Tell learners to write down eight words they would find in a text about dinosaurs. This could be done with the whole class or in pairs. (For example: *teeth, colour, feet, eat, big, extinct, plants, animals.*)

o Now, ask them to write down five words they <u>won't</u> find in a text about dinosaurs. (For example: *handbag, chocolate, gloves, alien, cheese.*)

o Learners read the text in **C** and check which of their words are in it. After they have read the text, learners suggest sentences using words they wrote down for dinosaurs that *weren't* in the text. They could also write sentences about dinosaurs using the words they didn't expect to find in the text. For example: *Dinosaurs love eating chocolate ice cream! A dinosaur needs a very big handbag!*

C Choose the right words and write them on the lines.

Reading & Writing **Part 4**

o Learners look at the picture of the dinosaur. Ask:
Is this dinosaur taller / fatter / funnier / friendlier than your dinosaur? Has it got more teeth than your dinosaur?

o Learners read the text about dinosaurs. Ask them, in pairs, to underline or circle any words they don't know. Teach/revise these words before completing the exercise. Words that learners may not know yet are: planet, ago, warm and drier.

o Tell learners to look at the first sentence of the text and at the three possible words for the gap (living, lives, lived). Ask which word is correct (lived). Explain why *lived* is correct. (Dinosaurs don't live now so we need the <u>past</u> tense.) Explain why 'living' and 'lives' are wrong. (We would need to put 'are living', which is a <u>present</u> tense, 'lives' is also <u>present</u> and singular but the word 'dinosaurs' is plural.)

o In pairs, learners choose words for the gaps in questions 1–10.

> **Check answers:**
> **1** looked **2** and **3** small **4** in **5** of **6** the **7** that **8** find **9** them **10** on

o Tell learners to close their books. Write the letter 'd' on the board. Each learner then takes it in turns to tell you the next letter to spell the word 'dinosaur'.

Note: There are four different vowels in this word. Only 'e' is missing. Pointing out patterns like this can help some learners remember difficult spellings.

D Do you know the missing word?

o Learners read the first phrase in the box. Ask them what the missing word is (of). Learners write *of* in the gap. Learners read the second phrase. Ask them what the missing word is (about). Learners complete the other six gaps with 'of' or 'about'.

> **Check answers:**
> **1** of **2** about **3** of **4** of **5** about **6** about

o Learners make sentences using these phrases and write them in their notebooks. For example: *There are lots of dinosaurs in this part of the story.*

E Play the game! Dolphins or bats?

o Give out one photocopy of page 129 to each group of 3–4 learners. Learners cut up the pictures and sentences (or you could do this in advance, if you prefer).

o For each pair of sentences (**a** and **b**), one is about dolphins and one is about bats. Learners match the sentences to the correct animal.

o Groups find the two animal pictures and put them face up on each of their tables. Learners put all the sentences in another pile and take it in turns to pick a sentence and to read it to the group. The group decides whether to put it next to the dolphin or the bat picture. Learners in the first group to correctly match all the sentences with the pictures are the winners.

> **Check answers:**
> dolphins: **1** b **2** a **3** a **4** b **5** a **6** a **7** a
> bats: **1** a **2** b **3** b **4** a **5** b **6** b **7** b

6 My things

Topics animals, clothes, family and friends

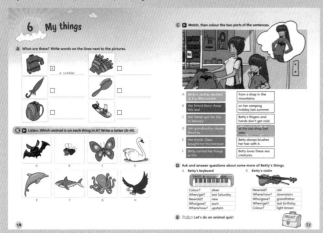

Not in YLE wordlists: *match*
Equipment needed
- Flyers audio 6B, 6C.
- Colouring pencils or pens.
- Photocopies of page 130 (one for each learner / pair of learners). See E.

(A) What are these? Write words on the lines next to the pictures.

- Say: *Look at the first picture.*
  Ask: *What's this?* (a sweater) Point to the words 'a sweater' on the line next to the first picture.
  Say: *This is an example. Now write the words for the other five pictures on the lines next to the pictures.* Help learners with any difficult words.

  Check answers:
  gloves, an umbrella, a brush, a rucksack/backpack, a snowboard

(B) ▶ Listen. Which animal is on each thing in A? Write a letter (A–H).   Listening Part 3

  Flyers tip
  In Listening Part 3, candidates only hear the words for each picture match once. If they aren't sure of the match, they shouldn't worry. They hear the conversation twice so can check or complete their answers when they hear it the second time.

- Learners look at the animal pictures.
  Ask: *Which ones do you know the words for?*
  Teach any words that are new.
  Ask: *Which of these animals do/don't you like?*
  Which of these animals is the smallest? (the fly)
  Which of these animals is the biggest? (the shark/dolphin)
- Play the first part of the audio.
  Ask: *Which animal can you see in picture A?* (a bat)
  Now look at the picture of the sweater in A. The letter A is in the box. Why? (Because Betty's sweater has got a bat on it.)

- Learners listen to the rest of the audio and write the correct animal letter in the box next to each picture in **A.**

  Check answers:
  brush – C   snowboard – D   gloves – G   umbrella – E
  rucksack – F

  Note: Point out that there are two animal pictures that are not used but that are heard: B fly and H eagle.
  Ask: *Where was the plastic eagle?* (on the shelf)
  Where were the flies? (inside the tent)

Audioscript

Listen and look. There is one example. Which animal picture is on each thing?

Girl: I love animals. Uncle Jack, I've got pictures of them everywhere. Look! Do you like my favourite sweater?
Man: Yes, it's great, Betty.
Girl: Mum bought it for me. She got it last year when we visited the zoo. It's got a bat on it. Look!
Man: I'd like one like that!

Girl: This is my favourite animal of all.
Man: The one on your snowboard?
Girl: Yes. Dad bought it for me last January when we were on holiday in the mountains. I love swans, don't you?
Man: Yes. I think they're amazing.

Girl: Here's my brush, too. My friend Mary gave it to me.
Man: Wow! What a lovely butterfly!
Girl: Yes, it's so pretty, isn't it? I keep it up there on my shelf next to that plastic eagle. I use it every day.
Man: Oh!

Man: Do you have any other animal pictures on your things?
Girl: Yes, Uncle Jack. I've got some on the backpack that I took on holiday with me when we went camping last summer.
Man: The sharks on the pockets look really dangerous.
Girl: They don't, Uncle Jack! I love them. But I hated the flies that came in our tent!

Girl: Do you like my umbrella? This has got animals on it, too!
Man: Let me see! Oh that's my favourite kind of animal.
Girl: Dolphins? I thought you liked octopuses best!
Man: No.
Girl: Well a friend of mine at school called Clare gave it to me. She went swimming with them once.
Man: That was very brave of her!
Girl: Perhaps.

Girl: And these are my new gloves.
Man: Grandma made those for you didn't she?
Girl: Yes. She wanted to make me something to wear to school in cold weather.
Man: Are they nice and warm?
Girl: Yes. And she put these purple octopuses on them. She's very clever! They were a great birthday present!

C ▶ Match, then colour the two parts of the sentences.

○ Learners look at the picture. Ask: *Where are these people?* (in a shop)
What are they buying? (sweater)
What can you see on the sweater? (a bat)
Who is the sweater for? The mother or the daughter? (the daughter)
What other animals can you see in the picture? (a goat, a lion)

○ Point to the halves of the sentences in the two green boxes: *Betty's mother decided to buy this sweater at the zoo shop last year.* Play the example on the audio again.

Point out that on the audio the information is in two sentences and is worded differently: *Mum bought it for me. She got it last year when we visited the zoo.*

○ Learners listen to the audio again and colour in the boxes round the second half of each sentence (using the same colour as the first half).

> **Check answers:**
> **B** Her friend Mary chose this and Betty always brushes her hair with it.
> **C** Betty's father got her this in January from a shop in the mountains.
> **D** Her grandma made these so Betty's fingers and hands don't get cold.
> **E** Her friend, Clare, bought her this because Betty loves these sea creatures.
> **F** Betty carried her things in this on her camping holiday last summer.

D Ask and answer questions about some more of Betty's things.

○ Write each of these five prompts on the board: *Colour, When/get, New/old, Who/gave, Where/now*
Say: *Let's ask and answer questions about the gloves in A using these words. Ask me a question about colour, please.* (What colour are the gloves?) *And what's the answer to this question?* (green)

Suggestions:
When did Betty get the gloves? (on her birthday)
Are they new or old? (new)
Who gave her the gloves? (her grandmother)
Where are they now? (on her hands)

○ Learners work in A and B pairs. Learner A looks at the information about Betty's keyboard. Learner B uses the prompts in B to ask questions about the keyboard. Learner A answers the questions. Then learners swap roles with Learner A asking and Learner B answering using the information about Betty's violin.

○ Say: *Now, choose a present that you really like. In pairs, ask and answer questions about your presents, using the questions in D.* Learners ask and answer questions about their things.

E Let's do an animal quiz!

○ Give out a photocopy of page 130 to each pair of learners. Pairs read and answer the questions.

○ Give a point for each correct answer. The pair with the most points are the winners.

> **Check answers:**
> **1** b **2** b **3** c **4** no (they're mammals) **5** hippo/hippopotamus **6** butterfly **7** yes (there are some sea animals that don't need light) **8** yes **9** a **10** c

📁 Animal fact file

○ Learners choose one of the animals in the quiz and research it either in the library or on the internet. They choose the most important information about the animal, for example its colour, size, food, where it lives and how it moves. They then write a sentence about each.

○ Learners can either draw or print out images of their animal to stick on their fact file.

○ Learners add their animal information and story to their project file. Alternatively, display learners' work on the classroom wall if possible.

7   Moving and speaking

Topics body and face, the world around us

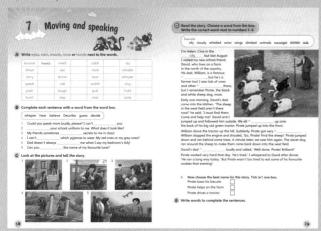

Equipment needed
o   Photocopies of page 131 (one for each learner / pair of learners). See E.
o   Pictures for Activity A.

A Write *eyes, ears, mouth, nose* or *hands* next to the words.

o   Mime bouncing a basketball and ask: *What am I doing?* (bouncing a ball)
    Which part of my body do I use to bounce a ball? (my hands)
    Point to the word 'bounce' in the first column of the table and to the word 'hands' next to it in the second column.

o   Now, 'throw' a learner the basketball and say: *(Michel) catch the ball!*
    Mime bouncing and throwing the ball again and ask: *What did I do?* (you bounced and threw the ball). *And what did (Michel) do?* (he caught the ball)
    Ask: *Can you find 'throw' and 'catch' in A?* (yes) *Which part of our body do we use to do these things?* (our hands) Learners write *hands* next to 'throw' and 'catch' in **A.**

o   Ask: *What other things can you do with a ball?* (pick it up, hit/kick it) *Everyone – stand up! Find a partner. You all have a ball. The ball's on the floor. Pick it up! Throw it to your partner! Hit the ball! Catch it! Put it on the floor. Kick it!*
    Say: *Are the words 'hit', 'pick up' or 'kick' in the box in A?* (no!)

o   Say: *Look at the monkeys in A* and ask: *What's one of the monkeys doing?* (whispering) *Do you whisper with your leg?* (no) *Do you whisper with your mouth?* (yes) *Find the verb 'whisper' in the table.*
    Ask: *Which part of our body do we use to whisper?* (our mouth) Learners write *mouth* next to 'whisper'.

o   Say: *Look at the man. What's he doing?* (smelling a flower) *What other things can you smell?* (food, plants, the sea …) *Find the verb 'smell' in the table. Which part of our body do we use to smell?* (our nose)

o   Learners write *nose* next to the word 'smell' in the table.
o   Learners look at the other verbs and write the word for the part of the body we use when we do them.
    Suggested answers:
    ears – hear
    mouth – speak, sing, shout, whistle, call, laugh, whisper, chat, taste
    nose – smell
    eyes – cry, watch, see
    hands – cook, carry, throw, push, pull, hold, catch, build, clap

o   Point to the picture of the boys in the stadium in **C**. Ask: *Where are these boys?* (at a sports match) *What are they doing?* (shouting) *Who are they shouting at?* (their team) *Do you shout when you go to watch your team?*

o   Ask: *Which part of our body do we use when we write?* (hands), *run?* (legs/feet), *eat?* (mouth), *read?* (eyes)

o   Divide the class into groups. One learner mimes a verb and the other learners in the group have to guess what it is.

B Complete each sentence with a word from the word box.

o   Whisper: *Can you hear me?* Do it very quietly so that learners can't really hear you. Ask: *Did you hear what I said?* (No!) *Why not?* (Because you were whispering.)

o   Point to 1 and to the verbs in the word box. Ask learners: *Which verb do you need to use to complete this sentence?* (hear) Learners write 'hear' on the line in sentence 1.

> **Check answers:**
> **2** Describe   **3** whisper   **4** decide   **5** believe   **6** guess

o   Read out question 6 and see if learners can guess your favourite tune. If they can't guess it, you could hum it! Then in small groups, learners take turns to ask the other people in their group question 6. You could find out which tune is the favourite for your class! (And everyone can hum it!)

C Look at the pictures and tell the story.

o   Point to the pictures in **C** and say: *These pictures tell a story. The name of the story is 'Kim can't talk today'. Just look at the pictures first.*

o   Point to the first picture and say: *Kim is going out. His mother is giving him a scarf. She says: ' Kim! You must wear your scarf today! It's really cold and very windy outside.'*

o   Point to picture 2 and ask: *Is Kim wearing his scarf?* (no) *Where is Kim putting his scarf?* (in his pocket)

o   Point to picture 3 and ask: *Where's Kim now?* (in a stadium) *Is his team playing well?* (yes) *Is he shouting a lot?* (yes) *Is he wearing his scarf?* (no) *Is his friend wearing a scarf?* (yes)

o   Point to picture 4 and ask: *Where's Kim now?* (at home) *What's the weather like?* (it's raining) *How does Kim feel?* (cold) *Where's Kim's scarf now?* (on the ground, outside his house)

o   Point to picture 5 and ask: *How does Kim feel today?* (not very well) *Who has come to see him?* (his friend) *What's Kim's friend giving him?* (the scarf)

- Learners act out the story.
- Learners tell the story in pairs. Then, two pairs work together in groups of four. One learner is the narrator and tells the story. The other three are the boy, his mother and his friend.

  Kim is going out. His mother is giving him a scarf. She says 'Kim! You must wear your scarf today! It's really cold and very windy outside.'

  But Kim isn't wearing his scarf. He's putting it in his pocket.

  Now, Kim's in the football stadium. He's shouting a lot. His friend's wearing a scarf, but Kim isn't.

  Kim's arriving home now. It's raining and Kim is very cold. His scarf is on the ground, outside his house.

  The next day, Kim doesn't feel very well. His friend comes to see him and gives him his scarf.

D Read the story. Choose a word from the box. Write the correct word next to numbers 1–5.

Reading & Writing Part 3

- Point to the dog in the picture and ask:

  Where do you see these dogs? (on a farm, in the countryside)

  Do you see dogs like these in your country?

  What names do people sometimes give dogs?

  What's a good name for this dog?

- Say: *Read the story and answer these questions:*
  1 *Which month was it?* (August)
  2 *What are the names of the people in the story?* (Helen, her friend, David, and his dad, William)
  3 *What's the dog's name?* (Pirate)
  4 *What's the dog's favourite food?* (cookies)

  Flyers tip

  In Reading and Writing Parts 3, 4 and 6, candidates should look both before and after the gaps to help them decide what kind of word is missing.

- Read out the start of the story. Point to the words in the box at the end of the story and ask:

  Can you see the word 'city'? (yes)

  Point to the word 'city' in the example in the text.

  How many more words are there in the box? (nine)

  How many gaps are there in the story? (five)

  So, how many words don't you need? (four)

- Learners read the story again and write one word next to numbers 1–5. When they finish, they check in pairs that their answers are the same.

- Check answers, reminding learners to look at the words before and after the gaps.
  1 Read the sentence: *His dad, William, is a famous …*

     Say: *We need a word for a person. Which of the words in the box is a person?* (actor)
  2 Do the same with gap 2: *lots of cows and other …*

     Say: *This needs to be followed by a …* (plural noun).

     Ask: *Which words in the box are plural nouns?* (animals, sausages and wings) Ask: *Which one is the right answer?* (animals)
  3 Ask: *What kind of word do we need here?* (a past verb) *Which words in the box are past verbs?* (climbed, built and whistled) Ask: *Can you whistle or build onto the back of a tractor?* (no) *Can you climb onto the back of a tractor?* (yes)

  4 Ask: *Which word comes before gap 4?* (very) *What kind of word comes after 'very'?* (an adjective or an adverb) *Which adjectives are in the box?* (cloudy and excited) *Can a dog be cloudy?* (no) *So 'excited' is correct here.*
  5 *What kind of word do we need here?* (a past verb) *Which past verbs are in the box now?* (whistled and built) *Can you whistle loudly?* (yes) *Can you build loudly?* (no) *So, 'whistled' is the answer.*

- Ask learners to choose the best name for the story. (Pirate helps on the farm)
- Ask: *Did Pirate lose his biscuits or drive a tractor in the story?* (no)

  Check answers:
  1 actor 2 animals 3 climbed 4 excited 5 whistled

E Write words to complete the sentences.

- Give out photocopies of the incomplete sentences from page 131 about the story (one to each pair). Ask learners to complete them using 1, 2, 3 or 4 words.

  Check answers:
  1 Pirate 2 early 3 the sheep 4 (big, old, green) tractor
  5 find 6 behind some trees 7 (favourite) cookies

  Optional extension:

- Learners read the text in **D** again and call out words that they find in it for moving and speaking. Write the words in the infinitive form on the board (or you could ask learners to come to the board and write the words).

  moving come, jump, follow, climb, drive, stop, run, come back

  speaking say, shout, whistle, call, whisper

- Ask learners to tell you which of the verbs on the board are regular and which are irregular when we talk about the past. For the irregular verbs, they should also tell you the past form.

  regular: jump, follow, climb, stop, shout, whistle, call, whisper

  irregular: come (came), drive (drove), run (ran), say (said)

Listen and find the words.

- Read out these sentences, one by one. Learners listen and find the words they describe in the first paragraph of the story in **D**.
  1 *This is the eighth month of the year.* (August)
  2 *This is not south, east or west.* (north)
  3 *This person lives on the sea on a boat.* (pirate)
- In pairs, learners choose two words from the rest of the story and define them. Then they join together with another pair, say which paragraph(s) the words are in and read the definitions. The other pair has to find the words in the story in **D**.

8   School subjects

Topics school, places

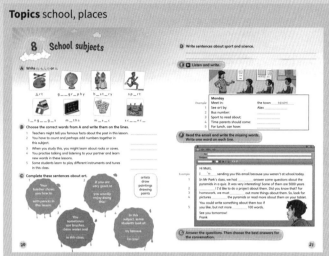

Not in YLE wordlists: *experiments, facts, partner*

Equipment needed
- Flyers audio 8E.
- Photocopies (one for each learner) of the activity on page 132 See G.

Ⓐ Write *a, e, i, o* or *u*.

- Ask: *What school subjects do you study?*
  What's your favourite subject?
  Which subjects don't you like?
  Which subjects are difficult?
- Learners look at the pictures of the school subjects and at the example. They then complete the words by adding the missing vowels.

> **Check answers:**
> geography, history, sport, languages, maths, music, science

Note: School subjects that are languages begin with a capital letter, for example *French, English*.

Ⓑ Choose the correct words from A and write them on the lines.

- Read sentence 1: *Teachers might tell you famous facts about the past in this lesson.* Ask: *Which subject is this?* (history)
  Which words tell us that the answer is history? (facts about the past)
- Learners write *history* on the line in 1. Learners read 2–5 and write the subjects.
  Say: *Remember to spell the words correctly!*

> **Check answers:**
> **1** history   **2** maths   **3** geography   **4** languages   **5** music

Ⓒ Complete these sentences about art.

- Learners look at the four paint circles. Ask: *What colours are these paints?* (orange, green, pink and blue)
  Learners look at the five words in the word box and use them to complete the four sentences about art.
  Ask: *Who's good at art? Is art one of your favourite subjects? Why? Why not?* (Learners answer.)

> **Check answers:**
> **1** draw   **2** drawing   **3** paints   **4** paintings … artists

Ⓓ Write sentences about sport and science.

Note: If you are short of time, this activity could be done for homework.

- Learners write two different sentences – one about sport and another about science, starting their sentences with two of the sentence starts in **C**. Write the sentence starts on the board for them to copy and complete:
  Your teacher shows you
  If you are very good at
  You sometimes
  In this subject, some students
- Useful words for learners to know when talking about science are 'experiment' and 'scientist'. Teach these words if learners do not know them.

Suggestions:

Sport

Your teacher shows you different ways to throw and hit a ball in this lesson.

If you are very good at running and jumping, you usually enjoy doing this!

You sometimes throw, bounce and catch balls in this class.

In this subject, some students learn to play different sports and games.

Science

Your teacher shows you different metals in this lesson.

If you are good at maths you might enjoy this lesson, too.

You sometimes do experiments in this class.

In this subject, some students learn about famous scientists.

Ⓔ ▶ Listen and write.   Listening Part **2**

- Point to the woman in the picture.
  Say: *This is Miss Bridge. What's her job?* (a teacher) *What's she doing?* (talking to the students) *What are the students doing?* (listening and writing)
- Say: *Listen to Miss Bridge. What is different about next Monday?*
  Play the example on the audio. Learners listen and answer the question.
  Answer: They don't have classes.
- Point to the example in **E** and to the word 'square' on the line.
  Say: *The children have to go to the town square on Monday.*
- Play the rest of the audio. Learners listen and write their answers. Let them listen twice.

> **Check answers:**
> **1** Magus   **2** 28   **3** tennis   **4** 4.30   **5** sandwiches

Audioscript

Listen and look. There is one example.

Woman: Now, on Monday, remember, we don't have any classes because we're going on a study trip that day. Have you got a piece of paper? I want you to write some things.

Children: OK!

Woman: We can meet at the town square.

Children: Right!

Can you see the answer?
Now you listen and write.

Woman: We can see some art by Alex Magus at the museum.

Boy: Can you spell that name for us?

Woman: Yes. It's M-A-G-U-S.

Boy: Thank you. Cool name!

Woman: Mmm. After that, we get on the bus and go to the library.

Girl: Which bus, Miss Bridge? The number 57?

Woman:	No. That bus doesn't go to the library.
Girl:	But the number 28 does. Should we catch that one?
Woman:	Yes, we should. And when we get there, you can find out about the history of the sport that we're playing this month.
Boy:	You mean tennis?
Woman:	That's right, Charlie.
Boy:	Yes. And I'm good at it. I've got a really great tennis racket …
Woman:	OK. And at three o'clock, we can go to the park!
Boy:	Great!
Woman:	And then please tell your parents to collect you back here at half past four, under the big tree outside the school.
Boy:	Right.
Woman:	Now, one last thing. We can't have lunch at school that day, so …
Boy:	Can we buy some pancakes? There's a fantastic place where you…
Woman:	(cuts in)No. Bring some sandwiches, Paul.
Boy:	OK.

Practise /s/, /ʃ/, /tʃ/, /dʒ/ /ɪz/.

○ Write on the board: *sandwiches   messages   buses*
Explain: *We say a sandwich, one message and a bus. Sandwich ends in the sound /tʃ/ and message ends in the sound /dʒ/. Bus ends in /s/. When we make these words plural, we add /ɪz/to the ends of the words.*

○ Say: *These words are plural words. They talk about more than one sandwich or bus. For example: two sandwiches, six messages, three buses. When we only have one of these things, we say a* (sandwich), *one* (message), *a* (bus). *These words end in /tʃ/ and /s/, so we add 'es' and say /ɪz/ to make them plural.*

○ *Can you find another word in sentence 3 in C that ends in the same /ɪz/ sound?* (brushes) Add this word to the board and say: *Brush ends with the sound /ʃ/. When we say 'brushes', we add/ɪz/to the end of this word, too.*

○ Add this word to the board. Circle the letters 'sh' and say: /ʃ/ *brushes.*

○ Write on the board: *a place / in some places.*

○ Explain: *This word ends in 'ce', but we say /pleɪs/. Words that end in 'ce' end with an /s/ sound, so we say the plural form like 'buses'.*

○ Say: *Look at the sentences in C. Let's find other plural words that don't end in /ɪz/.* (pencils, paints, students, paintings, artists)

○ Ask different learners to read out sentence 3: *You sometimes use brushes, clean water and paints in this class.* Make sure they say 'brushes' and 'paints' correctly.

Note: The /ɪz/ ending is also used at the end of verbs ending in the same sounds in the present simple with he, she, it. You might want to mention this here. Learners could practise the /ɪz/ sound by saying: *Mrs Bridges teaches Vicky's and Lucy's classes to make sandwiches!*

F Read the email and write the missing words. Write one word on each line.
Reading & Writing **Part 6**

○ Point to the boy in the picture and ask: *What's this boy doing?* (looking at / reading something on the computer)
Point to the email and ask: *What's this?* (an email) *Who wrote it?* (Frank) *Why?* Learners read the email and say why. (He's writing to tell Matt about what they did in history class and what Matt should do for homework.)

○ Learners read the email again and write one word on each line.

Check answers:
1 to   **2** old   **3** find   **4** of   **5** than

○ Ask learners how they find out about things like pyramids, etc:
Do you use the internet or an app? Do you read books? Do you watch DVDs or television programmes?

G Answer the questions. Then choose the best answers for the conversation.
Reading & Writing **Part 2**

> **Flyers tip**
> In Reading and Writing Part 2, candidates should read all eight possible answers before choosing which one goes in each gap. If they don't read all of them carefully, they may choose one which is wrong for the gap they are looking at, but right for another.

○ Give a photocopy of the activity on page 132 to each learner.

○ Learners read and write their answers to the questions in **A**. They talk about their answers in pairs.

○ Say: *Tell me the subjects you study.* Write the subjects on the board. Ask questions 2 and 3: *What's your best subject? Which subjects are the easiest?* Put ticks next to their best subjects and crosses next to the easiest ones.

○ Ask: *Which job do you want to do in the future?* Write the jobs the learners say on the board. Put ticks next to the jobs learners chose.

○ Ask: *Which is this class's best subject? Which subject do most people find easy? What's the most popular job? How many of you would like to go to university one day?*

○ Learners could draw bar charts for the different subjects and jobs to show the results for their class.

○ Learners read the instructions for **B**. Ask: *Who's talking?* (Michael and Mr Spring)

○ Learners read Mr Spring's side of the conversation. Ask: *What are Mr Spring and Michael talking about?* (Michael's school and future job)

○ Learners look at the example and then cross out *B Hello, Mr Spring.* in the box.

○ In pairs, learners choose the other answers and write the letters on the lines.

Check answers:
1 A   **2** E   **3** G   **4** D   **5** C

Optional extension:
Learners could then write their own answers to Mr Spring's questions and act out the conversation in pairs.

The school alphabet race

○ Ask: *Can you say the alphabet in English?* (yes) *What's the first letter?* (a) Go round the class, with different learners saying the next letter of the alphabet till the last learner says 'z'. Repeat until learners say the alphabet really quickly.

○ Say: *Now, we're going to have another race! You're going to think of things you do in class starting with the letters of the alphabet! Who can tell me something you do starting with 'a'?* (Suggestions: ask, answer) *Well done!*
Make teams of three or four learners. Each team races to write words for as many letters as possible (but not for q, x, y or z). After 5 minutes, or when a team has words for 16 letters, stop the race and check answers.

Suggestions: b borrow/bring; **c** change/clap/clean/colour/complete/count; **d** draw; **e** enjoy/explain; **f** fetch/find (out)/finish; **g** give/glue/guess; **h** hear/help/hold/; **i** invite; **j** join; **k** know; **l** laugh/learn/leave/listen; **m** move; **n** need; **o** open; **p** paint/point/put; **r** read/remember; **s** say/show/sit/smile/speak/spell/stand/start/stop; **t** take/talk/teach/test/tidy; **u** understand/use; **v** video/visit; **w** watch/win/work/write

9 In my classroom

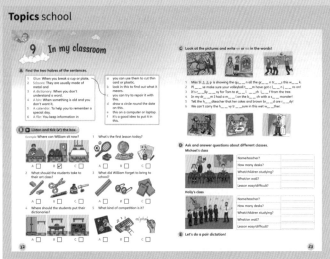

Equipment needed

o   Flyers audio 9B.

o   Six pieces of paper with a classroom object written on each one: a ruler, a bin, scissors, a book, a pen, a pair of glasses. See B.

o   Photocopies (one for each pair of learners, cut in half) of the activity on page 128. See E.

A Find the two halves of the sentences.

o   Ask: *What time is it now? What day is it today? What's the date today? Where can we look to find the time, day and date?*
    Suggestions: clocks, watches, phones, diaries, calendars, the internet.

o   Point to the names of the five things in the green box. Ask: *Is there a calendar in this classroom? Where is it? Do you have a calendar at home? Where is it? Where do you find glue, scissors, a dictionary and a bin?* (in a classroom)

o   Learners cover the orange box containing a–f with a piece of paper because they should begin by only looking at the first half sentences in the green box. Read: *Glue: When you break a cup or plate …* Ask: *How can we finish this sentence?* Write learners' suggestions on the board, for example: *You can use this to make it OK again.* Do the same with the other sentences. Teach/ revise: 'repair'.

o   Learners uncover the orange box and match the two halves of the sentences.

> **Check answers:**
> **2** scissors – **a**   **3** a dictionary – **b**   **4** a bin – **f**   **5** a calendar – **d**
> **6** a file - **e**

o   Learners look at their suggestions on the board. Ask: *Are any of these answers the same as the ones in your books?*

o   Explain that 'glue' is the word for the thing you use and also the verb for what you do with glue. Ask: *What do you use glue for at home?*

o   Ask: *Do you use an English dictionary? Have you got a digital dictionary? What kind of dictionary do you like most? An English-English dictionary or a dictionary that has words in English and in your language too?*

o   Write on the board: *glue, scissors, dictionary, bin, calendar, rubber, computer, glasses, paper, ruler, pen, notebook.* In pairs and as quickly as possible, learners write the list re-ordering it alphabetically.

o   Ask six volunteers to come to the front of the class. Give each of them a slip of paper with a classroom object written on it. Remember which learner has 'a ruler'. Say: *We have to find out (Peter's) word. It's something in this room and you can see it in the pictures in B.* Ask (Peter) *yes/no* questions, for example until the object is guessed.
    Suggestions: *Can you write with this? Can you cut things with this? Is this big? Is it made of metal? Have you got one in your school bag? Is it bigger than your hand? Is it thin? Can you draw lines with this? Is it a ruler?*

o   Continue with learners taking turns to ask questions about the other five objects.

B ▶ Listen and tick the box.   Listening **4** *Part*

> **Flyers tip**
> In a Listening Part 4 conversation, candidates hear the correct option as shown in one of the pictures. However, they also hear the two incorrect options as shown in the two other pictures. Make sure they listen carefully to the whole conversation before choosing their answer.

o   Learners look at the pictures. Ask: *Which of the things from A can you see in the pictures?* (scissors in picture 2B, glue in 2C)

o   Learners look at the questions and pictures. Ask: *Where's William?* (at school). *Who do you think is talking to William?* (a teacher)

o   Learners look at pictures in 1 A, B and C. Ask: *What subjects do you use these things for?* (sport, geography, maths)

o   Ask learners to look at the pictures in 4 A, B and C. Ask: *Where's the shelf?* (next to the cupboard, behind the table/desk, above the bookcase)

o   Play the example. Point to the answer (B – desk by door). Ask: *Did you hear about the other desks in the classroom, too?* (yes).

o   Play the rest of the audio twice. Learners tick the correct boxes.

> **Check answers:**
> **1** B   **2** C   **3** B   **4** C   **5** C

Audioscript

Listen and look.
There is one example.

Where can William sit now?

Boy: Can I sit on one of the new dark blue chairs today, Mrs White?

Woman: Not today, William. Sit at your normal desk by the door, please.

Boy: Can't I sit at the back of the classroom with my friend, Charlie?

Woman: Sorry, not this morning.

Can you see the tick?
Now you listen and tick the box.

1 *What is the first lesson today?*

Boy: Are we going to have a sports lesson today, Mrs White?

Woman: Not today, William. Your sports teacher is ill.

Boy: Oh no! Will we have Maths again, then?

Woman: No, you'll have a Geography lesson first this morning. Mr Jones will come and teach you in that class.

2 *What should the students take to their art class?*

Boy: What must we bring for our art class tomorrow?

Woman: You'll need to bring some glue. That's all.

Boy: But what about scissors? We're going to cut out some pictures from magazines again, aren't we?

Woman: Yes, but I'll give you those. I'll give you pencils and rubbers too.

3 *What did William forget to bring to school?*

Woman: Now, have you got all the things that you need at school today?

Boy: I've got all my books.

Woman: Well done, William, but you'll need other things too.

Boy: Well, I've got my new plastic ruler, but – oh no! My glasses aren't here!

Woman: Oh dear. Well, perhaps your mum can bring them for you.

4 *Where should the students put their dictionaries?*

Woman: Now take out your new blue dictionaries.

Boy: The ones in our desks?

Woman: Yes, William. And put them on that empty shelf.

Boy: The shelf that's next to the cupboard?

Woman: I mean the one above the bookcase.

Boy: Oh, OK!

5 *What kind of competition is it?*

Woman: Right! One more thing. There's a competition here in school next Tuesday.

Boy: Yes! There's a circle round that date on the classroom calendar. What kind of competition is it? Is it a music competition?

Woman: That's a good idea, but no. It's a spelling competition, William.

Boy: Does the winner get a nice prize?

Woman: Yes. A poster with all the planets on it!

Boy: Great!

C Look at the pictures and write *ee* or *ea in the words*!

○ Say: *Now we can have a kind of spelling competition!*

○ Write on the board: *see* and *sea*. Ask: *Do these words sound the same?* (yes) Underline 'ea' and 'ee'. Say: *In some words these both sound like /iː/.* Add *bread* to the board. Show learners that 'ea' can sometimes sound like /e/. Ask learners if they can think of other 'ea' words that sound like 'bread'. (weather, treasure, ready)

○ Learners look at the six pictures. Read out each sentence. Learners find its picture.

○ Learners complete the 'ea' or 'ee' words using their wordlists or dictionaries if necessary.

○ Drill the sentences. Point out that 'ea' in all the 'ea' words in sentences 2 and 3 sounds the same /i/, but sounds different from those in sentence 5 /e/.

○ Ask two learners to role play each sentence. Tell learners to add a suitable short reply. Write on the board: *Oh dear! Did they? That's wonderful! Well done! Thank you! Pardon? Great!* to help with ideas. For example, two learners mime carrying a heavy box of treasure in the rain. One puts it down and says, *We can't carry the heavy treasure in this weather!* The other learner says, *Oh dear!*

Optional extension:
For homework or in pairs, learners choose five 'ea' or 'ee' words from **C** and use them to write five different sentences.

D Ask and answer questions about different classes.

○ Say: *Listen to five questions about you and your classroom.* Read out the questions below pausing between each one. Learners write answers.
What is the name of your friend?
What's your favourite lesson?
How many children are there in your class?
Are your lessons long or short?
What can you see on the board?

○ Write the questions on the board. Learners give their answers.

○ Cross out the grammatical words to show learners how the questions might appear in the Speaking. For example: ~~What is the~~ **name** ~~of your~~ **friend**?

○ Learners look at the picture of Michael's class and the five question prompts. In pairs, they decide how to ask these questions. Write correct suggestions on the board: *What's the name of your teacher? How many desks are there? What are the children studying? What's on the wall? Is the lesson easy or difficult?*

○ Ask: *What might the answers be?* (a woman's name, three, a school subject, a map, easy)

○ Different learners now ask you the questions. Give them the following answers: It's Mrs Brown. There are 17 desks. It's a history lesson. A map. It's easy.

○ Learners could write your answers as notes, for example: Mrs Brown, 17, history, map, easy.

○ Point to one of the girls in the second picture. Ask: *What's her name?* (Holly)

○ Point to the teacher in the picture. Ask: *What's his name?* Each learner chooses a name and writes it on the dotted line. Ask: *How many desks are there?* (There are no desks.) Learners write *0* in the second box.

○ Ask the other three questions. Learners write their answers in the third, fourth and fifth boxes.

○ In pairs, learners ask and answer questions about Holly's class. When they finish, ask: *Were the answers you wrote and the answers you heard the same?*

E Let's do a pair dictation!

○ Learners work in A and B pairs. Give out photocopies (cut in half) of the activity on page 128 They should **not** show their texts to each other.

○ Learner A starts by reading out their text. When they reach the first gap, Learner B reads the next part of the text and Learner A writes the two missing words. Learner B then continues reading until they reach a gap. Learner A dictates the two missing words for Learner B to write.

○ Learners continue in this way until they complete the text. They then check their spelling by comparing the texts against what they have written.

10 Clothes, animals and school

Topic clothes, animals, school

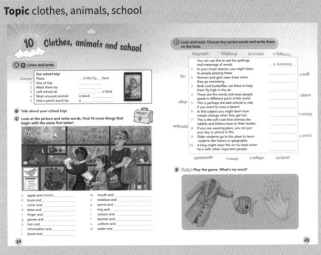

Equipment needed

O   Flyers audio 10A.

A ▶ Listen and write.

Listening Part **2**

O   Write on the board: *to the countryside   to the beach   to the mountains   to the city   to the forest*

O   Ask: *What did you do last weekend? Did you go somewhere?* Point to the board and ask: *Did you go to any of these places?* Tell learners they can choose one of the places and pretend they went there if necessary. Working in pairs, learners ask and answer the same question.

O   Ask further questions, giving suggested answers.
How did you go there? By helicopter?
What time did you leave home? At eight o'clock?
What did you see? An alien?
Where did you have lunch? On an island?
Give learners time in their pairs to think of real or invented answers.

O   Ask 2–3 pairs to tell the others about their real or imagined weekend trip.

O   Tell learners they are going to hear a girl telling her grandfather about her school trip. Learners look at the example. Ask: *Where did the girl go?* (to a butterfly farm) Explain that a butterfly farm isn't a place where they sell butterflies to eat! It's a place where visitors can go to see many different kinds of butterflies, other insects and sometimes birds and small animals, too. To help learners understand, they can see the children at the butterfly farm in the picture in **C**.

O   Learners look at the questions.

O   Play the audio. Learners listen and write the answers.

> **Check answers:**
> **1** Monday   **2** (school) bus   **3** nine thirty/9.30   **4** swan
> **5** waterfall

O   Ask: *Did the girl say they went by train?* (no) Ask if anyone can remember what she said. (The driver took us there in the school bus.)

O   Teach/revise 'by plane', 'by train', 'by boat' etc. (It's unusual to say 'by bike'.) Ask learners for other ways to say the same thing, for example, *We flew there on a big plane. We rode there on our bikes.* You could also teach 'on foot'. Note that in American English it's also possible to say 'by foot'.

Audioscript

Listen and look.
There is one example.

Girl: Grandpa, look at this picture on my phone. I took it on our school trip!

Man: Wow! It's lovely. Where did you go?

Girl: To a butterfly farm. It was brilliant there. Everything was so interesting.

Man: Good!

Can you see the answer? Now you listen and write.

Man: Which day did you go to the butterfly farm?

Girl: On Monday. We took some pictures while we were there and had to make a poster about it later in the week.

Man: I see. Was the butterfly farm far away? Did you have to go by train?

Girl: Not this time. The driver took us there in the school bus. It didn't take very long to get there.

Man: And were you there all day?

Girl: No. We left school at nine o'clock … sorry, it was half past nine.

Man: Quite early then. Tell me more. What did you see there?

Girl: Hundreds of really beautiful insects. I loved visiting the part where they had all the butterflies but they had a few unusual birds and other animals there, too. There was a black swan! That was the most unusual thing I saw there, I think.

Man: And did you give it something to eat?

Girl: No! They have to eat special food, Grandpa. But there was a surprise for us when my friends and I got hungry!

Man: What do you mean?

Girl: Our teachers gave us a picnic.

Man: Great! Did you eat your picnic outside?

Girl: Yes, next to a waterfall. It was really pretty but you can't swim there.

Man: Oh!

Girl: Come and look at my homework. I described everything I saw. My teacher said it was very good!

Man: In a minute! OK? I want to make a cup of tea first.

Girl: Ha ha. All right!

B Talk about your school trip!

O   Divide learners into small groups. Ask learners to invent an exciting school trip.

O   Groups talk about their trip and then write a list of the main details as if it was something they did last week. Write some questions on the board to prompt ideas if necessary.
Suggestions: *Where did you go? Who did you go with? What time did you leave? How did you get there? What did you see/learn there? Did you do a project before or after the trip? What was the trip like? What was the best part of the trip? Would you like to go there again? Why?*

O   Encourage learners to be creative with their ideas! They don't have to be realistic; for example: the trip could be to the moon to find out more about aliens or to a space station to learn about being an astronaut or travelling in space.

o   One learner in each group (with support from the others) then tells the rest of the class about their school trip.

o   Groups could draw pictures of the trip and write commentaries in present tenses, for example: *Leaving school! Look! We're on the moon!* or use the pictures to illustrate a summary of the trip which they write in the simple past tense.

C   Look at the picture and write words. Find 16 more things that begin with the same first letter.

o   Learners look at the picture. Say: *I can see something that begins with the letter 'b'. Can you?* Learners answer (box, belt, bat, butterfly etc).

o   Learners look at the list of words. In groups of 3–4, they find at least one more thing in the picture that begins with each of the letters and write them on the dotted lines.

o   If learners enjoy competitive games, say that for every word they find, their group gets one point. Acknowledge the highest scorers as winners.

o   After a few minutes, check answers. Accept any reasonable answer.

Suggested answers:

b   belt, bat, butterfly
c   coat, cage, cheese, countryside
d   dinosaur, drink
f   fish, flower, food, feet
g   glass, grape, glasses
h   hand, head, handbag
i   insect, internet
l   leg, light, leaf
m   mouse, moon, money
n   number, neck, nose
p   pencil, person, picture, pocket
r   rucksack, rock
s   screen, snake, spot, stripe, sweater, shell, star
t   tooth, tail, tree
u   umbrella
w   wing, watch, watermelon, water, wall

Learn about insects

o   To extend this practice, for homework, ask learners to research a type of butterfly or other insect they are interested in and to complete a simple fact sheet about it. They could do this by answering the following questions in complete sentences:

What kind of butterfly
or insect is it?   This is a ....
Where does it live?   It lives in ....
What does it look like? It's very .... / Its body is .... /
                         It's got ....
How big is it?   It's ....
Why do you like it?   I like it because ....

o   Learners add their insect fact sheet to their project file. Alternatively, display these on the classroom walls if possible.

D   Look and read. Choose the correct words and write them on the lines.

Reading & Writing Part 1

Flyers tip

In Reading and Writing Part 1, the definitions usually come from only three or four topic groups. Note that here the definitions are animal words, things you wear or school words. Make sure learners understand that the words above, below and to the sides of the definitions are the possible answers and they know they will not need to use all the answers.

o   Learners look at the sentences and possible answers. Ask: *How many questions are there?* (10 plus the example). *How many answers are there?* (15). Check that learners know they do not need to use four of these answers.

o   Look at the example together. Point out that because the definition contains 'This', the answer cannot be a plural noun.

o   Tell learners to draw a line through *a dictionary* to show this cannot be another answer.

o   To make the practice as authentic as possible, learners work on their own. They read the definitions and write the answers.

Check answers:

1 instruments   **2** swimsuits   **3** wings   **4** languages   **5** a camel
6 science   **7** fur   **8** a pocket   **9** a college   **10** a crown

E   Play the game. What's my word?

o   Learners look at the picture in **E**. Ask: *What can you see?* (a fish, a coat and a hand). Write these words on the board and ask: *What's the same about these words?* Learners guess. (They all have four letters.)

o   Ask learners to help you describe each word. Point to the fish and say: *This is an ... ?* (animal) Point to the coat and say: *This is something you can ... ?* (wear). Point to the hand and say: *This is part of your ... ?* (body)

o   Say: *Now I'm going to think of an animal, clothes or body word and you must guess it. You can ask questions about it, but I can only answer 'yes' or 'no'.*
Help learners by writing example questions on the board:
Is it an animal? Is it something you can wear on your head?
Is it on your face? Is it big? Is it red?

o   Point to the board and say: *You can ask questions like these, but in this game, the answer must be an animal, something you wear or a part of your body <u>and</u> the word must only be four letters long!*

o   Think of your word. Suggestions: *bear, bird, duck, frog, lion, boot, shoe, sock, belt, ring, foot, hair, neck, nose, knee.* Learners ask *yes/no* questions and guess what it is.

o   Divide learners into groups of 3–4. They play the same game in their groups taking turns to choose a word. If they need help, learners can look through units one to ten in the Student's Book for ideas.

o   Stop the game when everyone has had the opportunity to choose a word and answer the group's questions.

o   If you want to extend this game, include items that learners can see in the classroom.

11 Visiting different places

Topics the world around us, sports and leisure

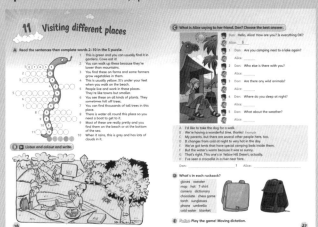

Equipment needed

- Flyers audio 11B.
- Colouring pencils or pens. See A and B.
- Two sets of questions. Each set should be written on different coloured strips of paper (eg blue and yellow). See E.

A Read the sentences then complete words 2–10 in the S puzzle.

- Learners read the first sentence. Ask: *What is this?* Point to the word 'grass'. Note that the last 's' of the word is already there in the snake. In pairs, learners think of another sentence that could describe grass. Write their suggestions on the board.
  Suggestions: *You walk on it. You can sit on it. You see it in parks. People play football/tennis on it. It needs water and sun. It's a kind of plant. Horses eat it.*
- In pairs, learners read sentences 2–10 and, in pencil, write the other letters of each word around the 's' in the snake. Tell them not to worry about the last word in the snake for now.

  > **Check answers:**
  > **2** hill(s) **3** field(s) **4** (s)and **5** village(s) **6** leave(s) **7** fore(s)t
  > **8** i(s)land **9** (s)hells **10** (s)ky

- Make sure learners have purple, orange, green, pink and blue colouring pencils. Read out these instructions, allowing learners time to colour each set of letters.
  Colour all the circles purple where you can see an 's'.
  Now find two 'n's and colour those circles orange, please.
  Can you find five 'a's? Colour those circles green.
  There's only one 'k'. Colour that circle pink.
  And now colour the six 'e' circles blue. Good!
- Learners now complete the puzzle by writing the colour-coded letters in the purple, orange, green, pink and blue circles to make the five-letter word 'snake'.
- Ask learners to look at the picture in **C**. Ask: *Where is the girl?* (in the desert) Ask: *Do some snakes live in the desert?* (yes) Learners write *desert* across the end of the snake's tail after 11.
- Say: *Look at your snake word pictures now! Let's make another snake word picture like this.*
- In pairs, learners make their own snake word pictures using the letter 'e' instead of 's'. They do not have to write the definitions, just the words crossing the snake's back.

- Give each pair a separate piece of paper. Say: *Draw a long snake. Put 10 'e's on its back.* Give learners time to do this, then say: *Now look at page 26 in your books again and find 10 words with the letter 'e' in them. Write them on your snake. Be careful! Put the 'e's in the right place!*
  Suggestions: green, gardens, vegetables, yellow, feet, beach, people, place, trees, water, sea, grey
- Learners add their snake patterns to their project file. Alternatively display the puzzles on a classroom wall if possible.

B ▶ Listen and colour and write.   Listening Part 5

> **Flyers tip**
> In Listening Part 5, candidates have to write a word from the vocabulary lists in the picture. The word will not be spelt out and is usually a noun. They need to write the word in the correct place and to spell the word correctly to gain the mark. The word they are told to write will make sense in the context – for example: *Write 'pens' on the box that you can see on the teacher's desk.*

- Learners look at the picture. Say: *These boys are on holiday.* Ask: *Where are they?* (in the country[side])
  What are the boys doing? (having a picnic on the grass) *What kind of animal can you see on the nearest hill?* (a goat)
  One goat is at the top of the hill. Where's the other one? (at the bottom of the hill)
- Play the example on the audio. Ask:
  What did the boy colour in the picture? (the rucksack)
  What colour did he use? (green)
  Whose rucksack is green? (the boy with the parrot)
- Play the rest of the conversation. Pause the audio to give learners 15 seconds the first time they hear each instruction. The second time, do not pause the audio (pauses in second listening are usually 10 seconds).

> **Check answers:**
> **1** Colour goat at bottom of hill – brown
> **2** Colour the boy on the right's cap – blue
> **3** Write 'White' on the board under the cloud
> **4** Colour empty plate - orange
> **5** Write 'Kiwi' on the box by the sandwiches

Audioscript

Listen and look at the picture. There is one example.

Woman:	Hi, Charlie. Do you like this picture?
Boy:	It's quite funny. Can I colour it?
Woman:	Of course. What would you like to colour first?
Boy:	Well, can you see the boy with the parrot on his shoulder?
Woman:	Yes.
Boy:	I'd like to colour his backpack. There! It's green now.

Can you see the green backpack? This is an example. Now you listen and colour and write.

1	Boy:	What else can I colour?
	Woman:	What about one of the animals?
	Boy:	Which one?
	Woman:	The goat at the bottom of the waterfall.
	Boy:	OK. Is the water in that stream deep?
	Woman:	I don't know! Use the colour brown for that one, please.
	Boy:	Sure!
2	Boy:	What can I do next?
	Woman:	Can you see the boys' baseball caps?
	Boy:	Yes. Can I colour the one that the boy on the right is wearing?
	Woman:	Good idea!
	Boy:	How about blue? Is that all right?
	Woman:	Yes, that's fine. Thank you.

3	Woman	Now I'd like you to write something.
	Boy:	OK. On the board under the cloud?
	Woman:	Yes.
	Boy:	Can I call that place Sky Hill?
	Woman:	We need a longer word than that. I'd like to choose the name, White Hill instead.
	Boy:	It isn't its colour, but OK …
4	Woman:	What would you prefer to colour next?
	Boy:	The empty plate, I think.
	Woman:	OK. Use purple, please. No, actually, orange is a better colour for that.
	Boy:	All right. No problem.
	Woman:	Great!
5	Woman:	And let's write another word now.
	Boy:	Where?
	Woman:	On the flat box by the sandwiches.
	Boy:	OK. Is it something you can eat? I can see the word 'Pie' on it!
	Woman:	Good guessing! Put the word 'Kiwi' above that.
	Boy:	Right… Does that taste good?
	Woman:	It's delicious! And this picture looks great now. Well done!
	Boy:	Thanks!

C What is Alice saying to her friend, Dan? Choose the best answer.

Reading & Writing Part 2

- Learners look at the picture. Say: *This girl is on holiday too*. Ask: *Where is she?* (in the desert)
  What can you see behind her? (a tent)
  What kinds of animals can you see? (camels and a beetle)
  How many camels are there? (two)
  One camel is standing next to the girl's tent. What's the other camel doing? (drinking water)
- Point to the girl and say: *The girl's name is Alice. What's in her hand?* (a phone). Say: *She's talking to a friend. What is she saying? Guess!* Learners make suggestions, for example: *It's really hot here! I'm having a great holiday! I can ride camels now!*
- Point to the instruction for **C**. Ask: *What's Alice's friend's name?* (Dan)
- Tell learners to close their books for a moment. Read the example: *How are you? Is everything OK?* Ask: *Who is asking this? Guess! Is it Dan or Alice?* (Dan) Say: *Listen to three answers. Which one is the best answer to Dan's question?* Read out Alice's first three possible answers: *I'd like to take the dog for a walk. We're having a wonderful time, thanks! My parents, but there are several other people here too.* Ask: *Which is the best answer?* (We're having a wonderful time, thanks!)
- Learners open their books again and see the example answer **B**. In pairs, learners now read the rest of the conversation. They choose Alice's answers and write the correct letters on the dotted lines.

  Check answers:
  1 G **2** C **3** H **4** E **5** D

- In pairs, learners think of one more question that Dan can ask Alice.
  Suggestions: What did you do yesterday? Which places have you visited? Is it easy to ride a camel?
  They write the question on Dan's last line.
- Learners change pairs and role play the conversation, taking it in turns to ask the questions. They add their own question at the end. The other learner replies.

D What's in each rucksack?

- Write the words *rucksack* and *backpack* on the board. Point to the spellings to show how similar the words are and make sure learners understand they mean the same. Explain that backpack is American English but that people often use this word in Britain now, too.
- Ask: *What do you bring to school in your bag?* Learners take it in turns to suggest objects that may or may not be listed in the box.
  Suggestions: scarf, gloves, books, pens, pencils, rubber, diary, letter, scissors, box, apple, sweets, sandwiches, memory sticks, ball, money, tickets, games.

- Write 12 suggested objects on the board. Learners choose eight things and write them in a list in their notebook.
- Ask one learner to say the eight things they wrote. As this learner lists items, the other learners put their hands up to show they also wrote this item.
- Learners look at the green and red rucksacks. Ask: *Whose rucksacks are these?* If learners don't recognise them from the pictures in **B** and **C**, say: *Here's the boy's green rucksack in picture B and the girl's rucksack in picture C.*
- Learners work in groups of 3–4. They look at the words in the box and choose which things to put in each rucksack. They must agree which eight things to put in each one. They write their chosen objects next to the green or red rucksack.
  Suggested answers:
  (green) umbrella, gloves, sweater, map, chess game, torch, chocolate, blanket
  (red) phone, sunglasses, T-shirt, cold water, camera, dictionary, hat
- Learners find and circle three nouns in this unit that have 'ch' in their spellings. (beach, chess, chocolate) Ask: *Can you remember the boy's name in B, too?* (Charlie)
- Say, making sure you model /tʃ/in the pronunciation of each 'ch': *I ate chocolate and played chess with Charlie on the beach!*
- Learners repeat the phrase together. Then, beginning with one confident learner, each learner repeats the sentence to the person next to them. Learners continue until everyone in the class has said the sentence to another person.

E Play the game! Moving dictation.

- Put each set of previously prepared questions in different parts of the classroom, face down.
- Divide the class into groups A and B. Then divide each group into pairs. Each pair must have a pencil and some paper. One learner in each pair collects a question from their set (a blue question for A learners and a yellow question for B learners). The first learner dictates the question to their partner who writes it on their shared piece of paper. The second learner in each pair then collects and dictates another question.
- Pairs from group A and group B, read, ask and answer their questions.

  Suggested questions:

Set A	**Set B**
Are you afraid of beetles?	Would you like to ride a camel?
What colour is your rucksack?	What colour is your phone?
Do you live in a town or in a city?	Do you live in a house or in a flat?
Who do you talk to on the phone?	Who do you go on holiday with?
What's your favourite place?	What's your favourite animal?
Do you sometimes go on picnics?	Do you sometimes go camping?

  For larger groups:

- Learners work in pairs. Give each pair a piece of paper and make sure they have pencils. Say: *Try to remember my eight questions! Listen carefully to each question and write down one word to help you.*
- Read out the first question (see above) adding extra stress to the key word 'beetles': *Are you afraid of **beetles**?* Continue asking the questions, stressing key words. Give pairs time between questions to talk quietly together and write their reminder words.
- Ask: *Can you remember any of my questions?* Learners look at their key words and ask you any questions they can remember. Prompt them with the first word to help them if necessary. Reply to their questions with simple short answers. Repeat any questions that nobody could remember.
- Learners ask and answer questions in a chain around the classroom.

12 A journey into space

Topics the world around us, names

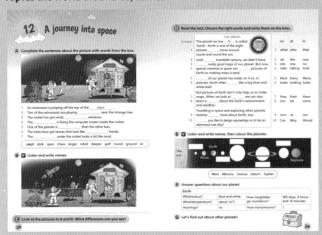

Not in YLE wordlists: *Celsius, degree*

Equipment needed

o Flyers audio 12B, 12E.

o Colouring pencils or pens.

o Photocopies of the tables on page 134 (one for each group of six learners, cut up) and 135 (one for each learner). See G.

Ⓐ Complete the sentences about the picture with words from the box.

o Learners look at the first picture and say what they can see. Write suggestions on the board, for example: *astronauts, planet, robot, TV, space, sky, tree, leaves, golf, spaceship*

o Read out sentence 1: *An astronaut is jumping off the top of the steps*. Ask: *Where is this astronaut now?* (in front of the rocket/spaceship)

o Learners complete sentences 2–7 about the picture, using the words in the box.

> **Check answers:**
>
> **2** golf **3** round **4** robot **5** larger **6** open **7** ground

Ⓑ ▶ Listen and write names.

o Learners listen and write the names of the robot and three astronauts on the lines under the picture.

o Play the audio. Check answers by pointing to the robot and the three astronauts in turn. Ask: *What's the robot's / this astronaut's name? How do you spell their name?*

o Check learners are understanding and pronouncing the five vowels, 'a', 'e', 'i', 'o' and 'u' correctly. Learners will usually hear the spelling of a name or place and have to write it on the form in Listening Part 2.

> **Check answers:**
>
> (from left to right): Glustida, Yebarchi, Paviol, Zenif

Audioscript

Can you see the robot in this picture? You can? Good! The robot's name is Zenif! You spell that Z-E-N-I-F. Now look at the three astronauts. The one in the middle is behind the net. His name's Yebarchi. I'll spell that for you. It's Y-E-B-A-R-C-H-I. The astronaut that's jumping out of the rocket has a really unusual name, too. He's called Paviol. That's P-A-V-I-O-L. Can you see the third astronaut? She's at the front of the picture. Look! She's playing badminton too! Her name's Glustida. Write her name now. You spell it G-L-U-S-T-I-D-A.

Ⓒ Look at the pictures in A and B. What differences can you see?

Speaking Part 1

> **Flyers tip**
>
> In Speaking Part 1, the examiner says something about his/her picture first. Candidates should listen carefully. The examiner's sentence will help them to form their own sentence. For example:
>
> Examiner: *In my picture, there are two cars.*
>
> Candidate: *In my picture, there are three (cars).*
>
> Examiner: *In my picture, the children are sitting down.*
>
> Candidate: *In my picture, the children are running.*

o In pairs, learners look at the two pictures in **A** and **B** and talk about the differences. Ask: *How many differences can you see?*

o Read out the following sentences about the picture in **A**. Learners listen and say how picture **B** is different.

In my picture:

There are two astronauts who are playing golf. (The two astronauts are playing **badminton**.)

There are two trees with leaves. (The two trees have **flowers**.)

The robot is watching television inside the spaceship. (The robot is **cooking** inside the spaceship.)

We can see three other planets in the sky. (We can see **one** other planet.)

There isn't a rocket in the sky. (There **is** a rocket in the sky.)

The astronauts are wearing orange gloves. (Their gloves are **white**.)

Note: There are a total of nine differences between these two pictures. Other differences are: rock behind / not behind the tree, jumping astronaut looks happy/sad, robot's head is square / robot's head is round.

In the test, candidates will only be asked to talk about five differences.

Ⓓ Read the text. Choose the right words and write them on the lines.

Reading & Writing Part 4

o Write the following questions on the board. Learners read through the text quickly to find the answers.

1 *What is the name of the planet where we live?* (Earth)

2 *How many planets move round and round our sun?* (eight)

3 *What does our planet look like from space?* (a blue and white ball)

o Ask: *How many words are missing from the text?* (ten plus the example) For each gap, learners choose from three words (on the right) and write one word in each gap.

> **Check answers:**
>
> **1** that **2** the **3** any **4** take **5** Most **6** looks **7** them **8** lot
> **9** us **10** Would

E ▶ Listen and write names, then colour the planets.

o Point to the planets in the picture.
   Ask: *What are these?* (planets)
   How many planets can you see? (eight)
   Where is our planet? (Learners point and say: *here*)
   How many planets are there between Earth and the sun? (two)
   What colour does our planet look from space? (blue and white)

o Say: *You are going to listen to a man and a girl talking about this picture.*
   Play the first part of the audio. Stop the audio and check learners understand that the planet which is nearest the sun is called Mercury.

o Play the rest of the audio. Learners listen and find the names of the planets in the box, then copy them above or under the correct planet. Play the audio again. This time, learners listen and colour the planets.

> **Check answers:**
> (from left to right)
> First planet from the sun: Mercury (brown)
> Fourth planet from the sun: Mars (red)
> Fifth planet from the sun: Jupiter (a red spot and orange and yellow stripes)
> Sixth planet from the sun: Saturn (yellow)
> Seventh planet from the sun: Uranus (light blue)

Audioscript

Listen and write the names of the planets and then colour the planets.

1 Girl: Dad, I have to write the names of the planets and colour this picture. Can you help me?
   Man: All right. Find the planet that's nearest the sun.
   Girl: Do you mean the smallest planet?
   Man: Yes. Colour it brown. That's the colour of Mercury in space.
   Girl: Mercury? OK!

2 Man: Now, look for the biggest planet. Its name is Jupiter.
   Girl: And what colour is Jupiter?
   Man: Well, first, draw a red spot on that planet.
   Girl: And then what must I do?
   Man: Put some orange and yellow stripes on that planet.
   Girl: All right!

3 Man: Four of the planets have rings round them? Can you see?
   Girl: Oh yes! What's the name of this planet, the one with the most rings?
   Man: That's Saturn.
   Girl: And I know what colour Saturn is! It's yellow!
   Man: That's right! Use that colour!

4 Girl: Which planet is between Saturn and Neptune?
   Man: That's Uranus. And Uranus is the same colour as Neptune.
   Girl: So, it's light blue, then?
   Man: That's right! Make it that colour.

5 Man: The last planet to colour is Mars.
   Girl: Wait a minute! Mars is the red planet, isn't it!
   Man: That's right!
   Girl: Great. I've got the right pencil here then. Thanks, Dad. That's the end of my homework!

F Answer questions about our planet.

o Revise or teach learners how to say temperatures in English.

o Write on the board: *16°C.* Ask: *How do you say this temperature?* (sixteen degrees celsius/centigrade)

o Do the same with this temperature: *-75°C.* (minus 75°C / 75 degrees below zero)
   Practise saying other temperatures.

o Point to the table in **F**. Say: *Look at the five questions about Earth. I don't know anything about this planet, but you do, so I'm going to ask you some questions.*
   Ask different learners these questions:
   What colour is the Earth when you look at it from space? (blue and white)
   How many moons has Earth got? (one)
   What's the temperature on Earth? (about 14°C)
   Has Earth got any rings round it? (no)
   How long does it take for Earth to travel round the sun? (365 days, 6 hours, 16 minutes)

o Repeat this once or twice more, asking different learners to answer.

G Let's find out about other planets!

o Ask: *Would you like to travel in space? Why / Why not?*
   Which planets would you like to visit?
   How long might the journey be? Guess!

o On the board, write the questions you asked in **F** removing the word 'Earth'.

o Cut up the six tables with the information about the planets on page 134. Divide the class into groups of six learners. Give one table to each learner in the group. Then give each learner in the class a copy of page 135 with six empty tables too.
   In their groups, learners take it in turns to answer questions about the planet in their table. All six learners write the information in the appropriate box in their empty tables.

o Write questions about the six planets on the board. In pairs, learners write the answers, without looking at the tables, then in groups of six, they look at the tables to check their answers.
   How many of the six planets have got rings? (three)
   Which planet is the hottest? (Venus)
   Which planet takes the longest to go round the sun? (Neptune)
   Which planet has got the most named moons? (Jupiter)

> **Planet poster**
>
> o Learners choose one planet and make a poster about it.
> o They name, draw and colour the planet and write the information they have learned in this lesson on their poster. They can add any other information they find on the internet or in books.
> o Display the posters round the classroom.

Make the long space sentence!

o Say: *In these pictures, I can see trees.* A learner says your sentence and adds another word for something in the pictures in A or B. (*In these pictures, I can see trees and planets.*) Continue round the class, with each learner repeating the sentence and all the words that have been added, before then adding another word. See how long they can make the sentence!

Suggestions: *astronauts, doors, flowers, gloves, helmets, leaves, planets, rackets, robots, steps, windows; a net, rock, rocket, spaceship, TV, the ground, sky, badminton, golf*

Optional extension

Learners could make a long sentence about things that are NOT in these pictures. For example: *In these pictures, I can't see any clouds, waiters or tennis rackets.*

13   What horrible weather!

Topics weather, names

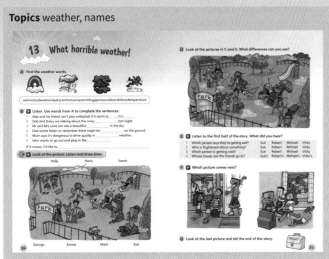

Not in YLE wordlists: *rainy, stormy, wellies*

Equipment needed
- Flyers audio 13B, 13C, 13E, 13F.
- Photocopies of page 133 (one per learner). See Project.
- Cards for Activity E.

(A) Find the weather words.

- Ask learners questions about weather: *What kind of weather do you like?*
  What do you do when the weather's fine / bad / horrible?
- Learners circle, then tell you, the weather words in the box. (warm, clouds, wet, wind, windy, dry, rain, hot, sun, sunny, storm, fog, foggy, snow, cold, ice, rainbow, temperature)
- Ask: *Which of these are in the pictures?* (a rainbow, a storm, clouds, ice)
- Write on the board: *kinds of weather* and *temperature*. Learners say which words from **A** to write under 'kinds of weather' and which to write under 'temperature'.

> **Check answers:**
> *kinds of weather:* clouds, wet, windy, dry, rain, sunny, storm, foggy, snow, ice, rainbow *temperature:* warm, hot, cold

- Point out the y-endings in the weather adjectives. Teach/revise 'cloudy' (and 'rainy' and 'stormy' which are not on the YLE wordlist). Add these three words to the board.

(B) ▶ Listen. Use words from A to complete the sentences.

- Learners read sentences 1–6. Tell learners that the missing words are all in **A**. In pairs, learners guess the missing words.
  Play the audio twice pausing after each conversation. Learners listen and check their answers. Ask: *Did you guess any of the answers?*

> **Check answers:**
> **1** rain **2** storm **3** rainbow **4** ice **5** foggy **6** snow

- Ask: *What can you do when it snows?* Write learners' ideas on the board, for example: *ski, make a snowman, make and throw snowballs, play on sledges.*
  Learners choose their favourite activity and complete the last sentence.

Audioscript

1 Girl: Oh no! Look at those big black clouds in the sky, Ben!
   Boy: If it's raining at the sports centre, we can't play volleyball outside.

2 Girl: Did you hear that storm last night, Dad?
   Man: Yes, Lily. I couldn't sleep because it was so noisy!

3 Boy: Look over there, Mum!
   Woman: Oh yes! What a lovely rainbow. It's beautiful.

4 Man: The temperature is still below zero so be careful when you ride your bike to school today, Helen.
   Girl: Don't worry, Dad. I know there might be ice on the roads.

5 Boy: It's really late, Mum. Can't you drive any faster?
   Woman: Not in this fog, Fred. It's too dangerous.

6 Girl: Look at all the snow, John. It's falling really quickly now.
   Boy: Well, let's go outside and make snowballs!

(C) ▶ Look at the picture. Listen and draw lines.

Listening Part 1

- Learners look at the picture. To make this practice authentic, make sure learners understand the instruction and then play the audio twice.

> **Check answers:**
> Lines between:
> *Zoe* and seated girl with puppy, listening to music
> *George* and boy with pockets and curly hair
> *Emma* and girl pulling sledge with kite
> *Holly* and woman with magazine and sunglasses
> *Mark* and boy with red jacket and black T-shirt

Audioscript

Listen and look.

There is one example.

Girl: Do you like this picture, Grandpa? My friends and I often go to this playground.
Man: It looks great there!
Girl: Can you see the kid on the swing? The one with blonde hair.
Man: Yes. Why isn't he wearing any shoes?
Girl: I don't know. His name's Harry. He's one of my classmates!
Can you see the line? This is an example. Now you listen and draw lines.

Girl: There's Zoe!
Man: Where's she?
Girl: On the seat. She brought her puppy with her. It's so sweet.
Man: Ha! Has she got any other pets?
Girl: I'm not sure. She likes all kinds.

Man: And who's that?
Girl: That's George. He carries lots of things in all those pockets!
Man: He's got very curly hair!
Girl: Yes. He doesn't like it very much, but I think his hair looks amazing, Grandpa.

Girl: There's Emma. Look! She's pulling her sledge.
Man: Why? There's no snow on the ground.
Girl: I know, but she likes sitting on it sometimes.
Man: And she's carrying a kite.
Girl: Yes. She loves playing with it on windier days.

Man: I think I know that person. The one with sunglasses on …
Girl: The woman who's reading the magazine?
Man: Yes. Is her name Sarah?
Girl: Sorry, no. She's called Holly.
Man: That's a surprise. She looks like one of Grandma's friends.

D Look at the pictures in C and D. What differences can you see?

o   Learners look at the two pictures. Ask: *Is the weather the same in both pictures?* (no) Point at **C** and **D** and say: *In this picture, the weather's … ?* (sunny) *but in that picture, it's … ?* (cloudy and it's raining). Say: *Look at the people's faces. In this picture, the people look … ?* (happy) *but in this picture, they look… ?* (unhappy).

o   In pairs, learners find and talk about differences.
   1   There are two children / **no children** on the swings.
   2   The woman is holding a magazine / holding **an umbrella**.
   3   The man is sitting on a sledge / **pulling** a sledge.
   4   One puppy is sitting / **running**.
   5   The girl is pulling / **carrying** her sledge.
   6   A boy is not wearing / **wearing** his shoes.
   7   The boy in the black T-shirt is combing / **not combing** his hair.
   8   There's a comic on the ground / **in the boy's hands**.
   9   There's a dog outside / **inside** the park.

o   Ask each pair to tell the class about one of the differences.

E ▶ Listen to the first half of the story. What did you hear?

Flyers tip

In Speaking Part 3, the examiner starts the story by setting the scene and saying who the people are. If candidates forget the names, they should just ask: *What was his/her name?*

o   Point to the pictures in **C** and **D** again and say: *Let's listen and find out more about these people in the playground.*

o   Play the audio. Stop at the first pause and ask: *What are the children's names?* Write the names on the board: *Sue, Robert, Michael, Vicky.* Point to the girl on the slide in the picture in **C** and say: *This is Sue.* Point to the picture in D and the boy in the red T-shirt and say: *This is Robert.* Point to the boy in the green shirt with the comic and say: *This is Michael.* Point to the girl standing between the two boys and say: *And this is Vicky.*

o   Say: *Now look at the picture in D and listen. The four children are talking about the rain.* Learners listen to the rest of the audio. Say: *Now listen again, look at the questions in E and draw circles round the right names.* If necessary, play the audio a third time.

Check answers:
1 Sue   **2** Vicky   **3** Robert   **4** Michael's

Audioscript

Four friends are in the playground. Their names are Sue, Michael, Vicky and Robert.

Some other people are there too. It's a sunny day and everyone's happy.

The weather suddenly changes. It gets cloudier and then starts to rain.

'Brr! My hair's getting really wet,' says Sue to Robert.

'And I'm frightened of storms,' Vicky says to Sue.

'Well, I'm getting really cold. I haven't got a jacket,' says Robert to Michael.

'Come on,' Michael says to Vicky and the other two children. 'Let's run to my house.'

F ▶ Which picture comes next?

o   Say: *Now look at the pictures in F. What happens next? Does the weather get better again or does it get worse?* (learners guess). Play the audio, stopping after 'It's horrible out there!'. Learners identify the correct picture. (the TV picture)

o   Say: *Listen again. Michael and Robert have four ideas. What are they?*

o   Play the rest of the audio. Learners listen and answer.

Check answers:
watch cartoons, play chess, do some drawing, watch more TV

o   Ask: *How did Michael and Robert say these things?*

o   Write answers on the board, underlining the structures:
How about watching some cartoons on the internet?
We could play chess.
What about doing some drawing?
Shall we just watch some more TV then?

o   Point to the structures and ask different learners: *What shall we do now?* (learners offer suggestions, for example, *Let's have a break!*)
Say: *Shall we look at the last picture and tell the end of the story?*

Audioscript

Listen. Which picture comes next?
Woman: The children are watching TV in Michael's living room but they aren't enjoying themselves.
Vicky: What can we do?
Michael: The weather's worse now. Look! It's horrible out there!
Robert: How about watching some cartoons on the internet?
Sue: We can't do that! Dad turns the computer off when there's a storm.
Michael: We could play chess or what about doing some drawing?
Sue: No. That's boring, Michael.
Robert: Shall we just watch some more TV then?
Girls: Yes!

G Look at the last picture and tell the end of the story.

o   Pairs or small groups write the end of the story (the rainbow picture). Write questions on the board to help them.
   1   *What are the children looking at now?*
   2   *What are they saying?*
   3   *What do they decide to do?*

Suggested ending:

The children are looking out of the window. 'It's not raining now and look! There's a rainbow!' says Robert. 'Great!' say Michael, Sue and Vicky. 'Let's go back to the park!' Michael opens the door and they run outside again.

Write your own story now!

o   Give learners photocopies of page 133. Learners write a simple story and draw a final picture to create their own ending. The story can be a continuous text or conversations between the boy and the girl, or a mixture of both.

o   Learners add a title and their own name (as the author). Display their comic book stories on the classroom walls if possible.

When the weather's …

o   Say: *Listen! How many 'w's do you hear? When the weather's warm, we want to wear our swimsuits!* Say the sentence two or three times to allow learners to count the 'w's. (There are 7.) Say each half of the sentence again. Learners repeat. Say the whole sentence. Learners repeat.

Say: *When the weather's wet, we want to wear our wellies!* Ask learners what they think wellies are. (They are plastic boots we wear in the rain.) Say the sentence again. Learners repeat.

Divide the class into two teams – Team A says the warm weather sentence and Team B answers with the wet weather sentence.

14   Are you hungry? Thirsty?

Topics food and drink

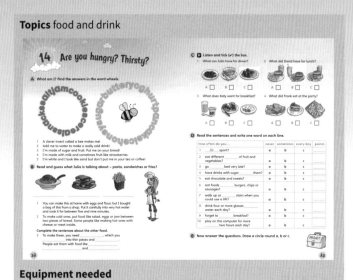

Equipment needed
- Flyers audio 13C.

Food word race

- Teach/revise 'flour' and 'yoghurt' then draw a table on the board with the following five headings: *fruit   vegetables   meat made with flour   made using milk*
- In groups of 4–5, learners copy the headings and write as many words as possible for the different categories. Give learners a time limit (3–4 minutes) for this. (All learners in each group write the words.)
- Groups call out the words on their list and write them on the board under the headings. The group with the most words (correctly spelt) wins.
- Read out the following words. If learners haven't written them already, they write them in the appropriate column.
  apple, banana, bean, biscuit, bread, burger, butter, cake, carrot, cheese, chicken, coconut, grapes, jam, kiwi, lemon, lime, mango, noodles, olive, onion, orange, pasta, pea, pear, pepper, pineapple, pizza, potato, sausage, strawberry, tomato, watermelon

> **Check answers:**
> (check learners' pronunciation)
> *fruit*: apple, banana, coconut, grapes, jam, kiwi, lemon, lime, mango, orange, pear, pineapple, strawberry, (tomato), watermelon
> *vegetables*: bean, carrot, olive, onion, pea, pepper, potato, (tomato)
> *meat*: burger, chicken, sausage
> *made with flour*: biscuit, bread, cake, noodles, pasta, pizza
> *made using milk*: butter, cheese, yoghurt

Ⓐ What am I? Find the answers in the word wheels.

- In pairs, learners circle all the words they can find in the two word wheels. Ask: *How many words did you find?* (11)
- Learners read the riddles and find answers in the word wheels. They can colour the circles with the answers in or write the answers in their notebooks.

> **Check answers:**
> **1** honey **2** ice **3** jam **4** yoghurt **5** salt

- Ask: *Which foods in the word wheels aren't answers?* (cookies, cereals, snacks, butter, pancakes, sugar)

Ⓑ Read and guess what Julia is talking about – pasta, sandwiches or fries?

- *What's your favourite? Pasta, sandwiches or fries?* Learners show which they like best by raising their hands. Learners read the first two texts and write the name of the food. (1 *pasta* 2 *sandwiches*)
  Ask: *Which words in the sentences helped you choose the answers?*
  Suggestions:
  Pasta: make, eggs and flour, hot water, cook
  Sandwiches: food, cold, … between two pieces of bread, cheese or meat inside
- Ask: *Which food did you not read about?* (fries) Learners write *fries* on the line beneath the 3rd picture. They then complete the sentences.
  Suggested answers: First sentence: potatoes, cut, cook
  Note: If learners ask you for the word 'fry', teach it here.
  Second sentence: burgers, chicken, eggs, sausages, etc.
- In pairs, learners think of their dream sandwich. They draw this, name their sandwich (for example 'Charlie's chocolate, chips and coconut sandwich') label the filling and show their dream sandwiches to the rest of the class. The class then vote for the best sandwich.

Ⓒ ▶ Listen and tick the box.

- Learners look at the pictures. Ask: *What do they all show?* (food and drink)
- Learners look at 1. Play the first part of the audio. Let learners listen twice. *Which is the correct answer?* Point to **A** – *Julia wants to have sausage and beans for dinner*.
  Note: Make sure learners understand that they will hear the food they can see in the other pictures too. (She had some soup and cheese for lunch and her father offers her meatballs with tomato sauce and rice.)
- Learners look at questions 2, 3 and 4 and name the food and drink in those pictures. The food shown is 2 burgers, chips, water, salad, banana milkshake; 3 orange juice, yoghurt, toast and jam, eggs and tomatoes; 4 sandwiches, birthday cake, pizza
- Play the audio. Learners tick the correct boxes. Play the audio a second time for learners to check their answers.

> **Check answers:**
> **1** A **2** C **3** B **4** C

Audioscript

Listen and look.

1 *What can Julia have for dinner?*
Girl: What can I have for dinner, Dad?
Man: Would you like a bowl of soup and some cheese, Julia?
Girl: Not really. I had that for lunch at Clare's house.
Man: Did you? Well, what about some meatballs with tomato sauce and rice?
Girl: Can I have beans with some sausages? I like those much more.
Man: All right.

2 *What did David have for lunch?*
Woman: What did you have for lunch at school today, David?
Boy: A burger.
Woman: What did you have with it? Fries?
Boy: No. I was very good. I had a salad.
Woman: Did you have a banana milkshake too?
Boy: No, just a glass of water today.

3 *What does Katy want for breakfast?*
Man: Good morning, Katy. Are you hungry?
Girl: Not very. What's for breakfast?
Man: I'm having eggs and tomatoes. Would you like some too?
Girl: No. Just bread with jam, please.
Man: OK. What about some orange juice or strawberry yoghurt too?
Girl: No, thanks.

4 *What did Frank eat at the party?*
Woman: Did you enjoy the party yesterday, Frank?
Boy: Yes. It was fantastic. We did puzzles and had a dance competition! But there wasn't any birthday cake.
Woman: Oh ... Were there lots of different sandwiches to eat instead?
Boy: No only pizza. But it was delicious. It was as good as yours, Mum!

D Read the sentences and write one word on each line.

o Look at the first question with learners: *How often do you do sport?*
Say: *All the questions start with How often do you …*
Ask: *Which questions have got lines in them?* (1, 2, 3, 4, 6, 7, 8, 9, 10)
How many questions have got missing words? (eight)

o Learners write one word on each line to complete the questions.

> **Check answers:**
> **2** kinds (sorts/types) **3** to **4** in **6** like **7** down **8** of
> **9** have/eat **10** than

E Now answer the questions. Draw a circle round a, b or c.

o Learners read the ten questions again and circle answers a, b or c.

o Learners pick up their books and a pencil.
Say: *Who chose 'a' for question 1? Stand up and move here.* (Point to a part of the classroom. Learners who chose 'a' move there.)
Who chose 'b'? Move here. (Point to a different part of the classroom. Learners who chose 'b' move there.)
Who chose 'c'? (Point to a different part of the classroom. Learners who chose 'c' move there.)

o Say: *Learners in group a – sorry, you don't get any points! Learners in group b – you get one point. And learners in group c – great, you get three points!*

o Do the same with the other questions. Learners write the points they get for each question. They then sit down and total their points.
Points for each question:

1 a 0	b 1	c 3
2 a 0	b 1	c 3
3 a 3	b 1	c 0
4 a 3	b 1	c 0
5 a 3	b 1	c 0
6 a 3	b 1	c 0
7 a 0	b 1	c 3
8 a 0	b 1	c 3
9 a 3	b 1	c 0
10 a 3	b 1	c 0

o Learners look at page 129 of their book and read the text which corresponds to the number of points they got.
Ask: *Who got between 15 and 24 points? Put up your hands. Not bad! Who got 25 points or more? Well done!*

> 📦 **Food poster**
>
> o In groups of 3–4, learners do a project on food.
> o They choose a food (for example: a type of fruit, rice, chocolate, honey, yoghurt, pizza, pasta, cereal, strawberries, pancakes, meatballs, milkshake) and find out about it: where it comes from, what colour it is, how it is made/cooked, how long it takes to grow, etc.
> o They find information online or in books.
> o Learners in groups produce a short text and poster about their chosen food. They add this to their project file after giving a short spoken presentation about their chosen food to the rest of the class.

15   What's for dinner?

Topics food and drink, animals, time

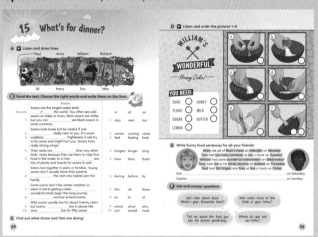

Equipment needed

O   Flyers audio 15A, 15D.
O   Internet or reference books. See A.

Listen and draw lines.

O   Ask learners: *What are your favourite animals? Why do you like them?*
O   Read out these questions. Learners look at the picture and answer.
    Where are these animals? (in the forest)
    What are they doing? (eating, dancing, skipping, cooking …)
    What kind of animals are they? (a panda, a spider, a kangaroo, an octopus, a bear, giraffes, a parrot, a swan)
    What's your favourite animal in this picture? Why do you like it?
O   Say: *I'm going to say some sentences about this picture, but the sentences are wrong. Listen and put up your hand to correct the sentences.*
    Sentences to read out:
    1   *An animal that's wearing a hat is cutting a cake into pieces.* (It's cutting a **pizza**.)
    2   *There are no animals with wings in this picture.* (There are **two** animals with wings.)
    3   *The umbrellas are different colours.* (They're the **same** colour.)
    4   *Five glasses are on the table.* (**Three** glasses are on the table.)
    5   *The table where the panda is sitting is round.* (It's **square**.)
O   Say: *Look at the names above and below the picture.* Play the example on the audio. Say: *Look at the line between Paul and the panda. What did you hear about this animal?* (He's sitting at the table. He's eating with chopsticks.)
O   Say: *Listen to the girl talking to her father about this picture.* Learners draw lines between five other names and animals.

> **Check answers:**
> Lines should be drawn between:
> 1 *Harry* and the kangaroo
> 2 *Eva* and the shorter giraffe
> 3 *Jill* and the spider
> 4 *Richard* and the octopus
> 5 *Anna* and the swan

Audioscript

Listen and look. There is one example.
Girl: I'm reading a funny book, Dad. It's for younger children really but I don't mind that. The story's about the animals in this picture.

Man: Oh! They're having a picnic. They look very strange! Some look quite scary, too!
Girl: Ha! Yes, they do. And all these animals have names. Can you see Paul? He's already sitting on one of the seats.
Man: Do you mean the panda with the chopsticks?
Girl: That's right. He borrowed those from one of the others.
Can you see the line? This is an example. Now you listen and draw lines.
Man: What are they eating? It's difficult to see.
Girl: Sausages, burgers and meatballs, I think, but the cook burned some of them.
Man: Oh dear! What's the cook's name?
Girl: Harry. He likes wearing that red baseball cap in sunny weather. He sometimes wears sunglasses too.
Man: Really? The two giraffes are having fun! Look!
Girl: Yes! The shorter one's called Eva.
Man: What's the other one's name?
Girl: I can't remember. Sorry.
Man: It's ok. I didn't know that parrots could skip!
Girl: Well, this one can!
Man: What kind of juice is that insect drinking?
Girl: It's mango juice, I think.
Man: Well, it's enjoying it! What's its name?
Girl: Jill. It's a really strange insect. If it wants to, it can change the colour of its body and legs.
Man: What a brilliant idea! I'd like to do that!
Girl: Dad!
Girl: And look! There's Richard!
Man: Which creature is that?
Girl: The one with the camera in its arms.
Man: Does it like taking photos?
Girl: Yes, videos too. It's looking at some on the little screen.
Girl: And here's Anna! She listens to rock music all day long.
Man: Is that why she's moving her wings up and down? Is it some kind of dance?
Girl: No. She's getting ready to fly off to fetch some more food, I think. I can't remember.
Man: I see. So what will all these animals do after their picnic?
Girl: Oh, I don't know yet. I have to read more of the story to find out!

What do these animals usually eat?

O   Say: *The animals in the picture are eating sausages, burgers, pizza and pasta and one of them is drinking … ?* (mango juice)
    Do these animals really eat and drink these things? (No!)
O   Write on the board: *spiders*. Ask: *What do spiders eat?*
O   In pairs, learners write what they think spiders eat in their notebooks. Ask the same question for the other animals in the picture (kangaroos, pandas, giraffes, bears, parrots, octopuses). Pairs whisper their ideas and write their answers. Two pairs then work together to compare their answers.
O   Different groups tell you what they think each animal eats.
    Suggested answers:
    kangaroos – grasses, plants
    pandas – plants, especially bamboo shoots
    giraffes – leaves
    spiders – insects
    bears – plants, insects, fruit, meat, fish, honey
    parrots – fruit, nuts, beans, vegetables
    octopuses – seafood

B Read the text. Choose the right words and write them on the lines.

Reading & Writing Part 4

> **Flyers tip**
> In Reading and Writing Part 4, candidates should read the whole text before they choose the correct grammatical words. This will give them a better idea of content and grammatical structures (for example, the main tenses used).

○ Point to the swan at the top of the text. Ask: *What do you know about swans?* Learners tell you things they know (where they live, what they look like, etc).

○ Learners read the text. Ask: *What other information about swans do you know now?* Ask further questions as necessary, for example: *What do swans eat? When do they fly to warmer places?*

○ Learners look at the words to the right of the text, and the example. They decide which of the three words is the right answer and then write it on the dotted line.

> **Check answers:**
> **1** also **2** comes **3** feels **4** longer **5** there **6** before
> **7** these **8** to **9** which **10** can

Note: The words tested in this part of the test are mainly verb forms, prepositions, conjunctions, adverbs and adjectives.

too and *also*

○ Learners look again at the first gap in the text. Say: *'Also' goes after the verb.* Ask: *Why can't we put 'too' here?* (Because 'too' doesn't go before the main verb. 'Too' goes <u>after</u> the main verb.)

○ Write the following two sentences on the board. Ask: *Are these sentences right or wrong?*
Sharks eat fish. Sharks too eat plants. (Wrong. Should be: Sharks eat plants too.)
Bats eat insects. Bats eat fruit too. (Right!)
Learners write both examples correctly in their notebooks.

○ Ask: *Where do we put 'also'? Before or after the main verb?* (<u>before</u> the main verb)
Learners write the same sentences, this time using 'also'.
Sharks eat fish. Sharks also eat plants.
Bats eat insects. Bats also eat fruit.
Learners could do a drawing of a shark and a bat!

C Find out what Grace and Tom are doing!

○ Make two groups – A and B. Group A looks at Grace on page 118 and Group B looks at Tom on page 120. Say: *Grace and Tom are making a special birthday cake today.*
The cake is a surprise! Whose birthday is it? Grace's mum's? Tom's grandma's? Write the person whose birthday it is on the line in the first box!

○ Group A reads the questions and writes Grace's answers on the lines.
For example: *Mum's. chocolate, flour, eggs, milk, sugar. brown. Grandma's kitchen. small.* Group B writes about Tom. For example: *Dad's. strawberries, yoghurt, biscuits, sugar. pink. Tom's kitchen. large.*

○ Learners work in A and B pairs and ask each other questions. Help them form full sentence questions from the prompts if necessary and then write them on the board. Learner A asks B about Tom and Learner B asks A about Grace.
Whose birthday is it? What kind of cake is Grace making? What colour is the cake? Where is Grace making her cake? Is Grace making a large or small cake?

D ▶ Listen and order the pictures 1–6.
William's Wonderful Honey Cake!

○ Ask: *What's your favourite cake? Do you ever make cakes at home? Where does your family buy cakes? When do you have special cakes?*

○ Say: *William loves Honey Cake. Look at the pictures. Which things does he use to make it?* Check learners have ticked: eggs, flour, sugar, honey and butter.

○ Ask: *Can you see an oven in these pictures?* (no) Explain that the pictures only show how William makes the cake before he cooks it.

○ Tell learners they will hear William saying how he makes his cake. Say: *Listen. What does William put in his bowl first?* Play the audio. Stop the audio at the first pause. In pairs, learners decide which picture comes first (b) and write *1* in b's small circle.

○ Tell learners that they will hear one of the pictures twice so that picture needs two numbers in it. Learners listen to the rest of the audio and number the pictures.

> **Check answers:**
> **a** 5   **b** 1   **c** 4   **d** 6   **e** 2   **f** 3 and 7

○ Say: *Can you remember? What must you do before you start making this cake?* (turn on the oven, wash your hands) *Which vegetable can you also put in William's cake?* (carrots) *How long must William cook his cake?* (half an hour / 30 minutes)

Audioscript

Hi! You might need some help but you could make this delicious cake by yourself. Right! You need a cupful of flour, some butter, two eggs, a large spoonful of honey and something else … oh, a cupful of sugar of course. To prepare, you should turn on the oven before you start and wash your hands!
First, put some sugar into a big bowl … you don't need very much because there's honey in this cake, too.
When the sugar is in the bowl, cut the butter into small pieces. Use a knife to do that. Then you can add the butter to the sugar. Mix these two things together with a big spoon. Find some flour and put that in next, then break the eggs and put those carefully into the same big bowl. Last you put the honey in. You don't need a lot. Then you mix everything together again with your big spoon.
Some people add carrots before they put the cake into the oven. That might sound really strange but carrots taste great in cakes.
You cook the cake for half an hour. Enjoy!

E Write funny food sentences for all your friends!

○ Read the five sentences aloud, emphasising the highlighted words to show stress and sentence rhythm. The whole class repeats each sentence. Explain what 'fish fingers' are.

○ In pairs, learners write their sentences for 'Sue' and 'Sophia' using as many words beginning with 's' as possible. Encourage learners to be creative. For example: *Sue ate sausage sandwiches and sweet soup for her supper on Saturday! Sophia had six salad sandwiches before she went swimming on Sunday!*

○ Ask 2–3 pairs to read out their sentences. Alternatively, pairs could dictate their sentences to other pairs.

○ For homework, learners write four more funny food sentences beginning with Betty, David, Helen and Robert.

F Ask and answer questions.

Speaking Part 4

○ In pairs, learners ask and answer the questions.

Optional extension:

○ Learners write their answers in complete sentences and add two additional pieces of information to create a short text about food about them / their family.

○ They find, download or draw pictures of their favourite food and of people cooking or eating their favourite food to illustrate their texts.
Example text: *My favourite food is fish! I love fish. Mum cooks most of our food. We usually eat in the dining room but sometimes we eat in the kitchen. My sister puts the plates on the table. Yesterday I had fish and chips. I ate 30 chips. I had an apple after my dinner.*

○ Alternatively, the class collects information about what learners had for dinner the previous evening. You could ask questions like: *How many of you had meat? Did anyone have fish? What kind of vegetables did you eat? How many of you ate potatoes? Rice? Pasta?*

○ Working in small groups, learners write a short text and find, download or draw pictures to illustrate their texts.

○ **Suggestion:** About half of us had meat for dinner. Nobody had fish. Ella and Kit had rice. Most of us had pasta. We really like pasta! Most people had some salad with their dinner. After their dinner, some people had yoghurt and some had fruit.

16   Let's have a picnic!

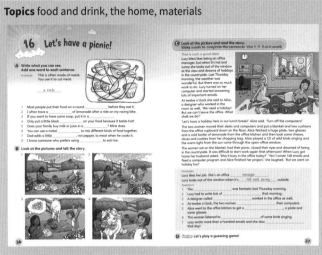

Equipment needed

O   Colouring pencils or crayons. See A and B.

O   Sentences for learners to mime. See D.

A   Write what you can see. Add one word to each sentence.

O   Make sure that learners have colouring pencils or crayons. Mime drinking a hot drink.
Say: *Mmm, this coffee is great! What's in my hand?* (a cup)

O   Mime eating something with a fork. Say: *I love eating chips! What am I picking them up with?* (a fork)

O   Learners look at the box of containers and cutlery in **A**. Say: *Find the cup. Can you see it? Colour it yellow. There's a fork in this picture too. Colour it blue.*

O   Look at the example (a knife). Say: *This is in the picture too. Can you colour it? Use your green pencil or crayon this time.*

O   In pairs, learners read the other sentences. They look for the objects in the box and write the answers on the lines.

> **Check answers:**
> **1** plate   **2** glass   **3** bowl   **4** pepper   **5** bottle   **6** spoon/fork
> **7** salt   **8** chopsticks

Optional extension:

Learners colour the other items, too. Tell them to do this using the instructions above, using colours of your choice. Check colouring.

B   Look at the pictures and tell the story.

O   This should be a whole class activity, so try to include every learner in the storytelling. First, learners look at the four pictures so they know the key parts of the story.

O   Say: *Let's tell this story together.* Divide the class into six groups. Say to group 1: *In a minute, choose the names and ages of the two children and write them down.*
Continue in the same way with other groups:
2 – the colour of the children's rucksacks and five things we think they carried in their rucksacks,
3 – their picnic place, the day they went there and the colour of the flowers,
4 – the weather that day,
5 – the colour of the cow, the cow's name and what it wants to do,
6 – six important words you can see in all four pictures.
When everyone knows what to do, learners begin exchanging ideas in their groups.

O   Ask groups for their information and write it on the board, for example:
Group 1: Maria, Tomas, 10 and 11 years old
Group 2: blue, plates, food, a blanket, a hat, a map
Group 3: the farmer's field, Friday, red
Group 4: warm and sunny, some clouds in the sky
Group 5: brown, Daisy, she's hungry, she wants to eat the apples
Group 6: butterfly, flowers, gate, apples, afraid, happy

O   Learners colour the cow, the flowers and the two rucksacks in the chosen colours.

O   Say: *Let's tell this story now.* Use the following prompts, pausing when you want learners to join in and fill the gaps with the key information on the board or mime a word, for example, 'rucksack', 'walking'.

O   In the pauses (shown here by the brackets), ask one learner in particular or everyone in the class to answer in chorus. Make this dramatic. Walk around and encourage a sense of fun while you are creating the story.
My cousins are called (Maria) and (Tomas). Maria is (10) and (Tomas) is (11).
They've both got big (rucksacks). The rucksacks are (blue) and inside the rucksacks they put things like (plates, food, a blanket, a hat and a map). They need their (rucksacks) because Maria and (Tomas) like going for walks and having picnics in (the farmer's field). Last (Friday) they put rucksacks on their (backs) and began (walking). The weather was (warm and sunny) with only a few (clouds in the sky).

O   Continue telling the story pausing for learners to fill the gaps. It's important to accept any appropriate words. For example:
When they got to the farmer's field, they <u>sat</u> down on the <u>blanket</u>, and started <u>eating</u>. They didn't <u>see</u> the <u>cow</u> that was behind the <u>gate</u>. Suddenly, Tomas saw a <u>butterfly</u>. It had beautiful <u>wings</u>. They were purple and <u>yellow</u>! He jumped up to look at it. Maria got up too. The cow, whose name was <u>Daisy</u>, opened the <u>gate</u> with its <u>nose</u> and looked at the children's <u>food</u>. Daisy wanted to eat their <u>apples</u>! Tomas was very angry. He was <u>afraid</u> too, but Maria said. 'Don't worry, Tomas!' She picked up some of the beautiful <u>flowers</u> and gave them to the cow! Daisy the cow <u>loved</u> the <u>red flowers</u>. Tomas <u>laughed</u> 'That was a really good <u>idea</u>!' he said. 'Let's look for that <u>butterfly</u> again, now.' 'OK!' said <u>Maria</u>. 'But shall we put the <u>apples</u> back in your <u>rucksack</u> first?'

O   Thank everyone for helping to tell the story. In pairs, learners then choose a name for their story. Write their suggestions on the board. Learners vote for the best one.

O   As an extension, groups of 3–4 learners could then take turns to tell a simplified version of the story, picture by picture. Each learner could say one sentence.
In Speaking Part 3, it is fine to tell the story in the present tense, for example: *It's a sunny day. Maria and Tomas are having a picnic. A cow is watching them. Tomas and Maria are watching a butterfly. The cow is opening the gate and looking at the apples. It wants to eat them. Tomas is looking at the cow now. He's angry and afraid. Maria is giving the cow some flowers to eat. Tomas is laughing now.*

C Look at the picture and read the story. Write words to complete the sentences. Use 1, 2, 3 or 4 words.

Reading & Writing **Part 5**

> **Flyers tip**
>
> In Reading and Writing Part 5, candidates shouldn't worry if they don't know the meanings of all the words in the story. They don't need to understand every word in order to answer the questions. Encourage them to enjoy reading stories and to guess at meanings that they don't know.

○ Learners look at the picture. Ask:
  Are these women in the countryside? (no)
  Where are they? (at work / in an office)
  Are they working? (no)
  Are they having a picnic? (yes)
  Is the window open or closed? (open)
  Is it sunny or cloudy outside? (sunny)
  What can you see on their desks? (computers, paper)
  What else can you see in the office? (chairs, desks, a clock, a blanket)
  Do they look bored / angry / happy? (happy)

○ Learners read the story and write any words that they don't know in their notebooks.

○ Teach/revise the words they don't know using the picture or explanations and actions. For example:
  An office *is a room in a building where business people work.*
  Mr West is Lucy West's **husband**.
  Tell one learner to **turn on** the classroom light and another to **turn** it **off** again.
  Fetch *means* **go and get**.
  Wonderful *means Great! Really good! For example The weather is* **wonderful** *today!*
  A break *is a short time when you don't have to work. Do you have a morning and afternoon* **break** *at school?*
  If an animal is **wild***, it doesn't live with people. It lives where it wants to live and has to find food by itself. Animals that live in zoos aren't* **wild***.*

○ Learners read the first paragraph of the story again and look at the two examples. Remind them that they can use 1, 2, 3 or 4 words to fill the gaps and that all the words they need are always in the story. In pairs, they find the example answers 'manager' and 'hot' and 'sunny' in the story and underline them.

○ In pairs or on their own, learners find the missing words for questions 1–7.

> **Check answers:**
> **1** weather **2** (important) emails **3** Alice **4** turned off
> **5** (cold) bottle of lemonade **6** a CD **7** fixed a (computer) program

So and such:

○ Teach/revise 'so' and 'such' to emphasise adjectives. Say: *Tell me the name of something you can see in our classroom?* (for example: desk) *What word can we use to describe a desk?* (for example: big) Write their suggestions on the board leaving a space between the words, for example: *desk   big*

○ Say: *I want to say that this desk is VERY big. How can I do that?* Write correct suggestions up on the board underlining the adverbs and using different colours for 'This' and 'is' if possible to help show the pattern: **This** desk **is** very big. **This** desk **is** really big. **This** desk **is** so big.

○ Say: *We can use another word too but we have to move some of the words.* Write the two words 'desk' and 'big' on the board again but this time put the adjective before the noun with no space: *big desk.* Then add: **This is** such a . Learners can now see: **This is** such a big desk.

○ Write on the board the following pairs of words:
  good story   long film   exciting game
  Ask different learners to use either 'so' or 'such a' with these words to make sentences. Check that learners understand they will need to use 'an' instead of 'a' before the vowel in 'exciting'.

○ Learners look at the title of the story. Ask them how to say this a different way, using 'so', 'very' or 'really'. For example: *That idea is so / very / really good!*

○ Write on the board: *What shall* **we** *do now? Let's … !*
  Ask: *What shall we do now?* Learners suggest answers using 'Let's'. Allow any classroom suggestions, for example: *Let's play games. Let's read another story. Let's learn some more words.* Write their suggestions on the board.

○ Say: *Those are all good ideas, but I've got a better one! Let's do some drawing and colouring now.*

Draw and colour.

○ Learners draw a large picture of a table in their notebooks or on a piece of paper. Tell them to draw the following things on the table. (Pause between each item to allow them time to draw.)
  Draw a big plate and a little plate.
  Draw a glass of water.
  Draw a big spoon and a little spoon.
  Draw a knife and fork.
  Draw a bowl of salad.
  Draw a bottle.
  Now colour all the things in your picture.

○ When learners have finished drawing and colouring they compare the colours in their pictures (orally). For example:
  Learner A: *In my picture, the big plate is blue.*
  Learner B: *In my picture, the big plate is yellow.*
  Learner A: *In my picture, the bottle is green.*
  Learner B: *In my picture, the bottle is green too.*

○ When learners have finished comparing pictures, say: *What shall we do now? Let's play a guessing game!*

D Let's play a guessing game!

○ Write the following situations on strips of paper:
  1 *You're carrying a bowl of hot soup.*
  2 *You're eating a bowl of rice with chopsticks.*
  3 *You're eating pasta with a fork.*
  4 *You're putting salt and pepper on your food.*
  5 *You're drinking a very small glass of water.*
  6 *You're cutting bread with a knife.*
  7 *You're putting some water from a bottle into a glass.*
  8 *You're carrying two huge, heavy cups of hot chocolate.*

○ Divide learners into two teams. One learner takes a strip of paper from you and has to mime the sentence for their team (the other team also watches). If they guess correctly, the team wins a point. If not, the other team has a chance to answer and win a point. Continue until all the sentences have been used. The winning team is the one with the most points.

17 A day's work

Topics work, places

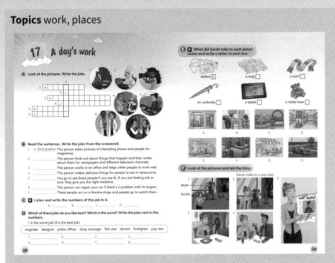

Equipment needed
○ Flyers audio 17C, 17E.
○ Cards with adjectives. See *What's my word?*

Ⓐ Look at the pictures. Write the jobs.
○ Say: *Look at jobs in these pictures. Talk in pairs. Which job is the most interesting / boring / difficult / the easiest?*
Say: *Now, write the words for the jobs in the crossword.*
Note: If necessary, point out that in pictures 6 and 7, there are two people so they need to use the plural of these words.

> **Check answers:**
> (check learners' pronunciation) **1** mechanic **2** cook/(chef)
> **3** photographer **4** journalist **5** manager **6** doctors **7** actors

Ⓑ Read the sentences. Write the jobs from the crossword.
○ Read out sentence 1. Point to the words 'a photographer' on the line.
Ask: *What other things do photographers take pictures of?* (animals, food, etc.) Learners read 2–7 and write the jobs on the lines.
Note: Remind learners to check if a singular or plural answer is needed. When it is singular, they should write *a* before the job. (See 1: a photographer.)

> **Check answers:**
> **2** a journalist **3** a manager **4** a cook/chef **5** doctors
> **6** a mechanic **7** actors

Ask questions about these jobs:
1 *Are you a good photographer?*
2 *Are there any TV programmes with famous cooks in your country? Do you watch these programmes?*
3 *Who's your favourite actor?*

Ⓒ ▶ Listen and write the numbers of the job in A.
○ Learners listen to four people talking about their jobs. They write the number of the picture (from **A**) next to each letter.

> **Check answers:**
> **a** 2 **b** 7 **c** 1 **d** 4

○ Write on the board: *I cook for people who come here to have meals.* Learners find this sentence in **B**. Ask: *Which job is this?* (a cook/ chef) Play the audio for **a** again. Learners listen and write down the words in the second sentence.

Ask a learner to come to the board and write the sentence: *I love making different meals for people to eat.* under the sentence from 4b.
Ask: *Who makes different meals in a restaurant?* (The cook/chef) *Who cooks in a restaurant?* (The cook/chef) 'Make meals' and 'cook' are different ways of talking about a cook's/chef's job. Point to the words 'have meals' and 'to eat' in the two sentences on the board. They are different ways of saying what people do in restaurants.
○ Say: *Listen to the cook again. How many sentences does he say?* (3) *When the cook speaks, how does he show us that he's finished each sentence?* Say the three sentences, making sure that your voice goes down at the end of each sentence.
Learners practise saying the three sentences. They could then practise more by reading out the sentences in 4 and 5 from **B**.

Audioscript

Listen and write the numbers of the pictures in A.
a I love my job. I love making different meals for people to eat. Our restaurant is very famous for its food.
b We have to work in theatres in lots of different places. But it's great because people like coming to see us.
c It's great when someone brings you a very old car. I have lots of fun with those. But most of our work is with newer cars. I like finding the problems and making everything right again.
d When something happens, we have to go and find out all the important things. Then we quickly send the news story to the newspaper office.

Ⓓ Which of these jobs do you like best? Which is the worst? Write the jobs next to the numbers.
○ Learners write the jobs in order of their own preference. (1 = least favourite, 8 = favourite) For example: 8 *a doctor*, 6 *an actor*, etc.
○ Write on the board: *difficult exciting dangerous important interesting boring*
Ask one learner to tell you which job they wrote next to 8 and why. For example: *I'd like to be a doctor because I think it's a very important and interesting job.*
○ In pairs or groups of 3–4, learners discuss why they like or dislike a job, using the words on the board.
○ The whole class finds the most popular job by adding up the number each job was given and finding the highest total.

Ⓔ ▶ What did Sarah take to each place? Listen and write a letter in each box.   Listening Part **3**
○ Point to the woman in the five pictures in **F** and say: *This is Sarah. She's a journalist for a very popular magazine. Yesterday, she had a very busy day.*
Point to the bottom set of pictures with places and say: *She had to take a different thing to each of these different places.*
○ Ask: *What different places can you see?*
Ask: *What can you do in these places? For example, what can you do in a bookshop?* (You can buy books there.)
○ Point to the top set of object pictures and say: *Sarah took these things to different places. How many things are there?* (six) *Which thing did she take to each place? Listen.*
○ Play the example on the audio.
Ask: *Why did Sarah take the letters to the office?* (because her computer program was not working)
Learners listen and write letters in the other five boxes.

Check answers:
teddy bear - C - funfair, scarf - G - café, umbrella - A - bookshop, map - F - hotel, tablet - E - castle

Audioscript

Listen and look. There is one example.

Where did Sarah take each thing?

Boy:	What's the matter, Aunt Sarah?
Woman:	I'm a bit tired, that's all. There was something wrong with one of my computer programs this morning. And I couldn't send any emails! I had to take a letter to an office instead because it was important. It was on the top floor of a skyscraper. The view was amazing.
Boy:	Well, the view sounds good.

Can you see the letter B? Now you listen and write a letter in each box.

Woman:	You know the prize I won on Saturday?
Boy:	You mean that silly teddy bear! It's huge!
Woman:	I know. I took it back to the funfair after my busy day at work.
Boy:	Why?
Woman:	Its fur wasn't very clean. They gave me another one. I'll give it to your cousin I think.
Woman:	Oh! I saw Helen at lunchtime, as well.
Boy:	I like her. She's really cool!
Woman:	She is, isn't she! I needed to give her back her scarf.
Boy:	The one she left in the car park last Sunday?
Woman:	That's right. I took it to the new café in High Street. We had some delicious apple pie and ice cream there!
Boy:	Wow!
Woman:	And I gave someone my umbrella today!
Boy:	Why?
Woman:	Well, I saw lots of people at the bookshop, the one next to the castle because Matt Eagle was there!
Boy:	The pop star? Amazing! Why was he there?
Woman:	He was just doing some shopping! I wanted to ask him some questions but he was too busy to talk to me. Then it started to rain so I gave it to him!
Woman:	I wanted to come home after that but I couldn't.
Boy:	Why not Aunt Sarah?
Woman:	Because I had to take a map to a hotel first. I met an inventor there yesterday. He was really nice. And he needed one. He doesn't like using his phone for that.
Boy:	Oh!
Woman:	I found one in the supermarket on the corner. He was really pleased when I gave it to him.
Boy:	So did you do any writing for the newspaper today?
Woman:	Yes. And I took some good photos earlier in the day. I used a new tablet to take those. I borrowed it from someone at work.
Boy:	Great! Where did you go to take the pictures?
Woman:	To the castle. A group of actors are making a film there. I asked them lots of questions because so many people are interested in the story. Yes ... it was a busy day.

F Look at the pictures and tell the story.   Speaking Part 3

o Ask: *What's Sarah's job? Can you remember?* (a journalist) *What do journalists do?* (Write about important people and news stories.)

o Point to the five pictures and say: *These pictures tell a story. It's called 'Sarah talks to a pop star'. Just look at the pictures first.*
   Then point to the first picture and say:

Matt Eagle, the famous pop star, is staying at the Sea Hotel. Sarah's standing outside the hotel. She wants to ask Matt some questions, but there are too many journalists and photographers on the steps there. Sarah can't get near him.

o You can continue in either of the following ways.
   1 To make this task as authentic as possible, in pairs, learners look at the four pictures and finding two or three things to say about each one, for example: (picture 2) *Sarah's unhappy. She can't talk to Matt Eagle. He's going into the building now.* Walk round and help if necessary. When learners have finished, two or three pairs tell their story.
   2 Alternatively tell the story in open class as follows.

o Say: *Listen to these questions about the second picture. Write two or three words to answer them. Don't write full sentences.*
   1 *Is Sarah near Matt Eagle now?*
   2 *What is Matt Eagle doing?*

o Ask the questions again. Different learners use their answers to continue the story.
   The story: *Sarah isn't near Matt Eagle. Matt Eagle is walking away from her on the stairs.*

o Do the same with the third and fourth pictures.
   Questions about the third picture: *What's Sarah doing now? What's she drinking? Who is coming into the café?*
   The story: *Sarah's in a café. She's having a cup of coffee. Suddenly, Matt Eagle comes into the café.*
   Questions about the fourth picture: *Who is Sarah talking to now? What do you think that they are saying?*
   The story: *Sarah is talking to Matt Eagle. He is answering all her questions about his job and hobbies.*
   Questions about the fifth picture: *What's Sarah looking at now? What can you read on the front page of the newspaper? Did Sarah talk to Matt Eagle?*
   The story: *Sarah's holding a newspaper. On the front page it says, 'Our journalist Sarah talks to Matt Eagle!' She talked to Matt Eagle and wrote about him for the newspaper.*

o Learners tell the story in pairs. They could also write it.

Play the game! *What's my word*?

o Prepare cards (One card for each group).
Card 1:	*delicious* *cool*	Card 2:	*enormous* *amazing*
Card 3:	*expensive* *soft*	Card 4:	*fun* *light (not heavy)*

o Write on the board: *sweet* Ask: *Which things are sweet? Is sugar sweet?* (yes) Write *sugar* on the board next to 'sweet'. *Is salt sweet?* (no) *What other things are sweet?* Write the words learners say on the board after 'sugar'.
   Suggestions: *apples, biscuits, cakes, candy, chocolate, coconut, cookies, honey, ice cream, jam, mango, melon, pears, pineapple, strawberries, watermelon*

o Write on the board: *a wheel, a tortoise shell, olives, Earth*
   Say: *These things aren't sweet! What are they all?* (round) *Which things are round?* (a bracelet, an eye, a ring, a plate)
   Give a card to groups of 3 or 4 learners. They write 3 or 4 things/ people to describe using each word.
   One team reads out its words. The other teams say the adjective.

Suggestions

delicious	chocolate ice cream, strawberry yoghurt, pizza, pasta
cool	trainers, jeans, program, app, band, pop star
enormous	elephant, whale, skyscraper, city, mountain, lake
amazing	view, story, person, holiday, film
expensive	necklace, ring, house, car, football player
soft	fur, cushion, blanket, towel, hair, sweater
fun	party, game, app, holiday, competition, funfair
light	leaf, balloon, cushion, plastic bag, fly, insect

18 Time and work

Topics time, work

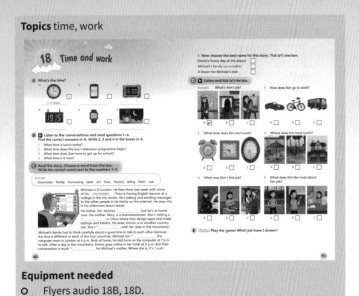

Equipment needed
- Flyers audio 18B, 18D.
- Job cards. See E.

A What's the time?

- Point to the pictures. Ask: *How many clocks can you see?* (4) *How many watches can you see?* (1) *And what's b?* (a phone)
  How do you find out the time? Do you use your watch? A clock? Your phone? Remind learners that we wear watches. Clocks are usually in rooms / on buildings, machines, etc.
- Point to the clock in **a**. Ask: *What time is it?* (3 o'clock) Point to the phone in **b**. Ask: *What time is it here?* (half past eight / eight thirty a.m.) Learners write the time on the line under picture **b**. Do the same with the other clocks and the watch.
- Draw an analogue clock on the board showing a quarter past nine. Explain that we can say: *a quarter past nine / fifteen minutes past nine / nine fifteen.*
- Change the time on the clock to twenty to eleven. Say: *We can say twenty to eleven or ten forty.* Explain: *If we want, we can use either 'a.m.' for the first 12 hours of the day (11 a.m.) or 'in the morning'. For the last 12 hours, we can use either 'p.m.' (11 p.m.) or 'in the afternoon / evening' or 'at night'.*

  Learners help each other to write the times under c, d, e and f. Say: *Now tell me these times in all the different ways.*

> **Check answers:**
> **c** four p.m. / four o'clock in the afternoon
> **d** seven fifteen p.m. / seven fifteen in the evening / quarter past seven in the evening
> **e** nine forty-five a.m. / nine forty-five in the morning / a quarter to ten in the morning
> **f** ten thirty-five p.m. / twenty-five to eleven p.m. / twenty-five to eleven at night

B ▶ Listen to the conversations and read questions 1–4. Find the correct answers in A. Write 2, 3 and 4 in the boxes in A.

- Point to question 1 and the '1' in the box next to the kitchen clock in **A**. Play the example on the audio. Make sure learners understand that lunch is going to be at 3 o'clock today.
- Learners listen and write the numbers 2–4 in the boxes next to the pictures in **A**.

> **Check answers:**
> **2 d** 19.15   **3 b** 8.30 a.m.   **4 c** 16.00

- Play 1 (the example) again. Ask: *Which other times do you hear?* (Half past three, and two o'clock.) (Sally wanted to come home at half past three. They usually have lunch at two.)
  Note: The two wrong times in the example question are the times that Sally wants to come home and the time that Sally's family usually have lunch (not the time that lunch is today!) See tip.

> **Flyers tip**
> In Listening Part 4, when there are questions about times, only the time shown in one of the three clock pictures will be the correct answer. But candidates will hear all three times in the conversation so they need to read the question very carefully.

Say: *You heard these times in question 2. Which questions do they answer?*
- Write on the board: *20.30   21.00*
  What time does the ....?
  Ask half the learners to listen to 2 again and complete the question for 20.30 and the other half to listen and complete the question for 21.00.
  20.30   *What time does the television programme finish?*
  21.00   *What time does the news begin?*

Audioscript

Listen and look. There is one example.
1 *What time is lunch today?*
Girl: Bye, Mum! See you at half past three!
Woman: Wait, Sally! You have to be back before that. Lunch is at three o'clock today.
Girl: That's late for lunch! We usually have it at two!
Woman: I know, but not today.
Can you see the number 1? Now you listen and write 2, 3 and 4.

2 *What time does the boy's television programme begin?*
Boy: There's a great programme on TV tonight.
Man: What time is it on? I want to watch the news at nine p.m.
Boy: No problem. Mine starts at quarter past seven and finishes at half past eight.

3 *What time does Zoe have to get up for school?*
Boy: Do you have to get up early, Zoe?
Girl: Not this week, because I'm on holiday. I get up at ten. But when it's school time, I have to get up at half past eight.
Boy: Do you? I get up at about seven o'clock every day!

4 *What time is it now?*
Man: Quick, May! It's late.
Woman: No it isn't. It's only four o'clock. The film doesn't start until four thirty.
Man: Oh sorry. My watch is wrong! It says 25 minutes past.
Woman: That's OK!

C Read the story. Choose a word from the box. Write the correct word next to the numbers 1–5.
Reading & Writing Part **3**

- Ask questions about the boy in the picture:
  What do you think the boy's doing on the computer – writing emails / talking to his friends / talking to his family?
- Learners read the first four sentences of the story to find out who the boy is and what he's doing. (His name's Michael and he's talking to his family on the computer.)

- Learners read the rest of the story and tell you why Michael is talking to his family in this way. (He's in London, his dad is at home, his mum is in China and his sister is in another country too.)
- Learners read the story again and write words on the lines.

> **Check answers:**
> **1** art **2** factory **3** skiing **4** use **5** later

- Learners choose the best name for this story. (Michael's family conversation)
- Ask: *Do you have friends or family who live in other countries? Do you use the computer to chat to your family and friends? Have you ever been to a place where the time was different?*

D ▶ Listen and tick the box.   Listening **4**^{Part}

- Say: *You are going to hear a girl talking about her sister's job.* Play the example on the audio and ask: *Why is there a tick in the box next to A?* (The girl's sister is an engineer and she works on roads and bridges.)
- Play the audio twice. Learners tick the boxes.

> **Check answers:**
> **1** A **2** C **3** B **4** B **5** A

Audioscript

Listen and look. There is one example. What's Kim's job?
Man: Hello. Is your sister working in an office now?
Girl: You mean Kim? Yes, but only for about an hour each day. She isn't a secretary.
Man: Is she an artist then?
Girl: She's an engineer. She designs skyscrapers most of the time but bridges as well.
Can you see the tick? Now you listen and tick the box.

1 *How does Kim go to work?*
Man: Does Kim take the bus to work?
Girl: She could do that, but she needs to drive there and to travel to different parts of the city each day.
Man: Can't she cycle? There's so much traffic!
Girl: I think she'd like to, but she needs to carry too much.

2 *What time does Kim start work?*
Man: What time does Kim have to be at work?
Girl: Well, she has to get up at a quarter past six. Then she has breakfast and leaves home at a quarter to seven.
Man: So when does she arrive in her office?
Girl: At half past seven. It's really early but she doesn't mind.

3 *Where does Kim have lunch?*
Man: Where does Kim take her lunch break? Does she go home?
Girl: She doesn't have enough time to do that, Mr Low.
Man: Is there a café in the building where she works, then?
Girl: Yes. But she usually takes sandwiches and eats them in the park. She likes doing that best.

4 *What was Kim's first job?*
Man: Is this Kim's first job? She told me she wanted to be the manager of a clothes shop!
Girl: Well, she didn't do that. But she worked at a police station once.
Man: Really?
Girl: Yes, but she didn't have to wear a uniform. She worked in the kitchen there.

5 *What does Kim like most about her job?*
Man: Is your sister pleased with her new job?
Girl: She had to study for a long time, but she loves it. She really enjoys being outside, too.
Man: Does she have to go to lots of meetings, too?
Girl: Yes, but she doesn't enjoy those very much. And she hates talking on the telephone!

What does she do? Ask and answer.

- Tell learners your answers to the questions about Kim. For example:
  I'm a teacher. I come to school by (bus) and I start work at (8.30). I have lunch (at school. I bring sandwiches with me). My first job was (in a big school in Madrid). What I like most about my job is (meeting lots of different people).
- Learners work in pairs. Each learner chooses a job they would like to do. Encourage them to be creative with their ideas. Check that learners know how to change the question forms to 'you'. Learners then take turns to interview each other asking the same questions in **D**.
- **Suggestion:**

Learner A: What's your job, Mario?
Learner B: I'm a cameraman. I make films about wild animals.
Learner A: How do you go to work?
Learner B: I go on my motorbike. It goes really fast!
Learner A: What time do you start work?
Learner B: At about ten o'clock. I don't like getting up in the morning!

- Ask 2–3 pairs to role play their interviews for the rest of the class.

E Play the game! Which job have I drawn?

- Write the jobs below on cards (one job on each card).
- Learners work in teams of 6–8. Two teams compete. One member of a team takes a card and draws a picture of the job on a piece of paper for their team. The team has two chances to guess the job. If they do not guess correctly, the other team has one chance to name the job. A team gets a point for every job they guess. Allow one minute to draw and guess each job.
- **Note**: Learners can draw pictures of a person doing the job or of things these people use in their job.
- **Suggested jobs**:

actor, artist, astronaut, bus driver, clown, cook, dentist, designer, doctor, engineer, farmer, film star, firefighter, journalist, manager, mechanic, nurse, photographer, pilot, football/tennis/hockey player, police officer, pop star, policeman/woman, singer, tennis player, waiter

19 Answer my questions

Topics the world around us, time, family

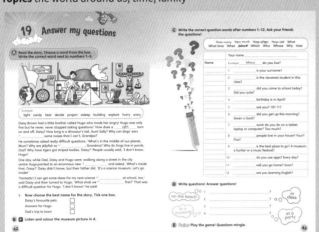

Equipment needed
o   Flyers audio 19B.
o   Question cards (one for each learner). See E.
o   Colouring pencils or pens.

A Read the story. Choose a word from the box. Write the correct word next to numbers 1–5.
Reading & Writing Part **3**

o   Write on the board: *What is plastic made of? Why is gold expensive? Who invented motorways?* Ask: *Do you know the answers to these questions?* (no) Say: *These are difficult questions! I don't know the answers!*

o   Ask: *Where can we find answers to difficult questions?* (on the internet, in books, in museums) Ask: *Have you ever been to a science museum? What did you learn/see there?*

o   Say: *This story is about a boy called Hugo Brown who asks lots of questions.* Learners read the story without inserting the missing words.

o   Ask questions:
How old was Hugo in the story? (five)
What was Hugo's sister's name? (Daisy)
Who were the children with when they saw the museum? (Dad)
What did Hugo want to look at first in the museum? (He didn't know! / He couldn't choose.)

o   Read out the example: *How does a light turn on and off?* Ask: *Why can't we put the word 'candy' here?* (We can't turn candy on and off.)
Say: *In pairs, write a list of machines and other things that you can turn on and off.* Give them 1–2 minutes to do this.
Suggestions: lamp, computer, television/TV, (digital) camera, (electric) guitar, radio, cooker, oven, fridge, video, computer screen, laptop, tablet, torch/flashlight, engine.
Note: Remind learners that we don't turn on/off things with engines (cars, motorbikes). We *start* them.

o   Learners choose words from the box to write in gaps 1–5. Tell them to look carefully at the words before and after the gap. They then choose the best name for the story.

> **Check answers:**
> **1** hear **2** scary **3** building **4** project **5** explore
> Best story name: Answers for Hugo

Note: If learners are familiar with terms like nouns, verbs and adjectives, explain why a certain part of speech is needed in the structure of the sentence too. (**1** 'can' + main verb **2** adjective **3** past continuous form **4** noun referring to 'museum' **5** main verb)

o   In pairs, learners think of one really difficult question. For example: *How long does an octopus live?* Pairs ask their question. Does anyone in the class know the answer? Suggest that learners try to find the answers in a library or on the internet and bring answers to the next class.
Note: An octopus usually lives for about six months, but a giant octopus can live for up to five years.

B   Listen and colour the museum picture in A.

o   Make sure that learners have colouring pencils, especially red, green, yellow and purple ones.
o   Say: *You're going to colour four different things in the museum picture.*
o   Play the audio twice. Learners colour the picture.

Audioscript

This is part of a museum and the boy's name is Hugo. Can you see the strange drums? Colour the smaller one. Colour it red, please.

Now, can you see the dinosaur? It's behind Hugo in this picture. Use your green pencil to colour that, but only colour its head. OK?

Hugo is looking at the big pyramid, isn't he? The one on the floor. It's made of glass, I think. Colour that now, please. Find your yellow pencil and colour it with that.

And find the flag! It's in the corner. It's big, isn't it? Colour it purple. Do that now, please.
Thank you!

> **Check answers:**
> Colour smaller drum – red, Colour dinosaur's head – green, Colour pyramid – yellow, Colour flag in corner – purple

o   Each learner chooses one more thing to colour in. In pairs, learners tell each other to colour one more thing in the colour of their choice. For example:
Learner A: *Colour the fish. Make it blue, please.*
Learner B: *OK!*

Optional extension:
Learners write words for all the other things in the picture. They might like to use dictionaries to find other words (for example: vase, jar, globe, unicycle).

C Write the question words after numbers 1–12. Ask your friends the questions!

o Tell learners they are going to ask and answer easier questions now.

o Look at the example question with the class. Learners then complete the 12 questions by writing the question words on the lines and crossing them out in the box. Tell learners to read through all the questions before they start writing. They should use all the question words.

Flyers tip

For Speaking Part 4, make sure that learners have plenty of practice in answering questions about themselves. Their answers can be short and simple but they will probably get better marks if they answer in complete sentences.

Note: If possible, learners sit in a circle.

o Say: *Write your name where it says 'Your name'.* When everyone has written their name, say: *Now, give your book to the person sitting on your right.*

o Learners look at the questions and choose one that they'd like to ask the owner of the book. They write their own name in front of that question.

o Learners pass the book they are now holding to the person sitting on their right again. Learners choose another question they'd like to ask and write their name next to it. Learners continue passing their books to the person on their right until all the questions have names next to them.

o The books are returned to their owners. Each learner then stands up, finds the person who has asked them each question, and answers it.

Note: Large classes: divide the class into groups of 12 for this activity. Small classes: learners choose two questions for each person to answer.

D Write questions! Answer questions!

o Learners work in groups of 4–5. Give each group one of the situations: *on the beach, in a museum, in class, at a party*. Learners tick the coloured bubble to show which situation they have been given and put crosses in the other three. Groups then think of four questions for each situation. They write the four questions on the lines. Encourage them to write a mixture of *yes/no* and open questions.

Suggestions:

(on the beach) Can we go for a swim now? Where's my towel? Is the sea cold? How deep is the water? Are the waves high? Do you prefer sailing or swimming?

(in a museum) Where's the lift? Do you like that strange pyramid? How old is this plate? What time does this museum close?

(in class) What are we going to study today? Which page must I look at? How do you spell 'library'? Can I borrow your pencil?

(at a party) How old are you today? What was your best present? What are we going to eat? Did you make those cakes?

o When they have finished, learners from one group role play their situation with learners from the other groups, asking and answering the questions.

E Play the game! Questions mingle.

o Prepare cards with one question on each (see suggested questions below)

o Give one question card to each learner. Learners stand up and move around and ask and answer questions. Tell them that they should answer in sentences, <u>not</u> with one word. No writing is necessary.

Note: Smaller classes: give learners more than one question, or put the questions face down on a table in the middle of the group. Learners take turns to turn a question over. Another learner answers it.

o After about five minutes, or when all questions have been asked and answered, learners sit down. Ask for some answers. For example: *Who asked the question about colour? What is most people's favourite colour? Who asked the question about skiing? How many people can ski?*

Suggested questions:

What's your favourite milkshake?

Have you ever entered a competition or a race?

What job would you like to do?

Can you roller skate?

How often do you go online?

Can you ski?

Who did you chat to last night?

Who's your favourite pop star?

What's your favourite hobby?

Who's the best football player in the world?

What time do you usually go to sleep?

Where did you go on holiday last year?

How do you spell your surname?

20 Calling and sending

Topics time, numbers, the home

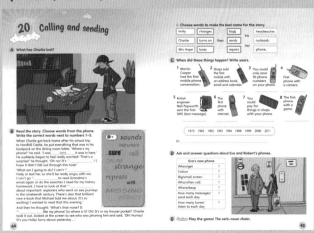

Not in YLE wordlists: *pay for, mobile (phone), SMS, connect*

Equipment needed
- Pencils and rulers.
- Photocopies of page 136. One per pair/group.

A What has Charlie lost?

- Point to the boy in **A**. Say: *This is Charlie. Listen, and answer questions about Charlie.*

  Ask these questions one by one, giving learners time to talk about their answers in pairs.

  1 *What's Charlie wearing? Are these his favourite clothes?*

  2 *He looks younger than you. How old do you think he is? When's his birthday?*

  3 *What did he study at school today? Which was his favourite school subject?*

- Ask three more questions about Charlie. This time, learners suggest answers. Write some of their answers on the board.

  1 *How did he travel home from school? Did he cycle, catch a bus or walk?*

  2 *What information is on those pieces of paper?*

  3 *You can see a baseball. Do you think that's his favourite sport?*

- *Look at Charlie's face and body. How's he feeling at the moment? Is he surprised, excited or worried?* (worried) *Why?* (he's lost something)

  Point to the hole in Charlie's backpack and ask: *What's he lost? What can you see on the table? What's he looking for?* Learners make suggestions. Write them on the board. Accept any reasonable suggestion and leave them on the board for later.

  Say: *Let's find out!*

B Read the story. Choose words from the phone. Write the correct words next to numbers 1–5.

- Learners read the text to find out what Charlie has lost. Ask: *Where did Charlie find his phone?* (in his trouser pocket!)

- Read the text aloud to learners up to: *on the dining room table!* Point to the backpack in the picture in **A** and ask: *Is Charlie's backpack full or empty?* (empty) *So does Charlie know that his phone isn't in his backpack?* (Yes – he's sure.) Point to the word 'sure' on the phone picture next to the text and on the line in the text. Learners read the text and choose words from the phone picture and write one word on each line.

Check answers:
1 missing   2 call   3 online   4 website   5 sounds

- Ask more questions about the text: *Who does Charlie have to phone today?* (Holly) *Who has given Charlie some homework?* (his history teacher) *What sounds exciting?* (a new e-book)

> **Flyers tip**
>
> In Reading and Writing Part 4, the last question tests understanding of the whole text, not just one part of the story. Candidates should not choose an answer because they see a word that is also in the text.

- Point to the three names in the boxes and ask: *Who is this story about: Holly, Charlie or Mrs Hope?* (Charlie). Learners put a cross in the boxes with Holly and Mrs Hope. Learners choose the words from one box in each group to make a sentence to describe this story. To do this, they cross out the words that are not correct.

  Answer: Charlie loses then finds his phone.

- Say: *We're going to write the start of Charlie's story. The story before the picture in A. Charlie came home.* Point to the answers to the first question on the board and ask: *How did he travel home from school?* Ask one learner to write a sentence using the words on the board.

  Suggestion:

  Charlie cycled home.

  Now you add a second sentence to the board: He opened the front door and went inside. Ask: *Where did Charlie go first?* (to the dining room) *What did he do with his backpack?* (put it on the table)

  Ask a different learner to add the third sentence to the board:

  Suggestion: He went to the dining room and put his backpack on the table.

  Do the same with more questions to produce sentences:

  Ask: *What couldn't he find? How did he feel? What did he do with the things in his backpack? What information is on those pieces of paper? You can see a baseball. Do you think that's his favourite sport?*

  Suggested story: Charlie cycled home. Then, he went inside to the dining room and put his backpack on the table. He couldn't find his phone. He was worried, so he took everything out of his backpack and put his book, sweets, pens, keys, pieces of paper and baseball on the dining room table. He always had a baseball and he wore a baseball cap, because that was his favourite sport!

  Say: *Look at the story on the board! It's fantastic! There are (68) words and it tells us how Charlie came home, what he did, how he felt and about Charlie and his favourite sport!*

C When did these things happen? Write years.

- Point to the text in **B** and say: *In this text there are seven things that you can do with a phone. Can you find them?* (call someone, text someone, go online, read emails, do a search, look at a website, read an e-book).

- Ask: *What other things do we do with our phones?*

  Suggestions: play and listen to music, take and send photos and make videos, send messages.

- Point to the years in the bottom box in **C**. Teach or revise how to say years: 1973 = nineteen seventy three (for years up to 1999, we say the year as two separate numbers). For 2001–2009, we use the word 'thousand' (two thousand and one) From 2010 on, we say 'twenty' (2011 – twenty eleven). In pairs, learners say the different dates at the bottom of **C** to each other.

- Say: *Now, choose two years that are important for you! Tell your parner why those years are special!* Learners talk about their special years.

○ Read the text in the first box: *Martin Cooper had the first mobile phone conversation.* Ask: *Which year do you think this happened? How long have people had mobile phones?* Different learners say the year this happened. Say: *Martin Cooper did this in 1973.* Learners write 1973 under 1.

○ Learners think about and decide the years that the other things happened and write them on the lines in pencil.

Check answers by asking the class to vote for the answer to each question, then tell them the correct answer to each question.

Check answers:
2 1993 **3** 1983 **4** 2000 **5** 1992 **6** 1999 **7** 2011 **8** 1994

○ Say: *There is one year that you have not used. Which one?* (1998) *In 1998, people could buy phones with screens that showed colours.* Repeat the sentence slowly. Learners listen and write this information on the line under the years box.

D Ask and answer questions about Eva and Robert's phones.

○ Ask again: *Who's got a mobile phone?* Learners who have one put up their hands. Ask different learners who put up their hands about their phones.

What colour's your phone?

Where do you keep your phone?

When did you get your phone?

Who do you often call on your phone?

Is the screen big or small?

How many messages do you send each day?

How many tunes do you listen to each day?

Note: The question prompts are not in the same order as the information.

○ Say: *I asked seven questions about your phones. Can you remember them?* Point to the prompts about Eva's phone in **D** to help learners. Explain: *You are going to ask or answer questions about Eva's phone.* Ask: *What questions do you need to ask?*

When did Eva get her phone? What colour is her phone? Is the screen big or small? Who does Eva often call on her phone? Where does Eva keep her phone? How many messages does Eva send each day? How many tunes does Eva listen to each day?

○ In A and B pairs, learners ask and answer questions about Eva then Robert's phones. Learner A looks at page 118 and Learner B at page 120.

E Play the game! The verb–noun chain.

○ Teach 'chat' and 'connect'. Give out photocopies of page 136 to each pair or group of three learners.

○ Say: *There are 25 verbs on this page. Can you find them all? Put circles round all the verbs!*

Check answers:
answer, begin, chat, connect, email, end, find, get, go, hear, join, lose, make, make, open, pick up, read, search, send, speak to, take, turn off, turn on, win, write

○ Point to the arrow between *answer* and *your phone.* Ask: *Which verbs are next to 'your phone'?* (*begin* and *find*) *Which verb comes after 'answer' in the alphabet?* (*begin*) *Draw a line from 'your phone' to 'begin'!* Learners draw the line.

○ Ask: *Which words are next to 'begin'?* (*a conversation* and *to your friends*) *What can you begin? A conversation?* (yes) *Draw a line between 'begin' and 'conversation'!* Explain that they should continue this way, moving from the second part of the phrase (your phone, a conversation) to the next verb in alphabetical order.

Check answers:
chat to your friends, connect to wifi, email your cousin, end a conversation, find an address, get a text, go online, hear your phone, join a group, lose a phone number, make a mistake, make a video, open a program, pick up emails, read your messages, search the internet, send photos, speak to your friends, take pictures, turn off the internet, turn on your camera, win a prize, write a text

○ Choose one of the actions and mime it to the class. For example: mime taking a phone from your ear and pressing the key to end a call. Learners watch and say what you are doing (ending a conversation). In groups of 4–5, learners take it in turns to mime an action. The other learners in their group say what they are doing.

Things I did yesterday.

○ Write on the board: *first   then   next   later*

Say: *Look at the words in the squares again. In pairs, use the words there and the words on the board to talk about what different things you do when you use your phone or computer.*

○ Learners talk in pairs.

For example: *First, I turn on my phone, then I connect to wifi and read my messages.*

21   The time of the year

Topics the world around us, weather, time

Equipment needed

o   (Optional) A calendar. See A.

Ⓐ How many words can you find on the calendar page?

o   Ask the following questions:

What day is it today? Is it a weekday or is it the weekend?
What month is it? Is it summer, autumn, winter or spring now?
What century are we in?

o   Point to the the page from a calendar in **A** and ask: *Which month can you see?* (September) *How many days are there in September?* (30) *Is September the first month of the year?* (No – it's the ninth month.)

o   Say: *This is a page from a calendar.* (If you have a calendar in the classroom, point to that too.) Ask: *How many time words can you see?* (15)

o   Point to the words 'a diary' in the 27th box. Ask: *What do people write in a diary?* (**Suggestions:** important dates, information, names, places)

Point to the word 'fall' in the first box. Explain that 'autumn' and 'fall' mean the same. 'Autumn' is used in British English and 'fall' in American English.

Draw 12 boxes across the board for the 12 months. Ask learners to copy it into their notebooks and colour: spring – yellow, summer – red, autumn/fall – orange, winter – blue. Once they have done this they can use it as a reference to help them order the words in blue.

Learners write the blue words from the calendar on the line – from shortest (in time) to longest.

> **Check answers:**
>
> **Note** The order of the seasons here will depend on which part of the world your learners live in.
>
> minutes, hours, days, a weekend, a week, months, fall, winter, summer, a year, a century.

Ⓑ Choose words from the calendar in A and write them on the lines.

o   Look at the example with learners.

Ask: *How many days are there in this year?* (365 or 366 if it's a leap year!)

o   Learners read sentences 1–11 and write words from the calendar page in **A** on the lines.

> **Check answers:**
>
> **1** fall   **2** summer   **3** midday   **4** minutes   **5** hours
> **6** a weekend   **7** months   **8** a century   **9** winter   **10** midnight
> **11** at the moment

o   Ask: *Where are you at the moment?* (in class/the classroom) *Who's speaking at the moment?* (the teacher/you!)

o   Ask: *Which words from A did you not use?* (a week, days) Ask learners to suggest sentences about these words.

Suggestions:

a week: There are seven days in one of these.

days: There are 24 hours in one of these.

Ⓒ Put the words in the spring, summer, autumn or winter boxes.

o   Say: *Look at the four boxes at the top of page 47.* Point to 'cold' in the winter box. Say: *In most countries it's cold in winter, isn't it? That's why 'cold' is in the winter box.*

> **Flyers tip**
>
> Encourage learners to write as clearly as possible. Marks are lost if letters and/or words are not legible. Answers should be clear enough to be read by someone who is not familiar with candidates' handwriting.

o   Learners look at the word box on page 46. In pairs, they talk about and then decide where to write these words (in the spring, summer, autumn or winter boxes). Ask 3–4 pairs where they put particular words.

Note: Answers will depend on which part of the world your learners live in.

Ask and answer questions.

o   Learners work in A and B pairs. Learner A looks at the questions on page 119 of their book and Learner B looks at the questions on page 121 of their book.

o   Learner A asks B their questions and Learner B answers. Learner B asks A their questions and Learner A answers. They write each other's answers on the lines.

Ⓓ Look at the pictures. What differences can you see?   Speaking Part 1

o   Point to the two pictures and say:

Here are two pictures. In both pictures, we can see … . (a forest)
In picture A, there are two birds in the trees but in picture B there are … . (four)

Ask: *What things do you think the people in the pictures can hear?*
(Picture A: the car, the birds, the sound of the snow)
(Picture B: the car, the birds, the water in the river, the wind, the fire)

Ask: *What can the people smell in picture B?* (their dinner!)

o   Say: *Picture A is nearly the same as picture B but some things are different. For example, in picture A the sky's dark blue, but in picture B … .* (The sky is light blue.)

o   Say: *I'm going to say something about picture A. You tell me how picture B is different.*

o Read out the following sentences about the picture in **A**. Learners listen and say how picture **B** is different.

In my picture:

Two people have made a snowman. (They've made a **fire**.)

The boy and girl are throwing snowballs. (The boy and girl are **sailing a paper boat down the river**.)

There's ice on the river. (There's **no ice** on the river.)

The man is wearing a brown sweater. (His sweater is **purple and white**.)

You can see lots of snow on the ground. (You can't see any snow, you can see some **grass**.)

The car is on the right of the picture. (It's on the **left**.)

E Read the message and write the missing words. Write one word on each line.

Reading & Writing Part 6

o Learners read the message and answer your questions:

Which picture goes with this message? (picture **B**)

Which person in the picture wrote it? (The boy playing with the paper boat.) *What's his name?* (Learners choose a name for this boy. For example, Jack.)

o Learners write words on the five lines.

Check answers:
1 of **2** bikes/bicycles **3** the/our **4** was **5** made/built

o Point to the text in **E** again and say: This text is about picture **B**. In pairs, you're going to think, talk and write about the day in picture **A**.

Ask these questions. In pairs, learners write short answers. Give them time to write their answers. Read the questions twice to give them time to check their answers.

1 What warm clothes did the children put on that morning?

2 Who brought the children to the forest?

3 How did they get to the forest?

4 Do the children live near these woods?

5 What did they do there first? Next?

6 When did they leave the forest?

7 What did they say when they arrived home?

In pairs, learners use their answers to make a short story about the day in picture **A**.

Suggested story:

That morning, the children put on boots, wool sweaters and hats and scarves. Jack's uncle drove him and his friends Julia and Mark to Appletree Forest, which is 5 kilometres from their house.

First, Jack and Julia made snowballs and threw them. Then, they helped Uncle George and Mark finish the snowman. They left the forest at 2 o'clock. 'What a fun day!' they said when they arrived home.

F Play time games!

o Learners work in pairs or groups of three. Give each group a sheet of paper. Ask one question from the list below, then give groups time to talk together and choose and write their answer. When a group is ready to answer they shout, 'Stop!' and the other groups must stop talking or writing. You then ask another question.

o Read out the following instructions:

1 *What are the first six months of the year? Write them in alphabetical order.*

2 *What are the names of the seven days of the week? Write the shortest name first and the longest name last.*

3 *Which of these words is different? Write it down. Tell me why it's different.*

a *hours, minutes, clocks, days* (clocks – the others are a length of time)

b *tomorrow, next week, yesterday, tonight* (yesterday – refers to the past, the others to the future)

c *quarter, midday, midnight, March* (quarter – doesn't start with 'm')

d *September, May, March, January* (May – doesn't have an 'r' in it)

Note: Accept any reasonable answers.

4 Which is longest: 5 weeks / 1 month / 30 days / 240 hours? (5 weeks)

5 What's the shortest: 50 weeks / 500 days / 1 year / 9 months? (9 months)

6 What's another way of saying 30 minutes? (half an hour)

7 How many hours are there in a week? (168)

📁 Special days

o Many days of the year are special for different reasons. Examples are: World Smile Day in October, Universal Children's Day on November 20th, the European Day of Languages (26th September) or World Water Day (22nd March).

o Learners choose a day and find out what's celebrated that day. Alternatively, give them a day to research.

o Learners find out: where it is a special day, why it's a special day, what people do on that day, what they eat or wear that day.

o Learners write a newspaper article describing the day.

o Learners add their article to their project file. Alternatively, display learners' work on the classroom wall if possible.

22 Important numbers

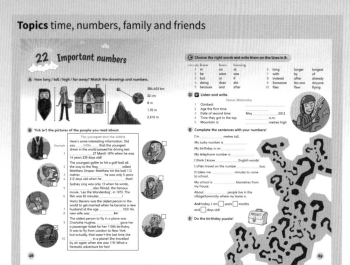

Not in YLE wordlists: *golfer, pass a test, became, get married, centimetre, metre*

Equipment needed

o   Flyers audio 22D.

o   Photocopies (one for each pair of learners) of page 137. See F.

Ⓐ How long / tall / high / far away? Match the drawings and numbers.

o   Learners look at the pictures. Ask them: *What's a good name for this man with the beard? And what name should we call the woman here?* Write the most popular names on the board, then learners choose a name for the man and woman.

o   In pairs, learners look at the numbers and decide which number measurement goes with which picture.

o   Ask different pairs questions in this order:
How high is the house? (8 m)
How long is (man's name)*'s beard?* (32 cm)
How tall is (woman's name)? (1 metre 70 centimetres) Write on the board: 1 metre 70 centimetres. Point out that this is the way we write metre and centimetres in British English. Ask: *How do you write these words in American English?* (meters, centimeters)
Say: *There is another way of saying this number.* Revise/teach saying numbers with decimals: *one point seven metres.*

o   Write on the board: *1,010   3,988*
Check learners know that we say 'and' before the tens in a number (one thousand and ten; three thousand, nine hundred and eighty eight). Also practise rising and falling intonation to indicate that we have/haven't finished saying a number. (one thousand ↗ and ten ↘) (three thousand ↗ nine hundred and eighty eight ↘)
Ask:
How high is the mountain? (2,616 m)
How far away is the moon? (384,403 km)

Ⓑ Tick the pictures of the people you read about.

o   Learners read the text through for a general idea of what it is about. They should not try to insert the missing words yet. Learners then look at the seven pictures.
Ask: *How many youngest or oldest people did you read about?* (5)
How many pictures of people are there here? (7)
Learners tick the drawings that show the five youngest and oldest people mentioned in the text and put crosses against the two that they didn't read about.

Check answers:
boy playing golf ✔   woman in plane ✔   woman with dog ✘
boy driving car ✔   boy filming ✔   woman climbing mountain ✘
man holding ring ✔

Ⓒ Choose the right words and write them on the lines in B.   Reading & Writing Part 4

Flyers tip
In Reading and Writing Part 4, candidates have to choose the correct word for each gap from three given words. They do NOT have to supply their own words. (They do this in Part 6.)

o   In pairs or on their own, learners read the text in **B** again and write words to fill gaps 1–10 in the text.

o   Ask different learners for the answers. Ask the rest of the class to stand up if they think the suggested answer is right, or to remain sitting if they think it's wrong.

Check answers:
1 on   **2** was   **3** but   **4** did   **5** and   **6** long   **7** of   **8** already
9 Someone   **10** flew

Ⓓ ▶ Listen and write.

o   Point to the picture of the woman and ask: *Did we read about this woman in the text in B?* (No) Point to the woman's name at the top of **D** and say: *This is her name. How do you say this name?* Learners try and say the name and surname.
Ask: *Where do you think she's from?* Learners suggest where. *Why do you think she's famous?* Learners suggest why. Play the first part of the audio (up to 'the highest mountain in the world.') Learners say her name, where she's from (Japan) and why she's famous. (she climbed Everest)

o   Learners listen to the whole audio and write words and numbers on the lines.

Check answers:
1 Everest   **2** 63   **3** 19th   **4** 7 / seven   **5** 8,850

o   Ask: *What other number did you hear?* (73) *What is it?* (Tamae's age when she climbed the mountain a second time.) Ask learners which mountain is the highest in the world. (Everest)

o   Ask: *Who can remember? How do you say the woman's name? How do you spell her surname? And her first name? How do you spell Tamae?* In pairs, learners say and spell the woman's first name and surname.

o   Say: *Tamae was very brave. Climbing Everest is really dangerous and very difficult as well!*
Write on the board: brave dangerous   very difficult
Learners think of something that they or someone they know or someone they have seen on TV has done that was brave, dangerous and very difficult. In small groups, they talk about these things.
Three or four learners could tell all their classmates how they felt after their brave, dangerous or difficult moment.

Audioscript

Girl:	Dad, I've found a great website with all the information I need to write about a special person!
Man:	So who are you going to write about?
Girl:	Someone I'm really interested in. Her name's Tamae Watanabe – the Japanese woman who climbed to the top of Everest!
Man:	You mean the mountain?
Girl:	Yes Dad! E-V-E-R-E-S-T – the highest mountain in the world!
Man:	Wow! That's a brave, dangerous and difficult thing to do!
Girl:	That's right! She's amazing. And you know, she didn't only do that once she climbed it twice!
Man:	Really?
Girl:	Yes. She was 63 years old the first time!
Man:	How wonderful!
Girl:	Then, she climbed it again on May 19th, 2012.
Man:	And how old was she the second time?
Girl:	She was 73! She's the oldest woman to ever climb that mountain!
Man:	How did she feel when she arrived at the top?
Girl:	I don't know. Very pleased perhaps!
Man:	Do you think her back, arms and legs were sore?
Girl:	Of course!
Girl:	For the last part of the trip, she and the other people in the group were climbing all night!
Man:	So, what time did they arrive at the top?
Girl:	At seven o'clock in the morning.
Man:	And how high is the mountain?
Girl:	It's 8,850 metres high!
Man:	That's a long way to climb and carry all the things they needed to get to the top!
Girl:	I know!

E Complete the sentences with your numbers!

o Write on the board: *0173 449 652   30/9/2010* (or *9/30/2010*)   *5.30*
o Ask: *What are these?* (a phone number, a date, a time)
o Drill the phone number. Each number should be said individually. *0* (as in the letter 'o' or zero), *one, seven, three, four, four, nine, six, five, two*.
o Ask: *How do we say dates? The thirtieth of September/September the thirtieth, two thousand and ten. We could also add the day to the date, for example: Wednesday, the thirtieth of September*.
   Note: In the United States, the month is written first, then the day. In Britain, the day always comes first if the month is written as a number, and usually comes first if the month is written as a word.
o Learners complete the sentences with their own numbers, selecting 'village', 'town' or 'city' as appropriate in the last sentence.
o Learners work in pairs or small groups. One learner says a number they have written in one of the sentences. The others have to say what that number refers to.
   For example: *Is that your telephone number?*

How old are you today?

o Ask: *What day is it today? What date is it today? When is your birthday? How old are you today?*
   Learners work out their ages in years, months and days or in years and days, then they write their names and ages in big letters and numbers on a big sheet of paper and hold it above their heads.
   Ask: *Who is the youngest in the class? Who is the oldest?* Learners turn round to see.
o Learners write their age in their books in years, months and days or years and days.

F Do the birthday puzzle!

o Give out one photocopy of page 137 to each pair of learners. Learners read the information about each person's birthday and write the dates. Remind them that in this puzzle, today's date is **Friday, 17th February.**

   Say: *Sentence 6 doesn't tell us the names of the two friends. Who are they?* (Kim and Emma)

   > **Check answers:**
   > **Anna** – 12th February, **Kim** – 17th August, **David** – 16th February, **Katy** – 18th February, **Paul** – 27th January, **Emma** – 17th August, **Harry** – 17th March, **Jim** – 29th January

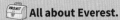 **All about Everest.**

o Each learner finds out five more facts about Everest. They can use the internet or library to do this.
   Suggestions:
   The first time Everest was climbed (1953). The youngest person to climb it. The quickest climb. The first person to snowboard and ski down Everest.
o Learners then work in groups of four and compare their facts. They choose the ten most interesting ones.
o Each group then makes a poster with a picture of Everest in the middle and their ten facts written around the mountain.

23   World, weather, work

Topics the world around us, weather, work

Equipment needed
o   Photocopies of 'My funny day at work' on page 138. See E.

A   Look and read. Choose the correct words and write them on the lines.

Reading & Writing Part 1

> **Flyers tip**
>
> In Reading and Writing Part 1, most of the answers are singular but some might be plural or uncountable. The possible answers are written in the correct form so candidates should make sure they include any *a / an / the* articles and not change the answers in any way.

o   Learners look at the sentences and possible answers. Ask: *How many answers have 'a' before them?* (8).

o   Ask: *How many have 'the' before them?* (2) *Can we say 'an internet 'a sky'?* (no) Explain that we always say 'the internet' because it's the name of something and 'the sky' because there is only one sky on our planet.

o   Ask: *How many of the answers are just one word?* (4) Explain why they don't have 'a' or 'an' before them. (websites is a plural, wifi, ice and fog are uncountables)

o   Check that learners know they do not need to use four of the answers.

o   Look at the example together. Tell learners to draw a line through 'an office' to show this cannot be another answer.

o   To make the practice as authentic as possible, learners work on their own. They read the definitions and write the answers.

> **Check answers:**
>
> 1 websites   2 a dentist   3 a cave   4 a storm   5 a pop star
> 6 fog   7 a desert   8 a screen   9 the sky   10 a wave

B   Add information to Mr Wild's business email! You choose!

o   Say: This is Mr Wild's business email. Learners decide which person Mr Wild might be in the first picture **C**. Perhaps the man in the striped trousers. Ask: *How old do you think he is? What kind of job might he do?* Accept any appropriate answers.

o   Learners read the incomplete email.

o   Ask: *Who is Mr Wild sending this email to?* (Dan) *Is Mr Wild having a busy day?* (yes) *Can he have lunch with Dan today?* (no) *Where is his house?* (in Stone Street)

o   Divide learners into groups of 3–4. Tell groups to think about Mr Wild's job. Ask: *What do you think he does at work each day?*
   Suggestions: answers the phone, writes messages, works on websites, talks to lots of people, tells people to do things, has meetings, thinks of new ideas, sells things, visits factories.

o   Ask: *What kind of business has he got? You choose.* Read out the suggestions. Learners choose their answers.
   Suggestions: he sells bicycles, rockets, hot air balloons; he makes chocolate, phones, computer apps, pasta, trainers, pyjamas, racing bikes.; he works in a theatre, a cinema, a restaurant, a bank, a museum etc.

o   Groups choose their own business contexts and words to complete the email. They should write one or two words in each gap.

o   This should be a fun exercise. Walk around and check answers are grammatically correct and encourage learners to be creative with their ideas.

o   Ask different groups to read out one or two sentences each so the text should be even funnier.

o   Accept any answers which might work in the context. For example, one set of answers might be:
   1 racing bikes   **2** eleven thirty   **3** new office   **4** wheels
   5 cartoon   **6** magazine   **7** DVDs   **8** cinema   **9** pizza   **10** taxi
   11 snow   **12** big supermarket

C   Look at the three pictures. Write about this story. Write 20 words or more.

Reading & Writing Part 7

> **Flyers tip**
>
> In the story in Reading and Writing Part 7 and Speaking Part 3, candidates can make their stories more interesting, and probably get better marks, if they add adjectives to show how the people feel and reasons why they might be doing these things. They can also include things that the people might be saying. A very strong example for a story for the pictures in C might be:
>
> *Mr Bell was late for work. He ran quickly along the street. Outside his office he fell over on some ice. All the things in his bag fell on to the ground. Some people came to help him get up again. And a bird gave Mr Bell his glasses and the last piece of paper. Mr Bell was very pleased and said thank you to everyone.* (66 words)
>
> Shorter, simpler stories are of course acceptable, but always encourage learners to be ambitious and to show what they know.

o   Learners have their books closed. Say: *Close your eyes. Listen. I'm going to ask you questions. The questions are about a picture.*
   Ask the questions. Learners say their answers, with their eyes closed.
   Say: *It's winter. What's on the ground?* (ice, snow) *There's a street in a town. What can you see in the street?* (shops, people, cars, a bus stop, a traffic light) *What clothes are the people wearing?* (coats, boots, scarves, gloves, hats) *There's a businessman in the street. What's he carrying?* (a laptop, phone, important papers) *You can see the businessman's office. What can you see in the office?* (desks, chairs, computers, phones, people)

o   Learners open their books and look at the first picture in **C**. Ask them if the picture is like the picture that they 'saw'.

o   Write on the board, reading out the sentences as you write them: *It was a very cold day. Mr Bell fell over in the street.*
   Write on the board, under this sentence: *winter ice street businessman fell over outside office*
   Ask learners to use these words to make the sentences you have written on the board better.

Suggestion

It was winter and there was ice on the street, so Mr Bell, a businessman fell over outside his office.

o Point to the second picture in **C**. Ask learners: *Which words might we need to talk about the story in this picture?* (children, come back, pick up, pieces of paper, man, help Mr Bell)

Ask learners to make a sentence about the story in this picture.

Suggestion

Two children came back and they picked up the pieces of paper and a man helped Mr Bell.

Write their sentence on the board.

o Point to the third picture in **C** and say: *Look! Who's helped Mr Bell as well?* (the bird) *What did the bird give Mr Bell?* (a piece of paper and his glasses)

Write on the board, under the other sentences: A bird gave Mr Bell his glasses and some paper.

o Point to the last two sentences on the board and say: *These sentences tell the story. But we can improve the sentences! How did Mr Bell feel at the end of the story? Pleased or unhappy?* (pleased) *Was the bird kind or horrible to Mr Bell?* (kind) *So, a kind bird gave Mr Bell his glasses and some paper. Mr Bell was really pleased. And what do you think Mr Bell said to the children, the man and the bird. He was pleased. They helped him and picked him and his papers up. What did he say?* (Thank you very much! You're very kind.)

o Say: *Let's give this story a name! In pairs, think of a name for this story!*

Give pairs time to choose a title for the story and then ask them to tell you their story names.

Suggestions

Help from people and a bird

Mr Bell gets his papers and glasses back

Helping Mr Bell

Kind people and animals

D **Two words or one word?**

o Write on the board: *There is a bird! Look!* Underline 'There' and 'is' and ask: *How can we write these two words so they look like one word?* (There's) Say: *We write 'there's' like this because when we speak, 'there's' sounds like one word. It's quicker and easier to say it like one word.* Point to a door in the classroom and say: *There's a door!*

o Point to other objects in the room.

Learners say: *There's a desk / light / bookcase / computer etc.*

o Using a blue pencil, tell learners to look at **B** and circle engineers' in line 1. Ask: *Is this really two words, like 'there's'?* (no). Make sure learners recognise that this is a possessive 's form (the meeting of the engineers).

o Using a red pencil, learners circle all other contractions they can find in **A** and in **B** (it's, don't, you're, I've, we're, I've, I'm, can't, it's, I've).

o Learners look at the contractions in **D**. (They could add 'I'm' and 'it's' to these.) Make sure they know that these are all two words contracted into one word. Ask what the two words are in each case and practise the pronunciation of each contracted form in short sentences, for example: *Who's that boy? I've got a new game. We're playing in the snow. I'm going home. It's raining.*

Note: 'who's' and 'whose' sound exactly the same and in 'who's' and 'there's' the 's' is pronounced /z/ but after the 't' in 'it's', the 's' is pronounced /s/.

E **Play the game. The verb–noun chain!**

o Give out photocopies of page 138 to each pair or group of three learners. There are 25 verbs and 25 nouns / noun phrases. The verbs are in alphabetical order.

o Point to the arrow between 'arrive' and 'at work'. Explain that the noun that goes with each verb is always in a square that is next to, above or below its verb.

o Ask learners which words that are next to or below 'brush' can follow it (*at work, a laptop, a model, your hair*). 'Brush your hair' is the logical combination.

o In the same way, learners continue moving to the next verb and find its noun.

Check answers:

Arrive at work. Borrow a laptop. Brush your hair. Build a model. Clean your teeth. Cross out a word. Dress up in a costume. Email a website. Enter a competition. Go up in the lift. Hurt your knee. Invent a machine. Laugh at a cartoon. Meet a film star. Open a computer program. Post a birthday card. Run down the stairs. Save a computer file. Search for information. Spend some money. Thank someone. Tidy your desk. Turn off the lights. Wait for a bus. Watch the news.

o Ask: *Which of these things are the most boring / fun / most interesting / easiest / most difficult etc.*

o Choose one of the actions and mime it to the class. For example: mime picking up a toothbrush, putting toothpaste on it and cleaning your teeth. Learners watch and say what you are doing (cleaning your teeth).

o In groups of 4–5, learners take it in turns to mime an action. The other learners in their group say what they are doing.

Things we did

o Write on the board: *first and then next later when while*

Say, then write on the board, under these words: *I hurt my knee when I was running down the stairs.*

Point to *hurt your knee* and *running down the stairs* and say: *These words are in the boxes. Can you see them?*

Now, you make sentences with two of the actions from the boxes. Point to the words *first, and then,* etc on the board and say: *Use these words to make your sentences. Let's see who can make the most sentences!*

In pairs or groups of 3, learners write sentences joining two of the actions.

Suggestions

First I cleaned my teeth and then I brushed my hair.

The people arrived at work and then they went up in the lift.

The teacher tidied her desk and turned off the lights.

That man built a model and later invented a machine.

I borrowed my sister's laptop to email the website.

My cousin entered a competition and later he met a famous film star.

An interview

o Learners choose someone they know or invent a person. They imagine they work for a children's website and need to interview this person about a day at work.

o They complete an interview script adding answers to the questions. They could then add a picture they have drawn or found online to illustrate the interview script.

o Learners add this to their project file. Alternatively display the scripts on a wall in your classroom.

Suggested script:

Hello! Please tell me about your day at work.

How do you travel to work?

....

What's the first thing you do?

....

Tell me about a special person that you work with.

....

Where do you usually have lunch?

....

What do you do in the afternoons?

....

Why do you like your job?

....

What time do you finish work?

....

Thank you!

24 Leaving and arriving

Topics transport, places

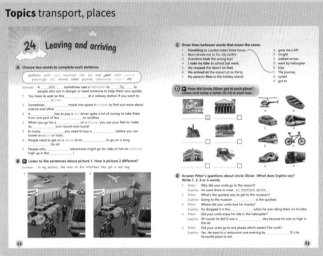

Equipment needed
- Flyers audio 24B, 24D.
- Photocopies of page 139 (one for each learner). See C.

A Choose two correct words to complete each sentence.

- With their books closed, ask learners: *How do you come to school? How many people come by bus / by car / on foot?* Learners put up their hands to show their answer. Count the number of hands to see how most children in this class travel to school each day.
- Ask: *If you want to travel to school or to another place that's far away, what can you get in or get on to take you there?* Write learners' suggestions on the board.
  Learners open their books. Ask different learners to call out one of the orange words in the sentences (*helicopter, train, rockets, taxi, bicycle, bus, plane, balloons*). Ask: *Is that word on the board?* If it isn't, add it to the other transport words.
- Point to the words on the board and ask: *Which do you think is the most exciting / most boring / slowest / fastest / safest / most dangerous way to travel?* Learners suggest answers such as: *by helicopter, in a truck, by bike, by train, by bus, in a rocket* etc.
- Learners open their books and look at the example in **A**. Ask them why 'pilot' and 'fly' are crossed out. (Because they are the answers in the example sentence.)
- Learners complete sentences 1–7 using other words from the box.

  > **Check answers:**
  > **1** platform, catch   **2** astronauts, planets   **3** passenger, city
  > **4** ride, wheels   **5** countries, ticket   **6** airport, journey
  > **7** love, sky

  Say: *There's another word for 'rocket'. Do you know it? It's made from two words – space and ship. Put them together, and you get a ….* (spaceship) *What do you call the people who travel in a spaceship?* (astronauts) *Would you like to be an astronaut? Why?/Why not?*
  Ask: *Would you like to go up in a hot air balloon? Why? Why not?*
- Ask: *Which two words were not answers?* (path, visit). In pairs, learners make two short sentences with these words.
  Suggestions: *We often visit my grandparents. Walk on the path, not on the flowers!*

B ▶ Listen to the sentences about picture 1. How is picture 2 different?

- Learners look at the two pictures. Ask: *Which words from the word box in A can you see in these pictures?* (sky, passenger, wheels, airport) *And which orange words from the sentences in A can you see here?* (helicopter, bus, bicycle, plane, taxi).

Say: *We can see wheels in these two pictures. And they all have tyres. Can you see the tyres? They're the black part of a wheel. How many tyres are there in the picture in 1? Can you count them? Be careful – you can't see some of the tyres on the taxis or the bus, but they are there!* (27 - 16 on the taxis, 2 on the motorbike, 2 on the bike, 4 on the bus, 3 on the plane on the ground)

- In pairs, learners find and circle differences between the pictures. Do not check the differences at this point.
  Note: There are 12 differences.
- Say: *Listen to the woman. She's describing the first picture. Write how the second picture is different.*
  Play the first sentence on the audio. Point to the example: *In my picture, the man on the motorbike has got a red bag.* Say: *This sentence says how picture 2 is different.*
- Play the other four sentences pausing after each one. Learners write how the second picture is different in their notebooks.
- Learners listen to the rest of the audio to check answers and compare them with their own. You may prefer to pause the audio for learners to say, not write, what the differences are.

Audioscript

Listen to the sentences about picture 1.
In my picture, the man on the motorbike has got a blue bag.
In my picture, there are four taxis outside the airport.
In my picture, the plane's on the ground.
In my picture, the bus doors are open.
In my picture, there's a helicopter in the air.
Now listen and check your answers.

Woman:	In my picture, the man on the motorbike has got a blue bag.
Boy:	In my picture, the man on the motorbike has got a red bag.
Woman:	In my picture, there are four taxis outside the airport.
Boy:	In my picture, there are two taxis outside the airport.
Woman:	In my picture, the plane's on the ground.
Boy:	In my picture, the plane's in the air.
Woman:	In my picture, the bus doors are open.
Boy:	In my picture, the bus doors are closed.
Woman:	In my picture, there's a helicopter in the air.
Boy:	In my picture, there isn't a helicopter in the air.

Find and talk about seven more differences.

- Say: *There are seven more differences that you didn't hear.*
- Divide the learners into two groups, A and B. Group A look at picture 1 and write a sentence about the person or thing that is different from picture 2. Group B look at picture 2 and write a sentence for each difference. They should NOT compare pictures. (For example, group A should write: *In my picture, a man is getting on a bus.* Group B should write: *In my picture, a man is waiting outside a bus.*)
- Learners work together in A and B pairs. Learner A reads out a sentence: *In my picture, a man's pushing a bicycle.* Learner B replies with the difference: *In my picture, a man's riding a bicycle.*

  1 A man is getting on a bus / **waiting outside** a bus.
  2 A man is pushing / **riding** a bicycle.
  3 A man and a woman / **two women** are running to the bus.
  4 The airport sign is red / **green**.
  5 It's cloudy / **sunny**.
  6 The man by the bus has got / **hasn't got** an umbrella.
  7 The man by the bus has got **blonde** / black hair.

C Draw lines between words that mean the same.

- Read out sentence 1: *Travelling to London takes three hours.* Point out that the word 'travelling' is in bold and that there is a line to F – *The journey.*

62

Say: *The journey to London takes three hours. Is this right?* (yes) *'Travelling' and 'The journey' mean the same in this sentence.*

○ Learners find the words that mean the same as the bold words in 2–7 and draw lines to the correct letters.

> **Check answers:**
> 2 A 3 B 4 G 5 C 6 H 7 D

○ Ask: *Which word didn't you need?* (trips) *How can we change sentence 1 to use 'trips' here?* (Trips to London <u>take</u> three hours.)

○ Give each learner a photocopy of the 'Funny trip' section of page 139. Learners sit in a circle.

○ Make sure everyone has a pencil and a sheet to complete.
Say: *In the top box, write the name of someone you know or someone who's famous, who's very young or very old or you can write something like 'The pop star' or 'The astronaut'.* Learners write in the top box. Say: *Now give your piece of paper to the person next to you.* Learners pass their sheet to another learner.

○ Say: *In the next box, put another person. You choose.* Learners write a name and then pass their sheet to the next person.

○ Say: *In the next box, write the name of a place you can travel to you know or somewhere you'd like to visit one day.* Learners write a place and then pass their sheet on.

○ Say: *In the next box, write a day of the week or any day you think is special. You choose.* The 'Funny Trip' sentence is now complete. Learners pass their sheet to the next person.
Learners take turns to read out sentences, for example: *The king travelled with our teacher to the moon by hot air balloon on my birthday.* Learners vote for the funniest sentence.

D ▶ **How did Uncle Oliver get to each place? Listen and write a letter (A–H) in each box.** Listening Part **3**

> **Flyers tip**
> In Listening Part 3, candidates should look carefully at both sets of pictures before they do the task. This will familiarise them with the context and help them predict words they are likely to hear.

○ Ask: *What places can you see in the small pictures?* (an airport, a museum, a castle, a forest, a police station, a restaurant). Learners write the names of the places on the lines.

○ Write on the board: *People go to this place when they want to ….*
Say: *This sentence is about an airport.* Ask learners to finish this sentence, for example: *catch a plane, fly somewhere, go on holiday.* Learners complete the same sentence for the five other places.

Suggestions:
A museum: … see old things / learn more about history
A castle: … see where kings and queens lived / visit a very old building
A forest: … see animals / climb trees and play
A police station: … tell the police about a problem / ask for help
A restaurant: … have a meal / meet their friends

○ Learners name the forms of transport in the pictures (a helicopter, boat, taxi, bus, train, bike/bicycle, car, lorry/truck).

○ Say: *You are going to hear a girl called Sophia and her uncle, whose name is Oliver, talking about where he goes for his job.* Play the audio. Learners listen and write a letter (A–H) to show how Uncle Oliver went to each place. Say: *There's one example (G).* Learners can listen to the audio twice.

> **Check answers:**
> museum – E, castle – D, police station – C, forest – A, restaurant – B.

○ Ask: *Which two pictures did you not need for your answers?* (F, the bike and H, the lorry)
Did you hear these words? (Yes, Oliver was on his 'bike' when he lost his money, and he saw 'lorries' from the helicopter.)

○ Ask: *What job do you think Sophia's uncle does?* (He's a journalist.) *What did you hear that helped you decide that?* (He wrote about places for the newspaper.)

Audioscript

How did Uncle Oliver get to each place?
Girl: Hi, Uncle Oliver! You have to do lots of travelling in your job, don't you?
Man: Yes, Sophia. I went to the airport yesterday. An important person was coming to see me.
Girl: Did you give him a lift back into town?
Man: That's right. In my new racing car! But there was lots of traffic on the motorway.
Girl So were you late?
Man Yes … by ten minutes! He was quite angry!

Can you see the letter G?
Now you listen and write a letter in each box.
Man: I wanted to find out some information at the museum in the city centre on Thursday.
Girl: Did you go by train?
Man: Yes, it's quick and easy. You buy a ticket from the machine and there are computer screens everywhere with all the information you need about times and platforms.
Girl: You go to such interesting places. You're so lucky!
Man: I know. I had to go and look at a castle last week. I'm writing about it for a newspaper.
Girl: How did you get there? By taxi?
Man: Not this time. I caught a bus but that was a bad idea! It took such a long time to get there, as well.
Girl: Oh dear!
Man: And I had to go to the police station one day.
Girl: Why?
Man: Because I lost my money when I cycled to the shopping centre last weekend. It was too far to walk, so I went by taxi.
Girl: Could the police officer there help you?
Man: Not really. He asked me several questions … Perhaps they'll find my money. I don't know.
Girl: Where did you go on Tuesday?
Man: Into the forest. Someone saw a bear there, so I wanted to write about that for the newspaper, too. It was a fantastic day!
Girl: Why?
Man: Because I flew there in a helicopter. I was very high in the air. I could see all the lorries on the road below me.
Girl: Did you stay there all day?
Man : No, I came home and then went out to dinner.
Girl: Where? To your favourite restaurant in Bridge Street?
Man: That's right! I went there by boat this time. It was lots of fun.
Girl: Wow!

E **Answer Peter's questions about Uncle Oliver. What does Sophia say? Write 1, 2, 3 or 4 words.**

○ Play the first part of the audio again. Uncle Oliver says: *I went to the airport yesterday. An important person was coming to see me.* So, the answer to 1 is: *He went there to meet **an important person**.* Ask: *How many words are there in this answer?* (three) *How many words can you write in the other answers?* (1, 2, 3 or 4)

○ Learners listen to Uncle Oliver again and complete sentences 2–5. Pause the audio to give learners time to write their answers.

> **Check answers:**
> 2 by train 3 shopping centre 4 fanastic 5 boat

Let's talk about you and transport.

○ Learners work in A and B pairs. Learner A looks at the questions on page 119 of their book and Learner B looks at the questions on page 121 of their book.

○ Learners ask and answer each other's questions. A writes B's answers and B writes A's answers.

○ Ask questions about the different things. Learners put up their hands if their answer is 'yes' or 'me!'.
How many of you have been in a helicopter?
How many of you enjoy flying in a plane?

25 What shall we do next?

Topics sports and leisure

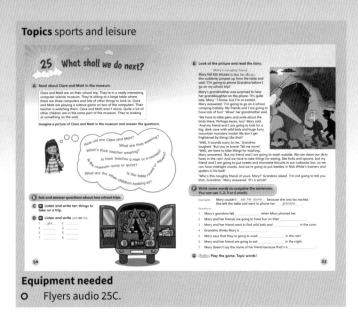

Equipment needed
- Flyers audio 25C.

A Read about Clare and Matt in the museum.

- Ask: *What places do you like going to? Do you like visiting museums?* If some learners answer *yes*, ask: *What kinds of things do you like finding out about?* Learners answer.

  Ask: *Can you use the internet at home? How often do you use the internet?*

  Say: *Read about Clare and Matt. They're at a museum. You don't have to answer the questions now so don't look at those yet.* Learners read the text.

- Teach/revise any key vocabulary so learners are confident they understand where Clare and Matt are / what they're looking at / how many other people are near them.

Imagine a picture of Clare and Matt in the museum and answer the questions.

- Say: *There isn't a picture of these children at the museum so you're going to try and see a picture of Clare and Matt in your head.* Make sure learners understand they are going to imagine the picture.

- Say: *Close your eyes and try to see the picture.*

  I'm going to help you to do this.

  I'm going to talk about Clare and Matt at the science museum now.

  I'm going to ask you some questions about Clare and Matt and about the museum.

  Don't answer the questions. Try to 'see' the answers in the picture you are making in your head.

- Read the following text slowly and quietly. Pause before you ask each question and pause for about ten seconds after each question. This will give learners time to 'answer' these questions in their imaginations.

  Clare and Matt are on their school trip. **How old are they?** (pause)

  What are they wearing? (pause)

  They're in a really interesting computer science museum. **Is the museum noisy or quiet?** (pause)

  They're sitting at a large table. **Is the table round or square?** (pause)

  There are three computers and lots of other things to look at on the table. **What else is on the table?** (pause)

  Clare and Matt are playing a science game on the computers. **What's on the computer screens?** (pause)

Their teacher is watching them. **Is their teacher a man or a woman?** (pause) **What's their teacher wearing?** (pause)

Clare and Matt aren't alone. Quite a lot of other children are in the same part of the museum. They're looking at something on the wall. **What are the other children looking at?** (pause)

- Say: *Open your eyes.* Wait in silence for few seconds more before continuing.

- In pairs, learners ask and answer the different questions in A to find out how different their imagined 'pictures' were.

- Learners could write answers to the questions in their notebooks for homework or create a table in their notebooks showing their own and their partner's answers.

B Ask and answer questions about two school trips.

Speaking Part 2

- Say: *Now you're going to ask or answer questions about the school trip that Clare went on last week and ask or answer questions about her friend's school trip, too. His name is George. He goes to another school.*

- Divide class into A and B pairs. Learner A looks at their set of questions and answers on page 122. Learner B looks at their set of questions and answers on page 124.

- Say to A learners: *You don't know anything about Clare's school trip, but your B partners do. Ask them questions about it.* Say to B learners: *Look at the answers about Clare's school trip. Find the right answer to each question.* Learners work in pairs, asking and answering the questions.

- Say to B learners: *You don't know anything about George's school trip, but your A partners do. Ask them questions about it.* Say to A learners: *Look at the answers about George's school trip. Find the right answer to each question.* Learners work in pairs as before.

- Ask questions in open class about both trips to check understanding.

C ▶ Listen and write ten things to take on a trip.

- Teach/revise: 'going to do' if necessary before doing this task.

- Say: *A class is going to go to the mountains for three days with their teacher. Guess what the children must take with them on their trip.* Write learners' first six suggestions on the board.

- Play the example on the audio. Say: *The children must take …* (pens). *Why?* (They must write with them.)

- Learners listen. In their notebooks, they write the ten other things the children should take. Pairs compare their lists before listening the second time. Check with the guessed objects on the board. How many objects did learners guess correctly?

> **Check answers:**
> **1** soap **2** toothbrush **3** comb **4** torch **5** towel **6** knife
> **7** fork **8** spoon **9** plate **10** phone

- In groups of 3–4, learners make sentences about the objects and the reasons for taking them. For example: *The children are going to take their toothbrushes so they can clean their teeth!*

Audioscript

Listen and write the things the students need. There is one example.

Man: Our class is going to go to the mountains next month. We'll be there for three days. I'm going to tell you ten things you need to bring with you. Write them in your books.

Girl: OK. What's the first thing, Mr Green?

Man: You need to bring a pen. You're going to do lots of writing.

Now you listen and write.

Man: Please bring some soap, too.

Boy: What? We have to take soap with us?

Man: Yes. You need to wash your hands before you eat! And I want you to clean your teeth twice a day, morning and night, so don't forget your toothbrush. And on our last trip, some of you forgot to bring a comb. Please remember to bring one this time.

Girl: Alright.

Man: And don't forget to bring a torch so you can see at night.

Girl: A big torch or a small one?

Man: It doesn't matter. You must bring a towel to dry yourselves with, too.

Girl: Just one towel?

Man: Yes. Now, for the things you need to eat with. Bring a knife and a fork. Bring a spoon too.

Boy: A knife, fork and spoon?

Man: Yes, that's right. What else? Oh, yes. A plate.

Boy: Should we bring a bowl too?

Man: No. Just a plate, please.

Boy: OK! What about my phone? Can I bring that?

Man: Yes, but you should only use it if you need to send a message or speak to your parents, OK?

D Listen and write *yes* or *no*.

O Ask learners to remain sitting if they prefer being at home or to stand up if they prefer going away.

Small classes: divide the class into two groups according to preference.

Larger classes: learners work in groups of four according to preference.

Groups think of four reasons why it's good to be at home or to be away. They write sentences in their notebooks. Learners from each group take it in turns to read out their reasons.

O Learners look at the picture of the car. Tell them that Mr and Mrs Hall and their children, Tony and Kim, are going to go on holiday in five minutes. Ask: *What can you see in the back of their car?* Teach/revise vocabulary if necessary (ball, bikes, camera, diary, magazines, map, mat, paints, paintbrush, tent, torch/flashlight).

O Give learners one minute to try to remember as much as possible about these things.

Note: 'Torch' and 'flashlight' are both on the Flyers wordlist but 'torch' is used more in British English and 'flashlight' in American English.

O Learners look at numbers 1–8 to the left of the picture. Say: *I'm going to talk about eight different things that you can see in the picture. Write 'yes' if the sentence you hear about the picture is correct. Write 'no' if the sentence is wrong.*

O Speak slowly. Say: *One. The Hall family are going to go camping.*

O Ask: *Can you see the 'yes' answer? This means the sentence was … ?* (right)

Say: *Now listen and write 'yes' or 'no' for the other sentences.*

Note: Pause for about ten seconds between sentences and repeat 2–8 if necessary.

Two. They're going to go skiing on their holiday, too.

Three. They're going to take lots of photos, of course.

Four. Tony and Kim Hall are going to take their bicycles with them.

Five. Their parents are going to take lots of newspapers to read.

Six. One person in the family is going to write about the holiday in a diary.

Seven. Another person in the family is going to paint some pictures.

Eight. Mr Hall is going to take his drum with him.

Check answers:
2 no **3** yes **4** yes **5** no **6** yes **7** yes **8** no

E Look at the picture and read the story.

O Learners read the story about Mary's friend. Revise: granddaughter, dark, brave, and secret.

O Ask questions: *What time of day did Mary phone her grandmother?* (evening) *What's Mary going to write about?* (birds) *What's Mary going to put in one boy's bed?* (spiders) *And what's she going to put in his trainers?* (beetles) *What's the name of Mary's friend?* (We don't know!)

F Write some words to complete the sentences. You can use 1, 2, 3 or 4 words.

Reading & Writing **Part 5**

O Read the first paragraph of the story again with learners. Say: *Remember, you can use 1, 2, 3 or 4 words to complete the sentences. All the words you need are in the story.* Learners complete the sentences.

Check answers:
1 surprised **2** (school) camping holiday
3 (huge) (furry) (mountain) monsters **4** (very) brave
5 our (dirty) faces **6** sweets and chocolate biscuits **7** secret

Note: The usual collocation is 'have a snack'.

G Play the game. Topic words!

O Say: *Think about words to say how you travel.* Divide the class into four teams. Each team has one minute to think of words on that topic.

O The first team says one word on that topic, for example: *by train.* The second team continues, for example: *in a space rocket.* The third, then the fourth team also say a word, for example: *drive, go by bike.* Continue like this. If a team repeats a word, they miss a turn.

O Teams get a point for every appropriate word. The team with the most points wins the game.

Suggested categories:

Things you can see in a road.

Things you can take on a journey to the countryside.

Things you can take on a summer/winter holiday.

Things you can see in an airport.

Things you can see in a railway station.

26   Where can we go on holiday?

Topics sports and leisure

Not in YLE wordlists: *surfboard*

Equipment needed

o   Flyers audio 26E.

Make crosswords.

o   Write the word *holiday* on the board vertically. Say: *Think of a word about holidays that starts with 'h' or has an 'h' in its spelling?* (suggestion: hotel) Write *hotel* on the board using the 'h' of *holiday*.

o   In small groups, learners think of words connected with holidays to fit around the other letters. Invite groups of learners to write their 'crosswords' on the board.

Suggested answer:

Hotel p**O**stcard **L**ondon **I**ce cream islan**D** be**A**ch sunn**Y**

Ⓐ Match four of the word circles with the pictures.

o   Learners look at the five word circles. In pairs, they find the three or four words in each one (sailing, view, island / climbing, sky, rucksack / tent, camping, torch / city, hotel, entrance / jungle, adventure, wild animals). Teach/revise vocabulary if necessary.

o   Learners draw lines between each word circle and its matching picture. Ask: *Which word circle doesn't have a picture?* (jungle, adventure, wild animals)

o   Check the other four matching word circles and pictures.

o   Ask three or four different learners: *Which of these five kinds of holiday might be the most exciting? Why?*

o   Learners look at the holiday word circles again and vote for their favourite kind of holiday. Ask: *Which holiday is the best? The worst?*

Ⓑ Complete the holiday diary. Write one word in each space.

o   Ask: *Do you write and tell your friends about your day on the internet?* If you have 'yes' answers, ask: *Do you write something every day? What do you like best, writing about your day on the internet or in text messages?*

o   Learners read the diary text and the example. Ask: *How long must each answer be?* (only one word) In pairs, learners choose words to fill each of the spaces.

> **Check answers:**
> **1** the   **2** which/that   **3** was   **4** sat/lay   **5** about   **6** on   **7** and
> **8** at/in

o   Ask: *What kind of holiday is this person having?* (a camping holiday). Learners choose the correct picture from **A** to go with this diary text. Ask: *Would you like to be on a holiday like this? Why / Why not?*

o   In pairs, learners write five things about a camping holiday that are fun and five things about a camping holiday that they might not like. Pairs share their ideas with the rest of the class. Ask: *Is there anything about camping that you think is fun? Is there anything that you don't like?*

Ⓒ Read the conversation and choose the best answer (A–H).   Reading & Writing Part 2

o   Point to the girl in the first picture in **D**. Say: *This is Helen.* Point to the other people and ask:
Who are these people? (Helen's mum and dad and brother.)
Are they going to go on holiday by plane? (no)
Are they going to go by car? (yes)

o   Learners read the conversation, look at the example and choose Helen's answers from A–H.

> **Check answers:**
> **1** G   **2** F   **3** E   **4** D   **5** H

o   Ask: *Where does Helen usually go on holiday?* (to the mountains)
Where is Ben going to go on holiday? (to London)
Have you ever been to London? Learners answer *yes* or *no*.

o   Write on the board: *Have you ever:*
stayed in a hotel?
slept in a tent?
climbed a mountain?
seen a wild animal?

o   In pairs, learners ask and answer these questions. Pairs could also ask each other more holiday questions, for example, Ben's questions 1 and 4: *Where do you usually go? What do you do during the day?*

o   Say: *Find the words 'science', 'tour' and 'building' in Helen's possible answers. Circle these words with your red pencil.*

o   Write on the board: *Will Ben go on a tour of that big science building in London?*

o   Say: *Listen carefully. When I say these words are there any letters that you don't hear?* Read the sentence out very slowly, pointing to each word as you say it and pausing for learners to suggest letters they can see but can't hear (ie: *Will Ben go on a tour of that big science building in London?*).

o   In pairs, learners make their own short sentence with the word *tour, science* or *building* in it. For example: *I had fun on the tour. I love science lessons. I live in a big building.*

Ⓓ Look at the pictures and tell the story.   Speaking Part 3

> **Flyers tip**
> In Speaking Part 3, candidates should use sequencing and linking words when they are telling the story. Using words like *now, next, then, but, because, so* make a story easier to understand.

- Ask questions about the first picture:
  How many people can you see? (four – and the man in the dream picture.)
  Where are they? (near their car)
  What are they looking at? (the things in the back of the car)
  Is everyone in the picture happy? (no, not the mother)
- Learners look at the first (line drawing) and picture 2 and write or say how the second picture is different.
  Suggestions:
  The family are in the countryside now. The mother looks happier now. The children are running in this picture. We can't see the things in the back of the car. We can see some tents and some trees.
- Point to all five pictures. Say:
  These pictures tell a story. It's called 'The day we forgot our tent'.
- Learners look at the first picture again and listen to you reading the first part of the story.
  Helen and her family are getting ready to go on holiday. They're putting all their things in the back of the car. They always go camping in the countryside. Helen's father loves camping, but her mother is thinking, 'I want to go to a hotel by the beach this year.'
- Learners look at picture 2 and continue the story. Ask questions to help them if necessary: *Where are they now?* (in the countryside / a forest)
  What can you see in the forest? (some tents)
  What are Helen and her brother doing? (running and playing)
  Helen's dad is going to open the back of the car. Why? (He's going to take out the things.)
- Do the same for pictures 3, 4 and 5.
  Picture 3
  What's Helen's dad doing now? (looking for something in the car)
  Does Helen's mum look happy? (no)
  Was the tent in the back of the car? (no)
  Picture 4
  What is Helen's dad thinking? ('I forgot/left the tent at home.')
  Is Helen's mother angry? (yes)
  Picture 5
  Where are the family now? (at a hotel by the beach)
  What are Helen and her brother doing? (swimming/playing in the swimming pool)
  What are Helen's parents doing? (lying in the sun)
  Is the father worried? (yes) *What's he thinking?* ('This is going to be very expensive.')
- Learners tell or role play the story in small groups. Learners could also write the story for the pictures. This would be useful practice for the writing in Reading and Writing Part 7.

E ▶ Listen and colour and write. 　Listening **5** _{Part}

- Learners look at the line drawing in **D** and listen to the example. Ask: *What colour is the tent now?* (orange)
- Say: *Now listen again. You are going to write something and colour more things in this picture.*
- Play the rest of the audio. Learners should hear 1–5 twice.

  Check answers:
  1 Colour rucksack with pockets green.
  2 Write 'happy' on man's T-shirt.
  3 Colour water in swimming pool blue.
  4 Write COUSIN on the board before Road.
  5 Colour torch – yellow.

Audioscript

Listen and colour and write.

Woman:	Hello! Would you like to colour some of this picture?
Boy:	Yes. Is this family ready to go on holiday?
Woman:	I think so. The father is thinking about sitting in the sun, isn't he?
Boy:	Yes, he is! And I can see the tent.
Woman:	Good. Colour it orange.

Can you see the orange tent? This is an example. Now you colour and write.

1
Woman:	Can you see the backpacks?
Boy:	Yes. There are two. They look very full.
Woman:	Colour the one with the two pockets.
Boy:	Right, I'll make that one green. Is that OK?
Woman:	Yes, that's fine.

2
Woman:	Now, I'd like you to write something, please.
Boy:	All right. What shall I write?
Woman:	Well, the father is feeling very excited about all the fun they're going to have on holiday so write 'happy' on the front of his shirt.
Boy:	OK! I'm doing that now.
Woman:	Thank you!

3
Woman:	Right, colour the water next.
Boy:	Do you mean the girl's drink? She's got a bottle in her hand.
Woman:	Not that. I mean the pool that the woman's thinking about.
Boy:	Oh OK. Shall I make it blue?
Woman:	Yes, please. That's a good idea.

4
Boy:	Can I write something else in this picture, too?
Woman:	Sure! Above the boy's head … the child with the baseball cap … you can see a board.
Boy:	Yes. I can see that.
Woman:	Good. Let's add the name of the road there. This road is called, 'Cousin' Road.
Boy:	Like the family word, you mean?
Woman:	Yes! It's the same spelling.

5
Woman:	Now, the last thing to colour. You decide!
Boy:	By myself? Oh OK. Can I colour the flashlight in the back of the car?
Woman:	Of course. Do you want to colour it purple?
Boy:	No. I prefer yellow. Is that all right?
Woman:	That's fine! Well done! This picture looks a lot better now!
Boy:	Thanks!

Play the game! Travel bingo.

- Tell learners to make a grid of nine squares, in three rows of three. They look at the wordlists for this unit and for Units 11 and 24 (pages 132, 133 & 136) and choose nine words. They write one of these words in each square. Read out these words, one by one. If learners wrote the word, they cross it out. The winner is the first person to cross out all nine words.

  Words to say: blanket, tent, torch, camera, camping beds, airport, boat, bus, helicopter, station, train, hot air balloon, motorbike, racing car, taxi, holiday, hotel, pool, tour, view

27   It's the holidays! Bye!

Topics transport, the world around us

Equipment needed

○ Flyers audio 27C.

○ Half a sheet of paper for each learner. See E.

Ⓐ Make a story with the seven pictures.

○ Ask learners what they can see in each of the seven pictures.
   Food, a beach, a cave, eyes, a pirate, a boy, the same boy with two girls on a (sailing) boat.

○ Ask: *Where do you find caves?* (in rocks / mountains / near the sea)
   In stories, what do pirates do in caves? (sleep, live, hide, hide / keep treasure) *When do people go sailing?* (when they're on holiday / at the beach / when it's windy / at the weekend)

○ Say: *The boy and the two girls are cousins. Choose names for them.*

   In groups of 3–4, learners write a story using the pictures in any order. They might find this easier if they include some conversation between the pirate and the children. When groups have finished their stories, they tell them to the class.

   For example: *Three children sailed to a beach. When they arrived, they saw a pirate. They were very surprised! 'Where are you going?' Sam asked the pirate. 'To my cave,' the pirate answered. 'Are you going to hide lots of gold and silver treasure there?' Pat asked. The pirate laughed. 'No,' he said. 'I'm going to go and get my picnic! I put it in there because it's too hot out here on the sand!'*

   Note: You could also display the stories round the classroom for groups to read.

Ⓑ Read the story. Choose a word from the box. Write the correct word next to the numbers 1–5.

Reading & Writing Part **3**

> **Flyers tip**
>
> In Reading and Writing Part 3, there are ten content words to choose from to fill the gaps, but candidates only need to use six. It should help them choose the correct answer if they recognise the different parts of speech found in this task: nouns, verbs, adjectives and adverbs.

○ Learners read the story about Jim and say if any of their stories from **A** were similar.

○ Ask questions about the story:
   1 *Did Jim go to a city for his holiday?* (No, to the beach.)
   2 *Who went there with him?* (his parents and two cousins, Emma and Alice)
   3 *How did they get to the island?* (They sailed there.)
   4 *Where did they eat?* (on the rocks)
   5 *Who came to find the children?* (Jim's dad/father)

○ Point to the word 'beach' on the line in the story and in the box.
   Ask: *Is 'beach' a verb, like 'write', or a noun like 'table'?* (a noun)
   Point to the words in the box and ask:
   Which other words in the box are nouns? (cave, strawberries)
   Which words are verbs? (touch, hid, collecting, watering)
   Which words are adjectives? (missing, wonderful, unkind)
   Note: 'missing' could be an adjective or a verb but is not listed as a verb in the YLE word list.

○ Ask: *How many words must we add to the story?* (five) Say: *Find the correct word in the box and write it on the line.* If appropriate to your teaching approach, learners should also think why a noun, verb or adjective is needed in each gap.

> **Check answers:**
> 1 strawberries (a noun – it follows in a list of other nouns after 'some')
> 2 cave (a noun – it follows 'a big dark')
> 3 hid (a verb – what pirates do with treasure)
> 4 collecting (a verb – this is what the children did)
> 5 wonderful (an adjective – it comes between 'What a' and 'place')

Now choose the best name for the story. Tick one box.

○ Learners choose the best name for the story. (Fun on the island)
   Ask: *Did we read about a sailing game or a pirate family?* (no) Say: *So the other two names are not right for this story.*

○ Write on the board: *dangerous exciting boring frightening wonderful interesting strange*

○ Ask: *What's the most dangerous thing you did on a holiday?*

○ In pairs or small groups, learners ask each other the same question. They then ask more questions using the superlative forms of the other adjectives on the board.

○ Walk around and check they are using the structure correctly.

   Note: If learners can already use the present perfect, use *What's the most dangerous thing you have ever done on holiday?* as the model sentence.

C ▶ Listen! What's Lily going to do today? Tick the boxes.

o Tell learners to close their books (so they can't see the options in **C** yet).

o Ask: *What are we going to do today?* Tell learners to begin their answers with *We're going to …* (have lessons, go outside, work on computers, have lunch, go home etc.)

o Say: *Listen to Lily. She's going to tell a friend what she's going to do today. It's the first day of her holidays so she isn't going to go to school.* Learners predict what Lily is going to do. Write their suggestions on the board. Learners open their books. Ask: *Are any of your ideas the same?*

o Learners listen and tick the things that Lily is going to do.

> **Check answers:**
> write messages, watch a TV programme, eat lots of biscuits, repair her bike, read an adventure story

o Ask: *How did Lily begin her phone call?* (Hi! It's Lily.)
Did you hear what the other person is going to do? (no)
What happened at the end of Lily's phone call? (The other person didn't say anything.)

o Teach/revise this use of 'working / not working' using examples that learners might say themselves, for example: *My computer's / phone's / pen's / DVD's working again now. This computer / phone / pen / DVD isn't working this morning.*

Audioscript

> Hi! It's Lily. Thanks for your message. I'm going to text all our friends. It's great to be on holiday, isn't it?
> After breakfast – I'm not dressed yet – I'm going to watch cartoons on channel five and finish all the chocolate biscuits that Mum bought yesterday!
> After lunch I'm going to take the front wheel off my bike and try to repair it. It won't be easy! I'd like to play chess too but there's no-one here to play with.
> After dinner, I'm going to finish that adventure story I'm reading. You know … I told you about it … the one about the journey into another world.
> What about you? Are you going to play video games or join the sports club?
> Hello? Can you hear me? Oh … Perhaps your phone isn't working. I'll call you again in ten minutes. Bye for now.

What about you?

o Ask: *Do you remember any of the things that Lily spoke about but isn't going to do?* Write learners' answers on the board. (play chess, go on a journey, join a sports club, play video games)

o Say: *Some of these are also interesting things to do. Would you like to do any of these things?* In groups of 3–4, learners choose one of these activities, talk about it and write about it in their notebooks. To help them, ask learners for their ideas in open class first if necessary.

o Write five question words on the board: (*why, who, where, when, how long*). Tell learners to use the words to give them ideas for things they are going to do and why. Make sure they understand that they don't have to use them in that order. For example:
I'm going to go for a bike ride today (why?) because I've got a new bicycle. I'm going to go for a bike ride with (who?) my best friend. We're going to ride (where?) through the forest. I'm going to meet her there (when?) after lunch and we're going to ride (how long?) all afternoon!

o After writing about their activity, learners in each group take turns to read out their plan to the rest of the class.
Note: This is an empowering exercise which will also help prepare learners for the storytelling activity in the speaking test. Allow learners full use of their imaginations to talk about their own plans and accept any reasonably appropriate answers.

D Decide what you are going to do tomorrow! Complete the sentences.

o Learners look at the cues in their books and complete the sentences. They can use their dictionaries to help them if necessary. If they can't find a word they need, tell them to ask you for help.
Note: Learners answers do not need to be realistic. They may find it more fun to invent activities using their imaginations. Encourage learners to be creative with their ideas.

o In pairs, learners tell each other about their fun day!

E Play the game. Really?

o Write on the board: *Really? If you want! Cool! I'm going to do that too! That's such a good idea! That's lots of fun! But that's so boring!*

o Point to the list of expressions. Ask: *What can you say when you are both going to do the same thing?* (I'm going to do that too!)
What can you say when you think it's a bad idea to do something? (But that's so boring!)
Which three things can you say when you think it's a very nice idea to do something? (That's such a good idea! Cool! That's lots of fun!)
What can you say if you agree to do something? (If you want!) *What can you say when you are surprised that someone wants to do something?* (Really?) Explain that 'really' can mean 'very', but like this, it means 'Are you sure?'

o On a piece of paper, each learner writes short sentences about the three activities they chose to do after lunch in **D**. For example: *I'm going to watch television. I'm going to play volleyball. I'm going to fly to the moon.* They also copy the responses on the board writing these underneath their three chosen activities.

o Learners move around the class finding different people to talk to. In their pairs, they tell each other what they're going to do. After each sentence the other learner replies, choosing an appropriate response from the list.

o At the end of the lesson, say: *Right! Now we're all going to close our books and say goodbye!*

28 I want to win!

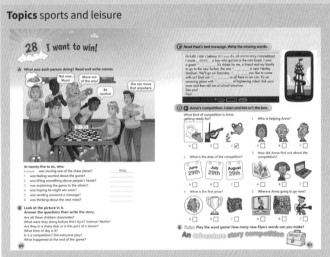

Equipment needed

o   Flyers audio 28D.

o   Pencils and colouring pencils or pens and card. See B and Project.

Ⓐ What was each person doing? Read and write names.

o   Learners look at the unit title. Ask: *Do you like winning when you play a game? How does it feel when you win / when you lose?*
    If someone who has lost a game is feeling sad, what can you say to help them feel happier again?
    Don't worry! Perhaps you'll win next time. It's only a game. It's not important!

o   Learners look at the picture. Ask some general then personal questions before they complete the activity.
    Are these children inside or outside? (inside)
    Two of the children are playing a game. What are their names? (Holly and Fred)
    How many of their friends are with them? (five)
    We can't see one boy's name. We can only see the first two letters of his name. What do you think this boy's name is? Learners suggest names beginning with P-A-. Say: *It's Paul!* Ask: *How do you spell 'Paul'?* (P-A-U-L)
    What game are Holly and Fred playing? (chess)
    Can you play chess? How old were you when you started playing chess? How often do you play chess?
    Do you play any other board games? Which ones? Who do you like playing with most? Do you play board games like chess on the internet sometimes? Is it more fun playing board games on a table with people you can see or on a phone / the internet?

o   Teach/revise how to use and form the past continuous. If necessary, write the forms: *I / he / she / it was doing … we / you / they were doing …* on the board. Ask: *What were you doing at six / nine o'clock this morning / ten minutes ago?* 2–3 learners give their answers.

o   Learners ask and answer the same question form in a chain. For example:
    Learner A: *What were you doing at nine o'clock this morning?*
    Learner B: *I was running to school. What were you doing at nine o'clock this morning?*
    Learner C: *I was playing in the playground. What were you doing at nine o'clock this morning?*
    Learner D: *I was talking to my friend.*

o   Ask: *What was Lily saying?* (Be careful!) Ask two learners to come to the front of the class. One mimes doing something dangerous, for example, climbing up something high. The other says: *Be careful!*

o   Ask: *What was Betty saying?* (Move out of the way!) Ask four learners to mime a situation in which someone wants to move through a crowd so needs to say *Move out of the way!*

o   Learners look at the example question. Explain that the different black and white things that we move across the chess board are called *chess pieces.* Ask: *So at 5.35, who was moving one of the chess pieces?* (Holly) Learners see the name 'Holly' on the example dotted line.

o   Learners read the other questions and write names. Learners can help each other by working in pairs or work alone then check their answers with a partner and talk about any differences.

> **Check answers:**
> 1 Lily   2 Betty   3 John   4 Fred   5 Paul   6 Sue

Note: If some of your learners are chess players, you may wish to ask them to help you explain to the rest of the class the names of the chess pieces, the different ways they can each move and the aim of the game.

Ⓑ Look at the picture in A. Answer the questions then write the story.

> **Flyers tip**
> In Reading and Writing Part 7, train learners to use connectors, for example: *and, but, or, because, when* or *while* to link their sentences together. Remind them that simple sentences are fine, but they may be given a higher mark if they can include a compound sentence.

o   Say: *These seven children were all wearing the same colour T-shirts. Why? Do they go to the same school?* (yes) *Are they classmates?* Learners say what they think.

o   Tell one learner to read out the second question in **B** and to choose three different learners in the class to answer it. (What were they doing before this? Gym? Science? Maths?) The other learners answer.
    A different learner reads out the third question and everyone in the class decides on one answer – a chess club or a lesson.

o   Say: *We already said what time of day it is, so now, in pairs, talk about the last two questions in B.* Pairs ask and answer these questions.

o   Write on the board: *while, when, because, so.* Point to these words and say: *These are great words for telling a story. I want you to write a story about the picture in A. Use the questions in B to help you and try and use these words in your story.*

Suggested story

When school finished at half past five, seven of the students from Holly's class went to the chess club. Today was the end of the chess competition so everyone was very excited. While Holly and Fred were playing, Betty took photos. Lily was worried so she said 'Be careful!' to Holly. Holly won the game and the competition too!

Ⓒ Read Paul's text message. Write the missing words.

o   Ask: *What was Paul doing in the picture in A?* (He was reading a text message.) Say: *Paul's always texting! Look at the first line of his message. Who is Paul going to send it to?* (Kim)

o   Learners read the whole of Paul's text message. Before learners write the missing words, say: *I'm going to ask a question and then give you three answers. Only one of the answers is right. Listen to all three answers first. When I say them again put up your hand when you hear the right answer.*
    Ask: *Why is Paul happy?*
    Because he went to a funfair.
    Because he is going to go to an amazing place.
    Because he's reading a story about a rainforest.

- Learners should choose the second answer. Ask why the other answers are wrong.
- Check learners' pronunciation of 'ture' in adventure. /tʃə/. Write on the board:
  Charlie took a picture of his teacher at the Future Adventure Park last Tuesday!
  Say: *There are four /tʃə/ sounds in this sentence. Where are they?* Learners to come to the board and underline the /tʃə/ sounds in pic<u>ture</u>, tea<u>cher</u>, fu<u>ture</u>, adven<u>ture</u>.
  Say: *There are two more /tʃ/ sounds in this sentence. Where are these?* Learners come to the board and underline <u>Ch</u>arlie and <u>Tu</u>esday.
  Learners repeat the tongue twister two or three times.
- Learners read the message again and complete the text by adding the five missing words.

> **Check answers:**
> **1** prize **2** that/which **3** Would **4** drive/take **5** lots

- Ask: *Have you ever been to an adventure park?* If some of your learners have, ask them to tell the rest of the class about their day there. If no-one has, ask learners where they would like to go for a special day out.

D ▶ Anna's competition. Listen and tick the box.

Listening Part 4

- Point to the girl in the pictures in the example. Say:
  This is Anna. What's she doing in each of these three pictures? (drawing a cartoon, playing a violin, watering a plant) Say: *Anna loves competitions. Listen! She's telling her friend, Jack, about a competition that she wants to win. What kind of competition is it?*
- Play the audio. Learners listen to the example then answer the question (a competition to grow the biggest watermelon) and tick box **C**. Ask: *Do watermelons grow in hot countries or cold countries?* (hot countries) *Do you think Anna will win the competition?* Learners guess *yes* or *no*. Teach/revise 'to enter a competition'. Ask: *Do you enjoy entering competitions. Why? Why not?*
- Learners listen to the rest of the conversation twice and tick the correct boxes.

> **Check answers:**
> **1** B **2** B **3** A **4** A **5** C

- Ask questions: *Do you have a garden? Have you ever grown fruit or a kind of vegetable? Do you like eating watermelon? What's your favourite fruit/vegetable?*

Audioscript

> *Listen and look. There is one example.*
> *What kind of competition is Anna getting ready for?*
> Anna: Hello, Jack. Hey! I didn't like standing on the stage but I won the music competition last week!
> Jack: Excellent, Anna!
> You're always entering competitions, aren't you? You're so good at art. Did you win that cartoon drawing competition?
> Anna: No, I didn't!
> Jack: Well, perhaps you'll win next time!
> Anna: Thanks. Actually, I'm trying to win another competition now! It's for growing the biggest fruit or vegetable. I planted some watermelon plants. They're getting really big!
> Jack: Wow!
> *Can you see the tick? Now you listen and tick the box.*
> **1** *Who is helping Anna?*
> Jack: Your dad knows a lot about growing plants. Is he helping you?
> Anna: He's too busy on the farm, but Grandpa's giving me lots of advice.
> Jack: That's lucky!
> Anna: Yes, He often helps Mum with her vegetable garden, too.

2 *What is the date of the competition?*
Jack: How much longer have you got before the competition date?
Anna: It's ends on the 29th … so I have to be ready by then … .
Jack: The 29th of June? That's in three weeks!
Anna: No, I meant July! Just before our August holiday from school.
Jack: Oh, OK. You've got lots of time then … .
3 *How did Anna find out about the competition?*
Jack: Who told you about the competition?
Anna: No-one. I read about it in our village magazine.
Jack: Is there any information about it on the village website?
Anna: There might be. I don't know. It won't be easy to win because lots of people know about it now.
4 *What is the first prize?*
Anna: The winner gets a great prize!
Jack: Let me guess. A meal for all the family in the new village restaurant?
Anna: That's right! It's more fun than money.
Jack: And better than one of those little silver cups!
5 *Where is Anna going to go now?*
Anna: But I've got to hurry now.
Jack: Why? Where are you going? To see if your plants are OK?
Anna: I'll do that later. I've got a guitar lesson before I do that.
Jack: Oh, OK! Well, I'm going to go and watch some cartoons. See you tomorrow and good luck!
Anna: Thanks! Bye!

E Play the word game. How many new *Flyers* words can you make?

- This activity will help to revise some Flyers vocabulary.
  In groups of 3–4, learners write down the heading *An adventure story competition* and find their wordlist in the back of their books.
  Say: *You have ten minutes to think of as many Flyers words as you can make from these letters. Write them down. You can use your wordlists to help you but make sure you know what the words mean. Your words must be three letters long or longer. No plurals! Go!*
- Check answers. The following Flyers words are all possible as are some other forms of the listed verbs here:
  act, actor, advice, air, anyone, art, artist, camp, card, cartoon, cat, cave, century, corner, cut, date, dear, deep, dentist, desert, diary, drum, east, empty, end, enter, entrance, ever, ice, insect, invent, married, may, medicine, meet, metre, mind, minute, money, nest, noisy, ocean, once, oven, over, painter, partner, past, piece, pond, poor, post, postcard, race, ready, repair, repeat, same, save, score, screen, secret, send, since, soap, soon, sore, space, spend, spoon, spot, spotted, stadium, stamp, stay, step, stone, storm, stream, stripe, striped, student, study, sure, surprise, tape, taste, team, tent, tidy, time, toe, tour, tune, turn, tyre, untidy, use, visit, yet.
- To the group with the most correctly spelt words, say/ask the following, giving learners in that group time to answer questions:
  Did you want to win this game? Well, you did! Well done! Today, you are the winners!
  To the groups who didn't win say: *Perhaps you'll win next time!*

🧳 Find out about chess

- Learners research chess on the internet.
- They draw and label all the chess pieces and draw arrows to show how each piece moves.
- They find a few facts out about the history of chess, who plays it now and where it is played. Learners add their chess fact sheet to their project file. Alternatively display learners' work on the classroom wall if possible.

29 Doing sport! Having fun!

Topics sports and leisure, body and face

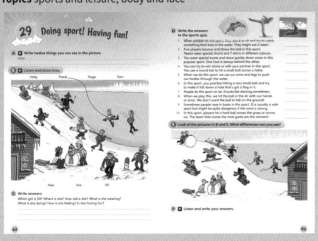

Equipment needed
Flyers audio 29A, 29B.

Ⓐ ▶ Write twelve things you can see in the picture.

○ Learners write twelve things they can see in the picture in **B**.
Suggestions: sky, hill, trees, forest, lake, ice, ice skates, skis, sledge, snowboard, snowball, snowman, house, windows, roof, door, balcony, jackets, trousers, scarf, hat, gloves, sunglasses, hair, arms, legs, faces etc.

○ Ask different learners to read out words. Write them on the board.
Note: Check that learners spell the plural of 'scarf' correctly. Show learners that 'snowboard' is 'snow' + 'board' as they already know both these words.

○ Say: *You are going to hear someone talking about different things you can see in this picture. What are they? Listen!* Play the audio. Pause after each description for learners to answer or for learners in pairs to point to where they can see the object in the picture and then write an answer in their notebooks.

Audioscript

1 You can see three of these and someone is sitting and going down the hill on one of them.
2 One boy is carrying these over his shoulder. Another boy is coming down the hill on his.
3 Two people are holding these in their hands. They're cold, round and white.
4 Two of the boys are trying to skate on this.
5 Most of the people are wearing these on their hands so they don't get cold.
6 Three people are wearing these round their necks.
7 When you ski, you put one foot on each ski. When you go snowboarding, you put both feet on one … ?

> **Check answers:**
> 1 sledges 2 skis 3 snowballs 4 ice 5 gloves 6 scarves
> 7 snowboard

Ⓑ ▶ Listen and draw lines.

Listening 1 Part

> **Flyers tip**
> In Listening Part 1, candidates won't hear a number before the speakers begin to talk about a different person, but there is a short pause between items. They shouldn't worry if they don't find all the answers during the first listening as they will hear the conversation a second time.

○ Learners look at the picture and take turns to say where each person is, what they are wearing and what they are doing, for example: *One boy is on the ice. He's wearing a green jumper and black trousers. He's skating.*

○ Play the audio. Learners listen to the conversation and draw lines from the names to the people in the picture. Learners listen to the conversation twice.

> **Check answers:**
> Lines should be drawn between:
> 1 *Vicky* and girl pulling sledge / wearing boots
> 2 *Hugo* and boy looking angry / getting cold
> 3 *Eva* and girl with snowman's hat / no gloves
> 4 *Tom* and boy skiing / wearing green jacket
> 5 *Alex* and girl with snowboard / wearing helmet

Audioscript

Listen and look. There is one example.

Man: It was such a cold day today. Can you see the ice on the balcony in this picture!
Girl: Yes, Dad. Are all those children in your class?
Man: Yes. I took them up the mountain for a sports lesson this afternoon. There's Frank.
Girl: The boy with the ice skates?
Man: That's right. He was a bit sore after he fell over… But he was OK!

Can you see the line? Now you listen and draw lines.

Girl: Who's that girl? The one with the sledge?
Man: That's Vicky. She's very good at most sports.
Girl: But it must be hard work, pulling it up that hill.
Man: Yes, but she had good boots on. That helped.

Man: Look at those two with the snowballs.
Girl: Yes! One looks quite angry! What's that kid's name?
Man: The girl?
Girl: I meant the boy, actually.
Man: Oh! That's Hugo! He was all right. He just didn't like getting cold.

Man: And Eva's here somewhere as well.
Girl: Is that her? The girl with the snowman's hat?
Man: Oh yes! There she is.
Girl: Did she forget to bring her gloves?
Man: Yes, she did! Silly girl.

Girl: Is that boy good at skiing?
Man: The one who's coming down really fast?
Girl: I meant the one in the green jacket. What's his name, Dad?
Man: That's Tom. He's having some lessons so, yes, he's really improving.

Girl: What about that girl. She looks really cool!
Man: Oh that's Alex.
Girl: Is her snowboard new? It looks new.
Man: I don't know, but her helmet is.
Girl: So you had a fun day, Dad!
Man: Yes. I was a bit worried about this lesson, but no-one needed bandages or x-rays so that was good!!
Girl: Ha ha!

C Write answers.

o Say: *There are two girls in the picture who don't have a line to a name. One of them is sitting next to the snowman. The other one is wearing a jacket. It's a nice colour. It's … ?* (red and white). *We can see a girl's name with no line to it. What's the girl's name?* (Jill)

In pairs, learners decide which girl to name 'Jill' and choose answers to the questions. Different learners read out their sentences about Jill.

Suggestion: Jill is the girl sitting on the ground. She's eleven and she's wearing a red hat, a yellow sweater and red gloves. She's feeling very happy. She's having lots of fun.

Who are you?

o Learners imagine they are one of the people in the picture. They should ask and answer questions in pairs.

Demonstrate this first with one learner in the class.

Teacher: *Are you a boy or a girl?* Learner: *A girl.*

Teacher: *Are you making a snowman?* Learner: *No.*

Teacher: *Have you got a sledge?* Learner: *Yes.*

Teacher: *Are you wearing a purple scarf?* Learner: *Yes.*

Teacher: *Are you Vicky?* Learner: *Yes.*

o Learners pretend to be another person in the picture. Their partner asks them *yes/no* questions to find out who they are.

D Write the answers to the sports quiz.

o In pairs, learners read the sentences and write the names of the sports on the dotted lines.

> **Check answers:**
> **1** fishing **2** basketball **3** snowboarding **4** table tennis
> **5** swimming **6** golf **7** ice skating **8** volleyball **9** sailing
> **10** hockey

o Ask: *For which sports do you need:*

water? (fishing, swimming, sailing)

cold weather? (skiing, snowboarding, ice skating)

In which sport can you play with a partner? (tennis, table tennis)

E Look at the pictures in B and E. What differences can you see?

Speaking Part **1**

Note: In Speaking Part 1, learners will only be asked about six differences.

o Learners look at the picture in **B** for a few minutes and try and remember what they can see in it.

o In pairs, learners look at the picture in **E** and talk about the things that are different from the picture in **B**.

o Say these sentences about the picture in **B**. Learners tell you how the picture in **E** is different.

In my picture:

The snowman is wearing a scarf with red and white stripes on it. (The scarf has **blue and yellow** stripes.)

The girl with the purple scarf is pulling her sledge up the hill. (She's **riding** her sledge down the hill.)

Two boys are ice skating. (They're playing **hockey**.)

The boy who's skiing is wearing gloves. (He **isn't** wearing gloves.)

There's ice on the balcony. (There **isn't** any ice.)

A girl is sitting on the ground next to the snowman. (**A dog** is sitting on the ground.)

The house is on the left of the picture. (The house is on the **right**.)

Two people are holding snowballs. (Two people are **pushing a snowball**.)

One boy is coming down the hill on a sledge. (**Two boys** are on the sledge.)

The girl is carrying a snowboard. (She's **snowboarding**.)

The bear is in front of the trees. (It's **behind the tree**.)

The girl in the red and white helmet is wearing sunglasses. (She **isn't** wearing sunglasses.)

F Listen and write your answers.

o Learners listen to the four questions and write their answers in their notebooks. Pause after each question to give learners time to write their answers. Read out the questions 2–3 times.

Listen and write your answers.

One. Which sports do you do at school?

Two. Is there a sports centre near your home?

Three. Which sports do people in your family watch on TV?

Four. Tell me about your favourite sport.

o Learners repeat the four questions to you. Write them on the board.

o In pairs, learners ask and answer the questions.

o Talk about learners' preferences in sport as a whole class.

Which is the most popular sport in this class? Put up your hand if you prefer football / basketball / tennis (etc).

o Write the suggested sports on the board and count how many learners like each one. Ask: *So, which is the most popular sport?* Learners answer. Ask further questions, for example: *How many people are in a football team? In a basketball team? And in a hockey team? Which is bigger – a volleyball or a baseball team? Have you ever been to an important game or sports match?*

Enter the sports words race!

o Ask: *Which of the sports in D do you need a ball to play?* (basketball, golf, hockey, table tennis, volleyball) Write these words on the board then ask: *Which other sports do you need a ball to play?* (baseball, football/soccer, tennis) Add the sports words that learners say to the board.

o Add these other sports to the board: *American football, cricket, handball, rugby.* Ask learners if they know how to play any of these sports.

o Ask: *How many players bounce and throw the ball in basketball?* (five – see **2** in **D**) Point to the words on the board and say: *Now, say the sports on the board in alphabetical order! What's the first sport?* (American football) *In pairs, say the words!*

Words in alphabetical order: American football, baseball, basketball, cricket, football, golf, handball, hockey, rugby, soccer, table tennis, tennis, volleyball

o Say: *Now, let's have a competition! This time, I want you to put the sports words in order from the sport that needs the fewest players on a team to the sport with the most players! The first one is easy! Which sport can only one player play?* (golf) *Which sports need only one player on a team?* (tennis, table tennis) *If you have access to the internet in the classroom, learners can go online and find out about the sports. If not, they could do this for homework.*

Answers: golf – 1 player; table tennis, tennis – 1 player; basketball – 5 players; ice hockey, volleyball – 6 players; handball – 7 players; American football, football/soccer, cricket – 11 players; rugby – 15 players

30 Summer and winter sports

Topics sports and leisure, transport

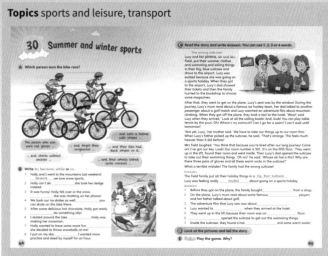

Equipment needed

o Photocopies of page 139 (one per pair) 'The swimming race'. See D.

Ⓐ Which person won the bike race?

o Ask questions: *Do you enjoy being in races? Who can ride a bike / swim / run / ski really fast?* Ask personal or impersonal questions about winning and losing: *If someone wins a race, how do they feel? What about if they lose the race? How do they feel then?* Learners answer.

o Write *bicycle* on the board. Cross out *bi* to leave *cycle* on the board. Explain that this is another way to say 'ride a bike'. Practise using 'cycle' as a verb. Say sentences which learners repeat using the correct form of 'cycle'. For example: *I ride a bike to school. > I cycle to school. I love riding my bike. > I love cycling. I rode my bike home yesterday. > I cycled home yesterday.*

o Point to the five cyclists. Say: *These five people are on racing bikes. They're cycling very fast because they're in a cycling race. Who won the race?* In pairs, learners read the five speech bubbles to find the answer (cyclist number 4). Ask: *What colour helmet was the cyclist who won the race wearing?* (purple) *How do you think he felt at the end of the race? Pleased?* (yes)

Note: You might also want to teach 'cyclist'.

Ⓑ Write *to, because, while* or *so.*

o Ask different learners: *Last night, while you were having dinner, did you watch TV?* (yes/no) *This morning, while you were having breakfast, did you talk to the other people in your family?*

Say: *We use 'while' or 'when' to talk about two things that happen or happened at the same time. While I'm speaking, what are you doing?* (listening)

o Revise 'to' for purpose. Write on the board (miming 'bat' if necessary):

Pat cycled to the shopping centre … buy a bat. Point to the gap and ask: *Which word can we put here?* (to) Add *to* to the sentence. Explain that when we're saying why we do something, we use 'to' before the verb.

o Revise 'because'. Add a second sentence to the board, next to the first: *Pat wanted to play table tennis.* Say: *Make one long sentence from these two shorter sentences*. (Pat cycled to the shopping centre to buy a bat because he wanted to play table tennis.)

o Teach/revise 'so'. Now write the same two shorter sentences on the board reversing the order: *Pat wanted to play table tennis. He cycled to the shopping centre to buy a bat.* Say: *Make one long sentence from these two now.* (Pat wanted to play table tennis so he cycled to the shopping centre to buy a bat.)

o Point out that there are complete sentences either side of 'because' or 'so'. If we use 'because' to join the sentences together, we put the sentence that explains the reason (the answer to 'Why?') last. If we want to use 'so', we need to put the reason (the answer to 'Why?') first.

o Read out sentence 1 in **B**. Make sure learners understand why we use 'because' in this sentence. (We can't use 'to' because the second part of this sentence doesn't begin with the verb. We can't use 'so' because the reason ('We love snow sports') doesn't come first.)

o Learners write *to, because, while* or *so* in sentences 2–8.

> **Check answers:**
> **2** so **3** while/because **4** because **5** to **6** while/because
> **7** so **8** because

Ⓒ Read the story and write answers. You can use 1, 2, 3 or 4 words.
Reading & Writing Part **5**

> **Flyers tip**
> In Reading and Writing Part 5, all the words candidates need for their answers are in the story and these words must not be changed. For example, if a word in the story is singular, it should appear in the answer in the same form.

Note: This story is slightly longer than in Reading and Writing Part 5.

o Tell learners to read the first sentence in the story. Ask: *Is this family going to go on a summer sports holiday or a winter sports holiday?* (a summer sports holiday). Learners read the rest of the story.

o Look at the first example: The Field family put all their holiday things in a big, brown suitcase. Ask: *How many words are in this answer?* (3). *How do you know this answer? Which part of the story tells you this?* (Lucy and her parents, Mr and Mrs Field, put their summer clothes and swimming and sailing things in their big brown suitcase …)

Look at the second example: Lucy was feeling really excited about going on a sports holiday. Ask: *How many words are in this answer?* (1). *How do you know this answer? Which part of the story tells you this?* (Lucy was excited because she was going on a sports holiday.)

o Learners complete sentences 1–7 using no more than four words in each sentence.

> **Check answers:**
> **1** some magazines **2** ice hockey **3** mountain climbing
> **4** go for a swim **5** the fifth **6** Lucy's father/dad
> **7** three pairs of gloves

o Ask questions relating to the story:

Have you been on a long journey? Where did you travel to?
Would you like to travel somewhere on a plane? Why? Why not?
Would you enjoy sitting next to the window? Why? Why not?
Do you like doing lots of sports? Why? Why not?
Which three things would you like to take with you on holiday? Why?

Ⓓ Look at the pictures and tell the story. **Speaking** Part **3**

o Learners work in pairs. Give each pair a photocopy of page 139, 'The swimming race'. In pairs, learners look at the five pictures to see what this story is about. Ask: *What's this story about?* (a swimming race) Say: *Yes! This story is called 'The Swimming Race'.* Learners write the title at the top of their page.

o To make this as authentic as possible, point to the first picture and say: *Peter and his two friends are going to swim in a swimming race today. Peter isn't good at swimming. His friends Paul and Anna can swim much faster than he can. Peter's worried about the race. But Peter's Dad says, 'Don't worry, Peter. Winning isn't important. Just have fun!'*

- Ask: *Which person is Peter in the first picture?* (the boy who's looking worried on the left) *What are Peter's friend's names?* (Paul and Anna) *Which person is Peter's dad?* (the man who's wearing glasses)
- Prompt learners to think about ways to tell the story by asking questions about each picture. In pairs, learners think of answers in complete sentences. They don't need to write anything. Give learners time to exchange ideas then ask different pairs to say something about each picture.

Questions:

Picture two

Is it the start of the race? Who is jumping into the water? Is anyone watching the race?

Picture three

Is Peter winning the race? Is Peter's dad sitting on his seat? What is Peter's dad saying to Peter?

Picture four

Is Peter swimming faster now? Is Peter going to win the race?

Picture five

Is Peter happy? Who is Peter waving to? Are Peter's friends happy too?

Suggested continuation of story for pictures 2–5:

It's the start of the race. Peter, Anna and Paul are jumping in the water. Lots of people are watching them.

Peter isn't winning. Peter's dad is standing by the pool. He's saying, 'Just have fun, remember!'

Peter is swimming faster now! He's going to win the race!

Peter is really happy. He's waving to his father. Peter's friends are happy, too!

Alternative activity: Photocopy the following text and cut into strips. In groups of 3–4, learners put the strips in the correct order and tell the story. See the suggested continuation of the story for the correct ordering.

Peter's dad is standing by the pool.

Peter is really happy.

Peter, Anna and Paul are jumping in the water.

He's going to win the race!

Peter is swimming faster now!

Lots of people are watching them.

He's waving to his father.

It's the start of the race.

Peter's friends are happy, too!

He's saying, 'Just have fun, remember!'

Peter isn't winning.

Optional extension

To practise Reading and Writing Part 7, ask learners to write the story in the past, adding the words 'because', 'while', 'so' or 'to' where they can.

Suggested story

Peter swam in a swimming race today. He didn't want to swim because he isn't good at swimming. While Peter was swimming, his dad was saying, 'Just have fun, remember!' Peter swam very fast so he won the race! Everyone was really happy at the end of the race.

E Play the game. Why?

- Say: *I like doing sports when I'm on holiday. I was on holiday yesterday and I went to a sports shop. Why?*

  Learners guess why:

  Learner A: *Because you wanted to buy a table tennis bat?*

  Teacher: *No.*

  Learner B: *To get some swimming shorts?*

  Teacher: *Yes.*

- The learner who guesses correctly comes to the front of the class. Show this learner a situation on a piece of paper. (See below for ideas.) Other learners guess why they went. They should begin their guesses with 'to'.

  Suggested situations and answers:

You went to the beach	to go fishing.
You went to the park	to play badminton.
You went to the mountains	to go skiing.
You went to the shopping centre	to buy some new tennis balls.
You went to our hotel room	to watch a football match on TV.
You went to the pool	to go for a swim.

- Write on the board: *Maria went to London.*

  Ask: *Why did Maria go to London?*

- In pairs, learners think of four reasons and write two sentences with 'to' and two sentences with 'because'.

  Suggestions:

  to meet the queen / to learn English / to go shopping / to visit her grandmother

  because she likes visiting different cities / because she wanted to visit some museums / because she wanted to watch an important running race / because she wanted to learn more about England.

31   Here and there

Topics the home, weather

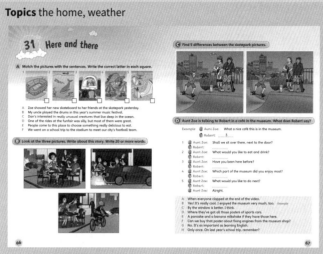

Not in YLE wordlists: *skatepark*

Equipment needed

o Photocopies of the sentences on page 140, cut up into cards. See 'Find your partner!'

Ⓐ Match the pictures with the sentences. Write the correct letter in each square.

o Point to the five places in the pictures in **A** and ask: *Which places can you see?* (a sports stadium, the sea, a music festival, a funfair, a skatepark). Teach any new words if necessary.

o Ask: *What can you hear in each of these places? You're in the stadium. What can you hear?* (people shouting and clapping) *You're next to the ocean! What are you listening to?* (the waves, sea birds) *If you go to the festival or for a ride at the funfair, what can you hear?* (music, people singing, shouting, laughing) *Now, you're at the skatepark. What noises do you hear there?* (the roller or ice skates, laughing, shouting)

o Point to sentences **A–F** and say: *These sentences are about these five places. Read sentence A. Which place is this sentence about?* (the skatepark)

So, where do we write A? (In the box under picture 5)

Learners read sentences **B–F** and write letters in the boxes under the pictures.

Check answers:

1 F   2 C   3 B   4 D   5 A

o Teach/revise *ocean* and *land*. Ask: *Which picture is different from the others?* (the ocean) *Why?* (It's not on the land.)

o Ask: *How many oceans are there?* (five) *Do you know their names in English?* (the Pacific, Atlantic, Indian, Southern/Antartic, Artic)

Do you know any unusual creatures that live in very deep water? (for example: some kinds of sharks and different fish)

Note: If your learners are interested and you have time, you could ask more questions about oceans and sea creatures or they could do a project about them.

Ⓑ Look at the three pictures. Write about this story. Write 20 or more words.
Reading & Writing Part 7

Flyers tip

In Reading and Writing Part 7, learners need to write about three pictures. The pictures show three stages of a short story. The instruction is to write 20 or more words. In most cases, stories of 25-40 words will be fine, but some candidates may write more than 50 words. To get good marks, train learners to look carefully at the pictures before they start so that they understand the general nature of the story. Then, they could produce one long or two short sentences about what is happening in each picture, like they do in the 'tell the story' task in the Speaking test.

o Point to the three pictures in **B** and say: *Look, these pictures show another place. Which place?* (a café) *What sounds do you think this family can hear?* (traffic, cars, bikes, people talking)

o Point to the three pictures and say: *These pictures tell a story. It's called 'The sports car and the racing bike.' Just look at the pictures first.* Then point to the first picture and say: *Mr and Mrs Banks and their children, Charlie and Clare, are having a snack at a café. They're on holiday and it's a sunny day.*

You can continue in either of the following ways.

1 To make this task as authentic as possible, learners now work in pairs looking at the other two pictures and finding two or three things to say about each one, for example: (picture 2)

A sports car is driving past the café. Charlie is pointing at the car and his parents are looking too. But Clare isn't looking because she doesn't like sports cars.

Walk round and help if necessary. When learners have finished talking, ask two or three pairs to tell their version of the story.

2 Alternatively tell the story in open class as follows.

Say: *Listen to these questions about the second and third pictures. Write two or three words to answer them. Don't write full sentences.*

Picture 2

What's driving past the café now? What colour is the sports car? Who likes the sports car most?

Picture 3

Can you still see the sports car? What's happening now? Why are the parents and the boy surprised? Who likes the racing bike most?

Ask the questions again. Different learners use their answers to continue telling the story.

o Learners write the story in their notebooks.

Suggested stories:

The family are having something to eat and drink at a café in the city. Two people in a sports car drive past. The boy points and smiles. But then an alien cycles past too. The family are really surprised!   (40 words)

A longer version of the story could be:

Mr and Mrs Banks and their children, Charlie and Clare, are having a snack at a café. They're on holiday and it's a sunny day. A racing car drives past. Charlie loves sports cars. He says, 'I'd like a sports car like that one day'. Then an alien cycles past on a racing bike. Mr and Mrs Banks and Charlie are really surprised. But Clare just says, 'And I'd like a racing bike like that one day.' (77 words)

Optional extension

Learners could role play the story.

C Find 5 differences between the skatepark pictures.

○ Point to the pictures in **C** and say: *We're at the skatepark again!* Point to picture **A** then picture **B** and say: *These pictures are nearly the same but some things are different. For example, in picture A, the girl's skateboard is red and white, but in picture B, the skateboard's purple and green. OK? In pairs, find and talk about five differences.*

○ Ask different pairs to say sentences about the differences they found.

Differences

In picture A:	In picture B:
The girl is wearing a helmet.	The **boy** is wearing a helmet.
The boy is looking at his phone.	The boy **isn't** looking at his phone.
The jacket is on the right.	The jacket is on the **left**.
The boy's shorts **don't** have pockets.	The boy's shorts have pockets.
The boy's wearing a yellow hat.	The boy's wearing a **red helmet**.
There's a bee above the lemonade.	There's a **butterfly** above the lemonade.
All the lights in the tallest building are on.	**Half** the lights in the tallest building are on.
There's a spaceship.	There **isn't** a spaceship.

Note: There are eight differences between these two pictures. In the Flyers test, candidates only need to talk about 5 differences.

○ Write on the board: *The girl's wearing a helmet. The boy's wearing a helmet. Say: We can talk about this difference like this or we can say: 'In picture A, the girl's wearing a helmet, but in picture B, she ...'* (isn't wearing a helmet.) *Make my sentences about picture A negative to talk about picture B!*

In picture A:

the jacket is on the left.	(The jacket is on the right.)
all the lights in the building are on.	(All the lights in the building aren't on.)
there's a bee above the lemonade.	(There isn't a bee above the lemonade.)

○ In pairs, learners talk about the differences between the pictures using affirmative and negative sentences.

D Aunt Zoe is talking to Robert in a cafe in the museum. What does Robert say?

○ Say: Read the first sentence in **D**. *Where are Aunt Zoe and Robert?* (in a café) *Is it the same café as the café in B?* (no – it's in a museum) *What kinds of museums do you know?* (science, history, art, transport, etc)

○ Read the example with learners. Ask: *Did Robert enjoy the museum?* (yes) Say: *Read Aunt Zoe's questions and find the best answer for each one. Write letters on the lines.*

Check answers:
1 C   **2** E   **3** H   **4** D   **5** F

○ Ask: *Which answers did you not use?* (A When everyone clapped at the end of the video. and G No. It's as important as learning English.) *Which of these answers is a good answer to this question: 'I don't think we need to study music.'* (G No. It's as important as learning English.) *And do you agree that studying music is as important as learning English?* (yes/no)

Find your partner!

○ Give out photocopies of the half sentences on page 140, cut up and stuck onto card if possible. Give each learner a card, making sure that you give out all three cards from each set.

○ Learners read what is written on their card. Ask: *Who has a card with a capital letter at the start of the first word?* Learners who have this on their card put up their hands. Say: *You have the first part of the sentence. You have to find two people who have the second parts of your sentence.*

○ All learners stand up and move around. When two learners meet, the learner with the first part of a sentence reads what is written on their card. If the second half of the sentence matches, the two learners stay together. They then both move together and the first learner reads out the first half of the sentence till they find an alternative second half. At the end, there should be groups of three learners who are standing together because their sentences match.

○ Ask all the groups to read out their sentences. They have two different sentences which start the same. The second halves should start with 'and' or 'but'.

32 Where?

Topics places, the home

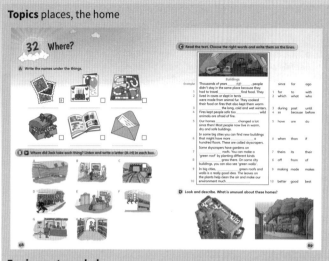

Equipment needed
○ Flyers audio 32B.
○ 12 cards with building words. See **D**.

(A) Write the names under the things.

○ Learners write the words for the objects under the six pictures. Teach/revise words as necessary.

> **Check answers:**
> **A** sweets/candy   **B** cards   **C** board game   **D** stamps   **E** book of cartoons   **F** letter

○ Ask: *When do people send cards?* (**Suggestions:** for birthdays, when someone has a baby, gets a new job, gets married) *Do you ever send cards? Do you ever get cards?*

○ Ask: *Do you play board games? Can you play chess?*
Does anyone in your family get letters? Who are the letters from?
Do you like candy? What's your favourite? Strawberry? Lemon? Do dentists like candy?

(B) ▶ Where did Jack take each thing? Listen and write a letter (A–H) in each box.

Listening Part 3

In towns

○ To introduce the topic, ask:
What's the tallest building near where you live? Are there any skyscrapers? Have you ever been to the top of a skyscraper? (If yes) *What was the view like? What could you see?*
Are there any shops where you live?
What other places can you find in towns or cities? Let's have a competition! Which team can write the most shops or other places you can find in a city? I'll give you a shop and a place to start: a library, a bookshop.

○ Teams of 3–4 learners write their lists.

○ Groups give their list of places/shops to another group to read out. Write their words on the board. Teams get a point for every correctly spelled place or shop.
Suggestions: an airport, a bank, bus station, café, car park, chemist's, dentist's, doctor's, factory, fruit shop, funfair, hospital, hotel, museum, offices, phone shop, playground, post office, restaurant, school, shoe shop, shopping centre, sports shop, stadium, station, store, supermarket, university

○ Say: *Which place would you like to go to this afternoon? Stand up if you want to go to these places!*
Come with me to the library!

Let's go to a museum!
Shall we go to the playground?
How about coming with me to the post office?
Who wants to come to the railway station?
Why don't we go to the university?

○ Divide the class into two groups, A and B. Learners in group A look at page 122 and learners in group B look at page 124. They read the five half sentences and write the name of each place on the line on the right. All the places are in the pictures in **B**.

○ Both groups of learners add another piece of information about each place to finish the sentences.

○ Learners move places to work in A and B pairs. They take it in turns to read out their definitions. Their partner says which place is being described and they compare their whole sentences to see if they are the same.

> **Check answers:**
> **Learner A: 1** a stadium   **2** a museum   **3** a station
> **4** a university   **5** hotels
> **Learner B: 1** hotels   **2** a stadium   **3** a station   **4** a museum
> **5** a university

○ Ask learners questions about the places they go to:
Where do you go after school?
When do you go shopping?
Which place don't you like in your town?
Tell me about your favourite town or city.
Note: You could also write these questions on the board and tell learners to ask and answer them in pairs.

○ Explain: *I'm going to say a sentence. Listen and tell me how many words you hear.* Say: *A postman is a person who takes letters and cards to people's homes.*
Learners: *13 words.*
Ask: *Which different words did you hear?*
Say the sentence again. In pairs, learners try to write the same sentence. One learner comes to the board and writes the sentence.

○ Say: *A post office is a place where you can buy stamps and send letters.*

○ Ask learners to finish this sentence: *A postcard is something you …*
Write their suggestion on the board. For example: *A postcard is something you write a holiday message on.*
Circle the words *person, place* and *something* on the board. These are important words for giving information about people, places and things!

○ Point to the picture of the library in **B**. Learners say a sentence about this place. (*A library is a place where you can read books and find information.*) Point to the book in **A**. Learners say a sentence about it beginning with: *A book is something …* (you read in school or at home).
Suggestion: *Books are things we read at school or at home.*

○ Say: *You're going to hear a man called Jack and the girl who lives next door talking about his day. Where did Jack take each thing?* Point to the pictures of the things in **A** and the places in **B**. Say: *Write the letter of the correct place in the boxes next to these different things.*

○ Play the audio twice. Learners listen and write letters in the boxes in **B**.

> **Check answers:**
> candy – **D** university   board game – **F** factory   cards – **G** bank
> invitation – **C** station   book of cartoons – **A** stadium

Audioscript

Jack is a postman. He takes things to different places in the town. Where did Jack take each thing?

Girl: Hi, Jack! You look tired. Are you OK?

Man: Oh hello, Julia. Yes, but I've been up and down so many steps today! I had hundreds of letters and some other quite interesting things to take to different places today. There were some special stamps. I needed to be very careful with those.

Girl: Where did you take them?

Man: To the museum. They're really old.

Girl: Wow! What did they look like?

Man: It's difficult to explain ...

Can you see the letter B? Now you listen and write a letter in each box.

Man: One of the largest things in my bag at the end of the day was a box. It was a funny shape and full of candy!

Girl: Where did you have to take that?

Man: To the university.

Girl: Oh! Who was it for?

Man: It was for someone important who teaches there. I like going there. It's full of such interesting people. But it's always difficult to find the right person to give things to!

Man: I had to take a board game that someone invented to an address that was quite difficult to find as well.

Girl: Really?

Man: Yes. Someone told me it was a prize.

Girl: Wow! For winning a competition?

Man: That's right. The people who entered had to design a poster for the New Railway station. The winner was the manager of the new shoe factory. I found him in his office. He was really pleased.

Man: After that, I had to take lots of birthday cards to Miss Pond at the place where she works. She's very popular.

Girl: I know her. She works at the library, doesn't she?

Man: She did, but she left about a month ago so I took it to the bank instead. She's got a really good job there now. I think she's going to have a party this evening!

Girl: Exciting!

Man: I had a lovely surprise for another person, too!

Girl: Really? What?

Man: A blue envelope which had an invitation inside. The address on the front was City Station so that's where I took it.

Girl: What was the invitation for?

Man: Dinner at that expensive hotel in Bridge Street!

Girl: Fantastic!

Man: And then I just had a book of cartoons in my bag…

Girl: I'd like one of those. It sounds fun!

Man: Yes, it looked great. Someone at the stadium bought it online. They were very pleased it arrived. It was a present for their daughter.

Girl: Oh! That's nice.

Man: I hope she likes it!

C Read the text. Choose the right words and write them on the lines.

Reading & Writing Part 4

○ Learners look at the picture and title ('Buildings'). Ask them to think of words they think will be in the text.

Suggestions: city, door, entrance, exit, factory, go in, house, live, roof, room, shop, town, wall, window

○ Learners read through the text quickly and see how many of their words appear. Building words: lived, floors, cities, garden, roofs, walls

Flyers tip

In Reading and Writing Part 4, candidates' spelling must be correct as they are copying the words from the options on the opposite page. They should check their spelling and that they have put each word on the correct line.

○ Learners choose one word for each gap from the three options and copy it into the gap in the text.

Check answers:

1 to   2 which   3 during   4 because   5 have   6 than   7 their
8 of   9 making   10 better

○ Say: *There are lots of words in this text that start with the letter 't'. Can you find a word with two letters beginning with 't'?* (to) Say: *Find other words in the text beginning with t.*
Suggestions: thousands, travel, tents, that, they, them, too, than, these, their, there, the.

D Look and describe. What is unusual about these homes?

○ Write each of these words on twelve small pieces of paper or card: *balcony basement elevator entrance exit front door garden gate grass roof stairs view*

○ Say: *Close your books, please.* Divide the class into three groups – 'inside', 'outside' and 'between'. The third group is 'between'. One learner picks up a card and reads out the word. If the word on the card is for something that is usually outside a building, the 'outside' group put both of their hands in the air and shout *'That's ours!'* If it is usually inside, the 'inside' group do the same. If the thing is <u>between</u> the inside and the outside, the 'between' group call out. Give each group the cards that belong to them.

Suggested answers: inside: basement, elevator, stairs
outside: roof, balcony, gate, garden, grass, view
between: entrance, exit, front door

○ Ask: *Is a roof usually on the top or on the bottom of buildings?* (the top) *Do you find lifts in high or low buildings?* (high)
Write on the board: *top / .... inside / .... high / ....*

Ask: *What's the opposite of top / inside / high?* (bottom, outside, low) Add these words to the board.

Learners open their books and look at the pictures in **D**. In their groups they talk about where they can see the things that are on their cards.

For example: *The pool is outside, on the top of this high building. The grass is outside this house, on the roof.*

○ Ask: *Which of the things in the text in C can you see in the pictures in D?* (a skyscraper, green roof, green wall, windows, doors, a lift)

○ Learners draw and describe their own unusual house, using the pictures in **D** to inspire them.

Optional extension:

○ Ask learners: *Have you ever moved to another house or flat? What things do you have to do before you leave the old house?*

○ Explain that you are going to move house and learners are going to help you. Give different learners one of the sentences below. Each learner reads out one sentence. All learners listen and mime the actions.

Note: They mime the actions without moving round the classroom.

1 *Go to the hall wall and take the large picture down, please! Put it on the floor.* (Learners walk to the wall and mime taking a picture off the wall.)

2 *Open the kitchen cupboard. Take the five cups and four small bowls out of the cupboard and put the things very carefully into the box on the floor.*

3 *Now, pick up the box. Careful! It's heavy! Go out of the kitchen door and carry it down the stairs.*

4 *Now, let's get the plants. Go back upstairs. Go into the bedroom.*

5 *Open the two big doors onto the balcony. Pull them open. In the left corner, there is a very tall plant. Pick it up! Carry it through the bedroom, through the door and down the stairs.*

6 *Finished? Not yet! Go back up to the bedroom. Put a chair in front of the bedroom cupboard. Stand on it! Pick up the big suitcase that's on the top of the cupboard. Now get down from the chair. Put the suitcase on the floor. Open it.*

7 *Now you can open the cupboard! Remember there are two doors. Pull them both open. Take the jackets and coats out of the cupboard. Put them into the suitcase, one by one.*

8 *Now, close the suitcase, pick it up and carry it downstairs.*

9 *Put it in the back of the car. Go to the front of the garden and open the gate. Get into the car. Let's go!*

○ Say: *Thank you for helping me!* (Clap your hands or shake different learners' hands, etc as appropriate.)

○ Read 1–19 again. Learners mime the actions again.

33   At the hospital

Topics health, body and face

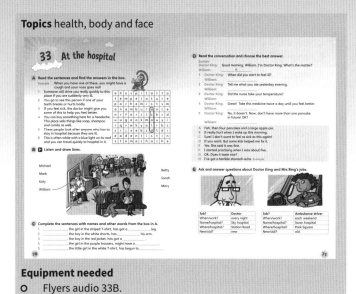

Equipment needed

○   Flyers audio 33B.

Hospital words

○   Write the word *hospital* in the middle of the board. Ask learners to tell you words connected with hospitals. Write the words on the board around the word 'hospital'.

    Suggestions: bed, nurse, doctor, ill people, visit, get better.

○   Learners look at the picture in **B** and name things they can see. Add more words to the board.

    Suggestions: sick, sore, broken, arm, stomach, foot, crying, temperature, headache, stomach-ache.

🅐 Read the sentences and find the answers in the box.

○   Read the example with learners and point to the words 'a cold' in the box. Learners read the sentences and find and circle the words for sentences 1–6 in the box.

    Note: Most of the answers are singular nouns with the article *a/an*, but there is one plural *(5 nurses)* and one uncountable noun *(3 medicine)*. The word 'these' in 5 tells us that this is a plural word.

> **Check answers:**
> **1** a hospital (1ˢᵗ line across)
> **2** a dentist (9ᵗʰ line across)
> **3** medicine (last line down)
> **4** a chemist ('s) (3ʳᵈ line across)
> **5** nurses (1ˢᵗ line down)
> **6** an ambulance (4ᵗʰ line across)

🅑 ▶ Listen and draw lines.

> **Flyers tip**
>
> In Listening Part 1, candidates hear two or three pieces of information to identify each person. The information might be about what the person is wearing, what they look like, what they're doing or where they are in the picture.

○   Learners look at the picture. They tell you where each person is and what they are doing. For example: *A girl is at the back of the room with a nurse. The girl's crying.*

○   Point to the line between the name *William* and the boy with the green face. Play the first part of the conversation.

    Ask: *What information do we hear about William?* (He's got a stomach-ache. He's with his mother. He has a green face.)

○   Play the rest of the conversation twice.

> **Check answers:**
> **1** *Sarah* and the nurse working on the computer.
> **2** *Mark* and the boy who's hurt his arm.
> **3** *Katy* and the girl with the broken leg.
> **4** *Betty* and the girl who's crying.
> **5** *Mary* and the girl who's having her temperature taken.

○   Say: *Listen again. You'll hear two things that describe Sarah and two things that describe Katy.* Play the audio again, pausing after each person has been talked about. Learners tell you the two pieces of information they heard. Write the information on the board and ask learners to make one or two sentences about each person:

    Sarah is working on her computer today. She's a nurse and she's got blonde hair.

    Katy broke her leg yesterday. She was cycling down a hill. She can't go up and down steps but she can sit and read her book.

Audioscript

Listen and look. There is one example.

Woman:	The hospital is full of people today. I know lots of their names.
Boy:	Do you?
Woman:	Yes. Can you see that boy with the stomach-ache?
Boy:	The boy with his mother?
Woman:	Yes, that's William. I give him piano lessons.
Boy:	Poor boy! Look at his green face!

Can you see the line? This is an example.
Now you listen and draw lines.

Boy:	Look at that woman!
Woman:	Which one?
Boy:	Over there. She's working on the computer.
Woman:	Oh, you mean the nurse with the blonde hair. That's Sarah.
Boy:	She looks busy.
Woman:	What's happened to Mark?
Boy:	I don't know. Which person is he?
Woman:	The boy who's hurt his arm. Look! He's just had an x-ray, I think.
Boy:	Oh yes. Where's his tennis racket?
Woman:	I'm not sure, but he can't play tennis today!
Woman:	And there's poor Katy! She broke her leg when she fell off her bicycle yesterday.
Boy:	Where was she cycling?
Woman:	Down a hill. It's difficult for her to go up and down steps now and it's very sore.
Boy:	Well she can sit and read. I prefer e-books, do you?
Woman:	Not always…
Boy:	What's the matter with that girl over there?
Woman:	Do you mean the girl with the nurse?
Boy:	No, the girl who's crying. The one in a skirt, not trousers.
Woman:	Oh, that's Betty. I don't know. But you're right. She doesn't look very pleased!
Woman:	And another nurse is taking Mary's temperature.
Boy:	The girl by the door?
Woman:	Yes. She had a really sore ear. She's touching it with her hand. Look.
Boy:	Oh, I get that sometimes. But it always gets better again quickly.
Woman:	That's good.

C **Complete the sentences with names and other words from the box in A.**

o Say: *There are six more words in the box in A. Can you find them?* Learners find and circle more words.

> **Check answers:**
> **Across:** (line 2) temperature (last line) stomach-ache
> **Down:** (line 5) broken (line 7) ill (line 9) hurt (line 10) cry

o Learners read the first half of sentences 1–5 and write the name of each person on the first line.

> **Check answers:**
> **1** Katy   **2** Mark   **3** William   **4** Mary   **5** Betty

o Learners read sentences 1–5 again and write one of the words they found in the box and did not use in **A** on the second line in each sentence.

> **Check answers:**
> **1** broken   **2** hurt   **3** stomach-ache   **4** temperature   **5** cry

Yes or no?

o Read out these sentences about the picture in **B**. Learners stand up if the sentence about the picture is correct and sit down if it is wrong.
  1 *A nurse is working at a computer.* (yes)
  2 *A nurse is carrying a girl who is crying.* (no)
  3 *The boy sitting next to the woman has got earache.* (no)
  4 *One of the nurses is taking a girl's temperature.* (yes)
  5 *The doctor is going into his office.* (no)
  6 *All of the nurses in the picture are wearing uniforms.* (yes)

D **Read the conversation and choose the best answer.**

o Ask: *What questions do doctors usually ask?* Write the questions on the board.
  Suggestions: *What's the matter? Have you got a temperature? When did you start to feel ill? When did this happen? Does it hurt?*

o Read out the example question and answer.
  Ask: *Which boy in the picture in B has got a stomach-ache?* (William)
  Say: *Read Doctor King's questions. Does he ask the same questions as the ones on the board?* (yes/no)

o Learners choose answers from the box and write the letters on the lines.

> **Check answers:**
> **1** B   **2** A   **3** E   **4** G   **5** C

Optional extension:

o In pairs, learners role play the conversation between Dr King and William. They can then write a conversation that Katy or Mark could have with the doctor.

E **Ask and answer questions about Doctor King and Mrs Ring's jobs.**

o Point to the picture of the doctor.
  Ask: *Can you remember this man's name?* (Doctor King)

o Say: *You are going to ask and answer questions about Doctor King.* Point to the word 'Job?' in the first box of the table. Learners tell you the question for this. (*What's his job?*) Write this question on the board.

o Do this with the other boxes in the table. Point to: *When/work? Name/hospital? Where/hospital? New/old?* and ask learners to make the questions. Write them on the board.
  Questions:
  When does he work? What's the name of the hospital?
  Where's the hospital? Is it / the hospital new or old?

o In pairs, learners ask and answer questions about Doctor King.

o Point to the picture of the woman.
  Say: *This is Mrs Ring, so we don't ask questions with **he**. Why not?* (Because she's a woman.)
  Point to the questions on the board and ask learners to tell you which questions they need to change. (*What's **her** job? When does **she** work?*)

o In pairs, learners ask and answer questions about Mrs Ring.

Optional extension:

o Learners can then draw another table and complete it about a person they know who helps people (for example: a dentist, a doctor, a nurse, a firefighter). Learners then ask and answer questions about these job information tables in groups.

Play the game! *What happened?*

o Say: *Listen to the 's' sounds! Are you ready? Alice's sister's shoulder was sore so an ambulance took her to the hospital in the city centre.* Say the sentence twice, then say it again, stopping and asking learners to say the words after you:
  Alice's sister's shoulder … was sore … so an ambulance … took her to the hospital … in the city centre.

o Ask: *Can anyone tell me the complete sentence?* Learners tell you the sentence. Write on the board: *Alice … .* Ask different learners to come to the board to write the next word in the sentence till you have the whole sentence on the board. Everyone says the sentence, quietly then loudly.

o Learners look at page 129. Tell them to choose words from the boxes to make a sentence about Harry or Helen.
  Suggestions
  Harry hurt his hand when he was hurrying/hopping home/helping with the horses.
  Helen hurt her head when she was hitting a hockey ball.

o Different learners say the sentence they made. Then, everyone says the sentence they made at the same time!

34   Oliver goes to hospital

Topics health, sports and leisure, time

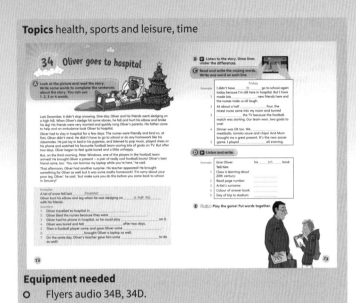

Equipment needed

o   Flyers audio 34B, 34D.

Ⓐ Look at the picture and read the story. Write some words to complete the sentences about the story. You can use 1, 2, 3 or 4 words.

Reading & Writing Part 5

o   Say: *Look at the picture.* Ask:
Who can you see? (a boy)
Where is he? (in hospital)
What is he doing? (maths homework)
Why is he in hospital? (He's broken his leg.)
How do you think he broke his leg? Let's read the story and find out!
(He fell when he was playing with a sledge in the snow.)

o   Learners read the story. Ask: *Which part of the story can you see in the picture?* (the end)

> **Flyers tip**
>
> In Reading and Writing Part 5, the picture will give candidates an idea of what they are going to read about, but it will not give them the information they need to complete the sentences. They have to read the text to find the words they need.

o   Say: *Read the first part of the story again.* Look at the examples together.
Point out that the information in the text is in a different order to the way it is given in the two example sentences.

o   Look at sentence 1 together. Ask: *How many words do we need to complete the sentence?* (2 – an ambulance)

o   Learners read the rest of the story and complete the sentences with 1, 2, 3 or 4 words.

o   Learners compare their answers in pairs. Then, ask different pairs to say which words they wrote.
Suggested answers: 1 an/the ambulance **2** friendly (and kind) **3** chess **4** a little unhappy **5** (really) (cool) football boots **6** Oliver's/His (best) friend **7** maths homework

o   Write on the board: .... *worried*
.... *bored*
.... *unhappy*
.... *lucky*

o   Ask: *Can you find these words in the text? Which word comes before each word?* Different learners come to the board and write the missing words on the lines.
(**very** worried, **quite** bored, **a little** unhappy, **really** cool)

o   Explain: *All of these words add something to the adjectives that come after them. Some words make the adjective stronger, meaning 'more'. Which words do this?* (really, very) *Others make the adjective less, weaker. Which words?* (quite, a little)
When we use these words, they are important and so is the adjective after them, so we say them clearly. Say these sentences (learners repeat them):
*His **friends** were **very worried**.*
*Oliver began to feel **quite bored** and a **little unhappy**.*

o   Then, say the sentences, omitting the adverbs and adjectives. Different learners say the sentences.

Ⓑ ▶ Listen to the story. Draw lines under the differences.

o   Learners listen to the story on the audio twice. The first time, they underline the differences between the two stories (there are 12). The second time, they write the different words in their notebooks. Ask learners to tell you the new word before they listen and check.

Check answers:	
1 December	February
2 stones	rocks
3 father	mother
4 nurses	doctors
5 classmates	friends
6 pop music	rock music
7 two days	three days
8 boots	shorts
9 best friend	cousin
10 laptop	tablet
11 maths	maths and history
12 January	March

Audioscript

Listen to the story. Draw lines under the differences.

Last **February**, it didn't stop snowing and Oliver and his group of friends had lots of fun playing with sledges on a high hill near their homes. But one afternoon, when Oliver's sledge hit some **rocks**, he fell and hurt his right elbow but also broke his leg in two places. His friends were really worried and one of them quickly rang Oliver's parents. His **mother** came to help and an ambulance soon arrived to take Oliver to hospital.

Poor Oliver had to stay in hospital for a few days. The **doctors** were friendly and kind and the food was great so, at first, Oliver didn't mind. He didn't have to go to school or spend time doing lots of homework like his **friends**! He just lay in bed in his pyjamas, and listened to **rock** music, played chess and other games on his phone and watched his favourite football team scoring lots of goals on TV. But after **three** days, Oliver began to feel quite bored and a little unhappy.

But then Peter Windows, one of the players in the football team came into his hospital room! He was carrying a present – a pair of really cool football **shorts**! 'To wear during football practice when your leg is better,' he said.

Peter Windows wasn't alone. Oliver's **cousin** followed him into the room. 'And you can borrow my **tablet** while you're here,' he said. Oliver began to feel much happier and very lucky! Then he had another surprise! One of his teachers appeared at the door! He brought something for Oliver as well, but it was some maths and **history** homework! 'I'm sorry about your poor leg, Oliver,' he said, 'but make sure you do all this work before coming back to school in **March**!'

C Read and write the missing words. Write one word on each line.

Part 6

o Point to the picture of the football game. Say: *This is Oliver's new game. What's he playing it on? A phone? A computer?* (no) Teach/revise: 'tablet' and ask: *Do you play games on a tablet sometimes? Would you like to play a game like this?* Learners answer. Ask: *A player is trying to score a … ?* (goal) *What's the number on his back?* (4) *What colour are his shorts?* (red) *Will he score the goal?* (yes/no!) If learners are interested, teach/revise 'goalkeeper' and ask: *What's the goalkeeper wearing?* (green shorts, a black T-shirt and blue gloves)

o Point to the text and say: *This is a page from Oliver's diary.* Ask: *Where's Oliver? How does he feel?* Learners read the diary page and tell you the answers (in hospital, very happy).

o Learners read the text again and write one word on each line, as in the example.

> **Check answers:**
> **1** of **2** past **3** on **4** had/ate **5** it/that

D ▶ Listen and write.

Listening **2**

o Point to the picture in **E**. Say: *Oliver knows both these people. Who do you think they are?*

o Play the first part of the audio. Ask: *Who are the people?* (The boy is a friend of Oliver's and the man is one of his teachers.)

o Learners listen to the rest of the audio and write words on the lines.

> **Check answers:**
> **1** paintings **2** 110 **3** Klee **4** blue **5** Monday

Audioscript

> *Listen and look. There is one example.*
> Man: Hi, Frank. You're going to visit Oliver in hospital this afternoon, aren't you?
> Boy: Yes, Mr Kind.
> Man: Good. I hope he's getting better. Can you take him a book? He'll need it for his homework.
> Boy: Of course! Which book?
> Man: His art book.
> *Can you see the answer? Now you listen and write.*
> Man: We're studying twentieth-century paintings in Oliver's class now. Can you tell him that?
> Boy: Yes. Our class studied that last year.
> Man: Which was your favourite painting?
> Boy: Erm, I can't remember.
> Man: Oh! Well, I'd like Oliver to read some texts.
> Boy: What page are they on?
> Man: Page 110. They're not very long, and there are only five of them.
> Boy: OK. I'll tell him. What are they about?
> Man: They're about one of my favourite artists. His name's Paul Klee.
> Boy: Sorry … How do you spell his last name?
> Man: K-L-E-E.

> Boy: Oh, yes. I remember him now.
> Man: And Oliver must answer some questions too. He can do that in his blue book, not the red one! Then perhaps his mum could bring it to school.
> Boy: All right.
> Man: And there's another important thing. We're going to go on a trip to the sports stadium next week, so it's important that Oliver does this work as soon as he can.
> Boy: Is the trip next Monday?
> Man: Yes, in the morning.
> Boy: OK.
> Man: And all the teachers are very sorry about his leg. Please tell him that.
> Boy: Sure! But Oliver's OK. He's got lots of computer games with him.
> Man: Good.

E Play the game! Put words together.

o Write on the board: *brush*. Ask different learners to tell you things that you can brush. Write their suggestions on the board (*your hair, your teeth, a horse, a dog*).

o Write these verbs on the board:

break	*feed*	*catch*	*send*	*plant*
grow	*turn on*	*look for*	*climb*	*repair*
practise	*close*	*wash*	*sell*	*collect*

o Form teams of 4–5 learners. Each team has to think of things which go with each verb.

o Give learners 3–4 minutes for this. For each correct combination, teams get a point. Acknowledge the team that has the most points as the winners.

Suggested answers:
break a leg, an arm, a glass, a cup, a window, a finger, a necklace
feed a baby, a horse, a rabbit, a tortoise
catch a ball, a train, a bus, a taxi
send a letter, a postcard, an email, a text, a message
grow plants, flowers, trees
turn on the light, the radio, a computer
look for a person, a telephone number, a toy, a website
climb a mountain, a hill, a wall
practise a song, a kick, an instrument
close the door, a window, a book, a gate
wash your hair, your hands, the car
sell a ticket, a newspaper, a bicycle, a snowboard
plant a tree, a flower, potatoes, onions, carrots
repair a car, a bike, a computer, a lift/elevator
collect comics, postcards, photos, shoes

35   What's it made of?

Topics materials, the home, the world around us

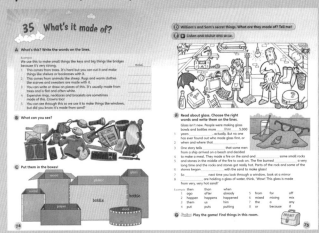

Not in YLE wordlists: *fan*

Equipment needed

○ A plastic pen or PC mouse, a wooden pencil, a metal spoon, a pair of glasses, a paper envelope, a drinking glass. See A.
○ Four cards, each with three categories written on. See F.
○ Colouring pens or pencils.
○ Flyers audio 35E.

Ⓐ What's this? Write the words on the lines.

○ Teach/revise 'gold' and 'wool'. Give examples of things made from these materials (pirate's treasure, wedding rings / gloves, socks, etc).
   Write *gold* and *wool* on the board. Say: *Gold is a kind of metal. Do you know the names of any other metals?* (silver [not on YLE wordlists: iron, steel, copper etc])

○ Give the six objects that you have brought in to learners to look at and pass to others in the class. Ask:
   What's the pen/mouse made of? (plastic)
   And the pencil? (wood)
   What about the spoon? (metal)
   This is an envelope. What's it made of? (paper)
   And now the glasses, what are they made of? (plastic/metal)
   What's this glass made of? (glass!)

○ Different learners tell you how to spell 'plastic', 'wood', 'metal', 'paper' and 'glass' and write these words on the board too. (All these material words are on the boxes in **C**.)

> **Flyers tip**
> In Reading and Writing Part 1, candidates can cross out the example answer and then other answers as they work through each task.

○ Look at the example sentence (metal) together.
○ In pairs or individually, learners read the other sentences and write the words on the lines. They can copy the words they need from **C** or the board.

> **Check answers:**
> **1** wood   **2** wool   **3** paper   **4** gold   **5** glass

○ Say: *Point to something in the classroom that is made of plastic.* Ask learners to point to items in the classroom that are made of the other named materials too.

Ⓑ What can you see?

○ Learners look at the pictures and tell you what they can see. Write the words on the board. Ask learners: *How do you spell bottle, comb, cupboard, knife, guitar?* Say: *In these words, there are letters which we can't hear. What are they?* (second 't' and final 'e' in bottle, 'b' in comb, 'p' in cupboard, 'k' in knife, 'u' in guitar)

> **Check answers:**
> (26 objects)
> a bottle, a bowl, a brush, a card, chopsticks, a comb, a cupboard, a (plastic) duck, an envelope, a fan, a fork, gloves, a guitar, a key, a knife, a lamp, a mirror, a computer mouse and keyboard, a newspaper, a pencil, a ruler, a sweater, a telephone, a toothbrush, a torch

Ⓒ Put them in the boxes!

○ Ask: *What is a bottle usually made of?* (glass) *What else can a bottle be made of?* (plastic)
○ Point to the word 'bottle' on the box labelled 'glass' and on the box labelled 'plastic'.
○ Working in small groups to encourage discussion, learners write objects (from the list on the board) on the boxes to show what they are normally made of.

> **Suggested answers:**
> *wood:* chopsticks, a bowl, a brush, a cupboard, a guitar, a lamp, a pencil, a ruler
> *plastic:* a bottle, a bowl, a brush, chopsticks, a comb, a duck, a fan, a fork, gloves, a knife, a lamp, a computer mouse and keyboard, a ruler, a telephone, a toothbrush, a torch
> *glass:* a bottle, a bowl, a lamp, a mirror
> *wool:* gloves, a sweater
> *metal:* a comb, a cupboard, a fork, a key, a knife
> *paper:* a card, an envelope, a fan, a newspaper.

Ⓓ William's and Sam's secret things. What are they made of? Tell me!   Speaking Part 2

○ Say: *I've got a secret diary at home. It's very old and I don't show it to anyone. I hide it behind the cupboard in my bedroom!* Say: *Put up your hands if you have a secret thing at home.* Learners may or may not put up their hands. Say: *Well, I'm not going to ask you what your secret things are. Don't worry! But now we <u>are</u> going to find out about someone else's secret thing.*

○ Divide class into A and B pairs. A learners look at their set of questions and answers on page 123. B learners look at their set of questions and answers on page 125. Help learners form the prompts if necessary.

○ Remind them that the words they see in the prompts should be in their questions and not be changed. For example: ***What's** ....'s **secret thing**?, **What**'s it **made of**? **Where** does .... **hide** it? **When** did .... **find** it? Is it **little** or **large**?*

○ Say to B learners: *You don't know anything about William's secret thing, but your A partners do. Ask them questions about it.* Say to A learners: *Look at the answers about William's secret thing. Find the right answer to each question.* Learners work in pairs, asking and answering the questions.

○ Say to A learners: *You don't know anything about Sam's secret thing, but your B partners do. Ask them questions about it.* Say to B learners: *Look at the answers about Sam's secret thing. Find the right answer to each question.* Learners work in pairs as before.

○ Ask questions in open class about William's and Sam's secret things to check understanding. For example: *Where is William's secret thing? What's Sam's secret thing made of? When did Sam find her secret thing? What's William's secret thing?*

E ▶ Listen and colour and write. 　Listening **5** Part

○ In pairs, learners look at the picture and, as quickly as possible, find four things that begin with the letter 'm', four things that begin with 'b', and four things that begin with 's'. They write the words in their notebooks.

Suggested answers:

M – man, map, mirror, moustache, mouse, music

B – ball, bat, bin, bottle, box, book

S – shelves, shorts, sledge, spider, suitcase, swan

○ Say: *You're going to listen and colour different things in the picture and write words somewhere in the picture.*

○ Play the audio twice, pausing for 15 seconds between instructions for the first hearing. Do not pause the audio for the second hearing.

> **Check answers:**
> **1** Colour sheet of music – purple
> **2** Colour square suitcase – red
> **3** Write 'books' on tall box
> **4** Write 'movies' on TV screen
> **5** Colour ball of wool next to castle – brown

○ Ask: *What's the octopus made of?* (plastic)
What's made of metal? (the box for books)
What can you see that's made of glass here? (the bottle, the light)
What about the girl's mirror? What's that made of?

○ If necessary, tell learners that most mirrors are made of glass with a kind of special silver paint on the back and ask: *What can we do with a mirror?*

Suggested ideas: Look at ourselves, write a message, read messages with it if they are written backwards, send messages (by catching light from the sun), watch other people in secret, make a fire.

Audioscript

Listen and colour and write.

Girl: This room is untidy!

Man: Yes, but Emma and her father are going to tidy it. No one usually goes there.

Girl: Oh! Can I colour the umbrella? The open one.

Man: That's a good idea! Make it green, please.

Can you see the green umbrella? This is an example. Now you listen and colour and write.

1 Girl: Shall I colour that piece of paper next?

Man: The one with music on it? Yes!

Girl: Can I use purple for that?

Man: Yes, you can!

Girl: Great! Thanks. That's my favourite colour.

2 Man: Would you like to colour the suitcase, too?

Girl: The round one?

Man: No, they never use that. Colour the square one. Colour it red.

Girl: All right. What's inside it?

Man: I don't know!

3 Girl: What's that octopus made of? That old toy that Emma's dad is holding?

Man: Oh, plastic, I think. But can you see the metal box behind him?

Girl: The tall one?

Man: Yes. Write the word 'books' on it, please.

Girl: All right! But it looks empty.

Man: Well, perhaps Emma's going to put some old toys in it soon.

4 Girl: Can I write something else here too? On the TV screen?

Man: Well, no-one has turned it on, but OK!

Girl: How about, 'Movies!' I love watching films.

Man: So do I. OK. You can write that word.

Girl: Thank you.

5 Man: Now, colour the ball of wool for me. The one next to the castle.

Girl: All right. Can I make that green?

Man: You've already used that colour. No, make it brown, instead.

Girl: All right! I'm doing that now. There!

Man: Excellent! Thank you.

F Read about glass. Choose the right words and write them on the lines.

○ Ask: *Can you remember what glass is made from?* (sand).
Learners read the text without filling the gaps. Ask: *Who made the first piece of glass? Was it a doctor, a cook or an engineer?* (a cook)

○ Learners read the first two sentences again. Point to the example 'than' in the first gap. Learners then write the correct words for 1–8 on the lines.

> **Check answers:**
> **1** ago　**2** happened　**3** us　**4** put　**5** for　**6** mixing　**7** the　**8** or

Materials

○ In pairs or on their own, learners can find out about another material on the YLE wordlists (card, gold, paper, plastic, silver, wood or wool) or about another material they are interested in.

○ They can find out where their chosen material is found or how it is made, what people use it for, how long people have used it for etc and then write a short text.

○ For example:

Wool grows on a sheep's body. Farmers usually cut the wool off their sheep once a year. The wool quickly grows back again. Wool is great because you can change its colour and it's very difficult to break or burn wool!

People have used wood for centuries. You can wear clothes made of wool on cold or on warm days. But you can use wool to make many other things in our homes too, like rugs and curtains.

The country with the most sheep in the world is China, but in Australia there are many more sheep than people. In 2010, there were 100 million sheep in that country.

○ Learners illustrate their texts with pictures, maps etc and add their material sheet to their project file. Alternatively, display their work on the classroom wall if possible.

How many can you remember?

○ Learners close their books. In pairs or groups of 3–4, learners try to remember all 26 things from activity **B** and write them down. The first pair/group that does this shouts 'Stop!'

G Play the game! Find things in this room.

○ Divide the class into four groups. Give each group a card with three categories written on it (see below). Each group writes a list of things they can see or that they know are in the classroom for each of the three categories on their card.

○ When the groups have finished, they read out the words they have written for one of the three categories on their card. They do NOT say what the category is. The other learners have to listen and say what they think the things have in common.

Find things in this room that:

1 are longer than one metre.

2 have corners.

3 are made of paper.

Find things in this room that:

1 are square.

2 are made of plastic.

3 are bigger than a balloon.

Find things in this room that:

1 are smaller than a computer mouse.

2 are made of wood.

3 are heavy to carry.

Find things in this room that:

1 are made of metal.

2 are lower than your desk.

3 are round.

36   Silver, plastic, glass, gold

Topics materials, the home

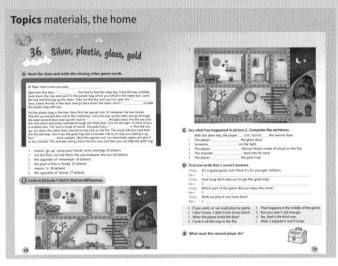

A Read the clues and write the missing video game words.

o   Ask: *Do you have any apps on your phone? What are they for? How often do you use them? Which is your favourite app? Why?*

o   Divide learners into groups of 3–4. Ask the following questions for learners to discuss in their groups: *Do you play video games? How often do you play them? Where do you usually play them? Do you play with other players or by yourself? Have you got a favourite video game? What's it called? If you don't like playing video games, why don't you like them?*
    (If you prefer, write these questions on the board.)

o   Say: *Look at A. Read what the player has to do in this video game. Find the missing words.* Point to the clues below the text. Say: *These will help you.* In pairs, learners decide what the missing words are and write them on the lines.

> **Check answers:**
> 1 climb   2 second   3 forget   4 break   5 inside   6 quickly

o   In pairs, learners choose a name for this game. Ask pairs to work together to choose the name they like best. Write the name each group has chosen on the board. Learners vote for the best name and write this on the dotted line at the top of the email.

o   Ask questions: *What must you put the silver key in?* (a plastic bag)
    Where can you find the special rock? (between the two lizards)
    What's in the metal box at the start of the game? (the plastic bag)
    What's the third door made of? (glass)
    What must you throw in the fire? (the box made of wood)
    What will try to stop you taking the golden ring out of the fire? (the monster)

B Look at pictures 1 and 2. Find six differences.

Speaking Part 1

Note: There are more than six extra differences between these two pictures, but in the Speaking test, there will also be more differences than the six that learners will be asked to identify.

o   Learners look at the two video game pictures. Point to picture 1 and say: *Is this at the start or the end of the game?* (The start of the game) *Where's the red player?* (Behind the green door) *Where's the orange player?* (Sleeping in its bed).

o   Point to picture 2 and say: *Is this the start or the end of the game?* (the end). *Where's the red player now?* (by the fire / outside the cave) *What's happened to the orange player? Is it still sleeping?* (No, it's woken up / it's awake.)

o   Say: *So the first picture is nearly the same as the second picture, but some things are different. For example, in the first picture, the lizards have got the special rock but in the second picture the monster has got the special rock. OK?*

o   Point to the first picture. Say: *This is my picture.* Point to the second picture. Say: *This is your picture. In my picture, it's half past three.* Encourage different learners to say how their picture is different. For example: *In my picture, it's a quarter to four.*

o   Do the same to talk about six other differences.
    Differences:
    The blue flower is in the water on the shelf. (It's **on the floor**.)
    The mirror is square. (The mirror is **round**.)
    There are two bats in the cave. (There is **one** bat in the cave.)
    The mat at the bottom of the stairs is blue. (The mat is **yellow**.)
    The key is in the tree. (It's **in the door**.)
    The fire is burning. (The fire **isn't** burning.)

o   Learners could write other differences for homework.

C Say what has happened in picture 2. Complete the sentences.

o   Say: *Look at the two pictures again.* Ask: *What can we say about the blue flower in the second picture?* (It's on the floor.) Say: *We can also say it has fallen on the floor.*

o   If necessary, revise the use and form of the present perfect before learners complete sentences 1–5. Make sure learners understand they can use this tense because they can see what has happened in the second picture in the time between the start and end of the game.

o   Learners look at the example. Read out the passage where they can find the verb they need in the game instructions in **A**: *Carry the key and the bag up the stairs. Take out the key and use it to open the second door.* Ask: *In picture 1, the player opened the second door with the key?* (no) *Look at the key in the second door in picture 2 now. Has the player opened the door with the silver key here?* (yes)

o   Say: *Now read sentences 1–5. Look for the part of the game where you can find the verb you need for your answers.* In pairs, learners complete sentences 1–5.

> **Check answers:**
> 1 has broken   2 has turned   3 has thrown/burnt   4 has gone
> 5 has taken/got

o   Ask: *What can we say about the spider?* (It has gone.) *What can we say about the metal box? The player … ?* (has taken it upstairs.) *What can we say about the plastic bag?* (The player has put it in the tree.) *And the second bat?* (It has flown up into the sky.)

o   Learners draw a player similar to the red one in the game. Ask two or three learners: *What have you drawn?* (I've drawn a player!) Say: *Now draw something next to your packman player.*

o   Ask two or three players what their partner has drawn. (He's/She's drawn a monster!) Draw something on the board, for example, a bat. Ask: *What have I drawn?* (You've drawn a bat!)

Rhyming words

o Write on the board: *head, key, door, bat, box, light, tree, mat, night, floor, rocks, bed*

o In small groups, learners find the rhyming pairs: head/bed, key/tree, door/floor, bat/mat, box/rocks, light/night.

o Groups then write a funny two line poem using the rhyming words at the ends of each line. Show them the poems below as an example.

o Alternatively, you could say the first line of each poem below. Groups choose a line to follow it.

Suggestions:

I don't know where to put my head.
I know I'll put it on my bed.

Where's the silver key?
Look! It's up in the tree.

Open the door
And sit on the floor!

Fly away bat!
Don't sit on my mat!

What's in that big box?
Six special black rocks!

Open your eye
And look up at the sky.
Now turn off the light.
OK. Goodnight!

D Find and write Ben's correct answers.

o Learners read Vicky's questions without adding Ben's answers. Ask: *Which game is Vicky talking about?* (the gold ring game / the name of the game learners chose in **A**)

o In pairs, learners choose the four answers from the ten options and write them on the lines. Check answers by asking three different pairs to read out one conversation turn each.

> **Check answers:**
> **1** Well, I enjoyed it and I'm ten.   **2** I don't know. I didn't look at my watch.   **3** When the player broke the door!   **4** If you want, or we could play my game.

o Divide learners into groups of 3–4. Say: *Write questions or other sentences that can go before all the other answers. Use your own ideas. Work quietly so other groups don't hear what you decide to write!*

Suggestions:

Where did you take the box made of wood? (I took it all the way to the fire.)

I'm going to drive Dad's car. (But you aren't old enough!)

Is your bike slower? (It's quicker actually.)

When does the player jump through the broken door? (That happens in the middle of the game.)

Is the second door made of glass? (No, that's the third one.)

Are you fourteen? (No, I'm younger than that!)

o A group takes it in turn to say one of their questions/sentences. Other groups quickly decide which answer to give and put up their hands to show they know.

o Ask all the learners in the first group to read their first question/sentence out together and all the learners in the second group to read their answer out together. Ask the rest of the class: *Is that correct?* before continuing in the same way with the other five sentences.

E What must the second player do?

o Learners continue to work in groups. Ask: *What does the message that's on the blue paper say?* Groups decide. Say: *Make it a funny message.* Write suggestions on the board. Learners vote for the funniest message.

Say: *The second player didn't do anything in this game. It woke up but it stayed in bed. What must it do?* Encourage learners to be creative. Ask for suggestions:
Put the flower back in the water. Eat the cheese. Read the message! Sit on the fatter lizard.

o In groups, learners imagine a series of tasks for the second player and write down instructions, telling it what to do. They should refer to **A** as a model. Give groups plenty of time to discuss this and to write their instructions. Groups then read out their instructions.

o Alternatively, one learner could give the instructions and the others in their group could mime them, for example: climbing trees, running down stairs, eating cheese etc.

Suggestion:

Get out of bed. Move quietly and slowly. There's a monster under the bed! Pick up the blue flower and the piece of cheese. Go downstairs. Take the plastic bag out of the tree and put the flower and cheese inside. Carry the bag carefully. Stand between the two lizards and take the message from behind the mirror. Walk past the lizards and stop on the yellow mat. Go up the stairs. Sit on the floor under the light. Read the message and then eat the message. Walk through the broken glass door and put the flower in the metal box. Walk through the door with the round window in it. Jump into bed and eat the cheese!

o Alternatively, learners can take turns to give their instructions in a chain with each subsequent learner miming the task. For example:

Learner A: *Get out of bed.*

Learner B mimes getting out of bed then says: *Pick up the flower.*

Learner C mimes picking up a flower then says: *Put it in the bowl of water,* etc.

Note: If you have the possibility to record sound in the classroom, groups could take it in turns to record their instructions for others to listen to and mime afterwards.

Video games

o Learners choose a video game and write about it. They either invent a game or write about a real game that they own.

o They say why they like it, what happens in the game, the age of players it is suitable for, how long the game takes, what is good about it, what is not so good about it, who gave it to them, where they play the game etc.

o They illustrate their game sheet with drawings or photos of the game. They then add their game sheet to their project file. Alternatively, display their game sheets on the wall after they have given a short presentation about their chosen video game.

37 Exciting days!

Topics work, clothes

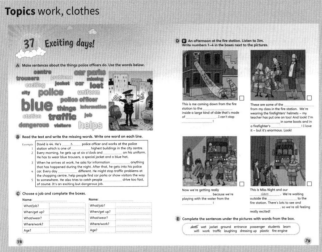

Not in YLE wordlists: *slide* (n), *visitor*

Equipment needed

- Flyers audio 37D.
- Photocopies (one for each group of 3–4 learners) of the text on page 141, the text cut up into 12 cards and the question sets into 4 cards. See E.

Ⓐ Make sentences about the things police officers do. Use the words below.

- Point to the picture and ask: *What can you see?* (police officer)
  Do you know anyone who is a police officer?
  What do police officers do?
  Explain: *We can say 'police officer' when we talk about a man or a woman who does police work.*

- Point to the word cloud. Learners use the words to make sentences about police work.
  For example: *Many police officers wear a blue jacket and trousers. This is their uniform.*
  Learners do this in pairs or different learners come to the board to each write a sentence there. Challenge them to use all the words in the box in their sentences.
  Suggestions:
  A police officer gives information to visitors.
  A police officer helps with traffic problems in the city centre.
  People go to the police station when their pet is missing.
  People who have lost things go to the police.
  Police stations are usually in the city centre.
  A police officer's job can be exciting and sometimes dangerous too.

Ⓑ Read the text and write the missing words. Write one word on each line.

- Learners read the text. They should not write anything yet. Ask: *Would you like to do David's job? Why / Why not?* Say: *Find the missing words.*

- Learners read the text again and write one word on each line.

  > **Check answers:**
  > **1** the **2** puts **3** about / on **4** is / seems / feels **5** who / that

- Ask and answer questions about David.
  Write the following on the board:
  What/job?
  When/get up?
  What/wear?
  Where/work?
  Age?

- Ask learners to tell you what questions they would need to ask for each of these pieces of information. Write the questions on the board.
  What's his job?
  What time does he get up?
  What does he (have to) wear?
  Where does he work?
  How old is he?

- Ask learners the questions about David. They tell you the answers from the text in **B**. Write the answers on the board.

  > **Check answers:**
  > Job: a police officer
  > Gets up: six o'clock
  > Uniform: blue hat and trousers, special jacket
  > Where: police station
  > Age: 44

Ⓒ Choose a job and complete the boxes.

- Say: *Choose a job and think of a person who does this job. It can be about someone you know or you can invent the details about an imaginary person. Write the name of the person on the line above the first box, then complete the boxes about the person's job.*

- In pairs, learners ask each other the questions and complete the second table about their partner's person.

  > **Flyers tip**
  > In Speaking Part 2, the examiner does not ask the questions in the same order as the information in the table. Candidates need to listen to the questions carefully and check which of the pieces of information they should use to answer.

Ⓓ ▶ An afternoon at the fire station. Listen to Jim. Write numbers 1–4 in the boxes next to the pictures.

- Point to the pictures in **D**. Point to the second picture and the shorter boy in the firefighter's jacket.
  Say: *This is Jim. Where is he?* (at the fire station)
  Point to the other people in the picture. Ask: *Who are these people?* (his cousins and aunt / his teacher and school friends …)

- Say: *These four pictures show the story of Jim's visit to the fire station but they're not in the correct order.*
  Play the first part of the audio and ask:
  Who is Jim talking to? (his grandma/grandmother)
  Where did Jim go today? (to the fire station)
  Play the rest of the audio. Learners order the pictures correctly by writing the numbers 1–4 in the boxes.

  > **Check answers:**
  > **1** Children and teacher outside fire station.
  > **2** Wearing firefighters' helmet. **3** Sliding down plastic slide.
  > **4** Playing with the water.

Audioscript

Listen and look. Write numbers.

Woman:	What did you do at school today, Jim?
Boy:	Today was a great day, Grandma. I went to the fire station with my class.
Woman:	Did you walk there?
Boy:	No, we got a lift on the school bus.
Woman:	What did you do there?
Boy:	First, a firefighter talked to us about the fire station. We were all outside. But it was a very hot day, so we went inside the fire station after that.
Woman:	Good idea! Today was very sunny.
Boy:	And the firefighters gave us their yellow helmets. They're very heavy! We put them on. I also put a firefighter's jacket on, but it was too big!
Woman:	Did you wear the hat and jacket all afternoon?
Boy:	No. We had to take them off – the firefighters needed to put them back in the fire engine. Next, we went up to the second floor of the fire station. This part was really exciting.
Woman:	Why?
Boy:	There was a kind of slide like you sometimes see in swimming pools. It was made of plastic. We sat down and went all the way down to the ground inside it. We had such a lot of fun!
Woman:	Yes. It sounds good!
Boy:	And after that, it got even better!
Woman:	Why? What happened next?
Boy:	Because the firefighters used the water in the fire engine to make a shower for us!
Woman:	Wow! And have you got any photos to show me?
Boy:	Yes. I'll send you them by email.
Woman:	OK! Great! Thanks!

(E) Complete the sentences under the pictures with words from the box.

○ Point to the pictures in **D** again and say:
These are the pictures that Jim sent to his grandma by email.
Point to the sentences under the pictures and say: *This is the email that Jim sent with his pictures.*

○ Point to the text under picture 1. Read out the first sentence: *This is Miss Night and our class.*
Point to the word 'class' in the box and on the line in this sentence.
Say: *This is an example.*

○ Learners read the other sentences under the pictures, choose words from the box and write them on the lines.

```
Check answers:
Picture 1: class, entrance, learn
Picture 2: students, dressing up, jacket
Picture 3: ground, plastic, laughing
Picture 4: wet, fire engine
```

Put the text about Emma the firefighter in order.

○ Give out one copy of the text on page 141 (cut up) to each group of 3–4 learners.

○ Say: *You have to put the 12 parts in order to form a text.*

○ Check answers by asking different learners to read the next part of the text aloud.

○ Ask: *Can you tell me two things that David the police officer and Emma the firefighter both do?* Write learners' suggestions on the board. For example:
They both have exciting jobs.
They both get up at 6 o'clock.
They both wear a uniform.
They both help people.

○ Ask learners to give you sentences about how David and Emma's jobs are different. Write them on the board.
Suggestions:
The police station is <u>in the city</u>, but the fire station is <u>just outside the city</u>.
David jumps into a <u>police car</u>, but Emma jumps into a <u>fire engine</u>.

How much can you remember?

○ Divide learners into four teams. Give each team a set of questions photocopied from page 141. Say: *These are about the different people you have read about in this unit*. Teams find the answers to their questions in the texts in **B**, **D** or the text about Emma.

○ Different teams ask the other teams their questions. The teams who are answering write their answers to each question and the team asking the questions give points for correct answers. Ask: *Which team got the most points?* Acknowledge that team as the winners.

```
Check answers:
1  a David    b Emma    c Jim    d Miss Night
2  a blue and yellow   b blue   c red and grey   d red and grey
3  a police station   b shopping centre   c fire station   d house
4  a in the police car   b by motorbike   c in the fire engine
   d on the school bus
```

38 Famous people

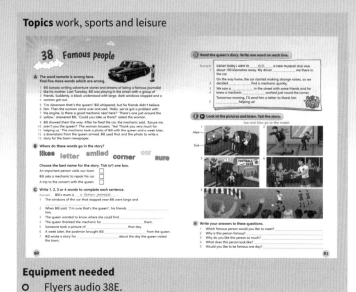

Equipment needed
o Flyers audio 38E.

(A) The word *tomato* is wrong here. Find five more words which are wrong.

o Point to the picture above the story and ask:
What can you see in this picture? (a boy and a big car that has a man in the front and a woman in the back)
What kind of car is it? (a Rolls-Royce)
Who do you think the woman in the car is? (Learners give their ideas.)

o Learners read the story and find out who the woman is (the queen).

o Read out the first sentence of the story: *Bill tomato writing adventure stories and dreams of being a famous journalist like his mother.* Ask: *Is this sentence correct?* (No – the word 'tomato' is not right here.)
Learners read the rest of the story and underline the words which are wrong.

> **Check answers:**
> Line 3: understood   Line 10: trousers
> Line 5: classroom   Line 12: downstairs
> Line 7: yellow

(B) Where do these words go in the story?

o Learners replace the words they have underlined with the correct words.

> **Check answers:**
> tomato – *likes*, understood – *car*, classroom – *sure*,
> yellow – *corner*, trousers – *smiled*, downstairs – *letter*

Choose the best name for the story. Tick one box.

o Learners choose the best name for the story. (An important person visits our town) Explain: *The other two are not good answers. 'Bill asks a mechanic to repair his car' is not right because it wasn't <u>Bill</u> who asked the mechanic to repair the car and it wasn't <u>his</u> car. (The queen asked the mechanic to repair <u>her</u> car.) It does not say anywhere that Bill and the queen went to a concert.*

(C) Write 1, 2, 3 or 4 words to complete each sentence.

o Look at the example sentence with learners. Point out that 'mother' in the text changes to 'mum' and that the words needed to complete the sentence appear at the start of the text in **A**.

> **Flyers tip**
> For Reading and Writing Part 5, make sure candidates read the instructions carefully. They should remember that they never write more than four words in one answer.

o Point to 'a famous journalist' on the line in the example sentence and ask: *How many words are here?* (three) *Is that a correct number of words for this part?* (yes)

o Learners complete the sentences 1–7 about the queen's visit.

> **Check answers:**
> **1** dark   **2** didn't believe   **3** a (good) mechanic   **4** helping
> **5** Bill (with the queen)   **6** a letter   **7** the (town) newspaper

(D) Read the queen's diary. Write one word on each line.   Reading & Writing **Part 6**

o Tell learners to read the text and to tell you:
Who wrote it? (the queen)
What did she write about? (her problems with the car and how Bill helped her)

o Learners complete the text by writing one word on each line.

> **Check answers:**
> **1** took/drove   **2** to   **3** boy/child   **4** that/who   **5** for

(E) ▶ Look at the pictures and listen. Tell the story.   Speaking **Part 3**

o There are two ways to tell the story.
1 To make this Speaking Part 3 as authentic as possible, tell learners to look at the five pictures, then play part 1 only of the audio. Learners listen to the start of the story then work in pairs pointing to each picture and saying two or three sentences about what they can see happening in each one.
2 To give learners more support, continue as follows.
Say: *Look at the five pictures. A man is going to tell the first part of the story. Look at the first picture now and listen.* Play the first part of the audio and ask:
What are the girl and her brother's names? (Sue and Alex)
Who's the footballer? (Oliver Quick)
What do Sue and Alex want to do? (go and watch Oliver Quick when he plays in his next match)

o In pairs, learners practise telling the rest of the story. Walk round and help them with ideas and words they need.

- Use the following prompts to help learners:
  Picture 2:
  Where is Sue now? (in the street.)
  Who's running past her? (Oliver Quick)
  What is Sue picking up? (some of Oliver Quick's money)
  Picture 3:
  Where is Sue now? (at home)
  Who is Sue talking to? (her brother Alex)
  What is Sue showing to her brother? (Oliver Quick's money)
  Does Alex have an idea? (yes)
  Picture 4:
  Where are Sue and Alex now? (in a (football) stadium)
  Who are they giving the money to? (Oliver Quick)
  What is the footballer giving them? (some tickets to watch the match)
  Picture 5:
  What are Sue and Alex watching? (a football match)
  Who are they waving to? (Oliver Quick)
- Two pairs join together and compare their stories.
- Play the second part of the audio. Learners compare their stories with this one.

Audioscript

Part 1
Man: These pictures tell a story. It's called 'Sue and Alex go to the match!' Just look at the pictures first.
Sue and her brother, Alex, love football. They're watching Oliver Quick on TV. Oliver is their favourite football player. Sue and Alex want to go and watch Oliver Quick when he plays in his next match. But they haven't got enough money to buy any tickets.
Now you tell the story.

Part 2
Man: Sue's walking in the street now. Oliver Quick is running past Sue! Oliver's dropping some money and Sue's picking it up!
Man: Sue's at home now. She's showing Oliver's money to Alex. Alex has got a good idea.
Man: Sue and Alex are at the football stadium now. They're giving Oliver his money. Oliver is very happy. He's giving Sue and Alex two football tickets.
Man: Sue and Alex are sitting and watching Oliver's match now. They're shouting and waving to Oliver. They're having a great time.

F Write your answers to these questions.

- Ask: *Would you like to meet an important person? Who?* Learners suggest different people. Ask: *What questions could you ask them?* Learners suggest questions, for example: *How old are you? What do you do each day? Do you live in a really big house? Have you got any pets? What are your hobbies? Do you drive an expensive racing car?*
- Learners work in small groups. They choose an important person they would like to meet, for example, a famous sports personality, actor or pop star.
- Learners read the questions and write their answers.
- Groups think of five or six questions they would like to ask this person and the answers their famous person might give.
- Still working as a team, learners then write an interview between themselves and their famous person, perhaps each learner asking one or two of the questions. They could add extra information between Qs and As, for example: *Would you like a cup of coffee? Yes, please. OK. I'll go and make one for you.*
- The group could then role play the interview to other groups in the class. All learners should take part if possible.
- They could freeze frame the role play with one learner asking prediction questions for example: *What happens next? What will she/he say?*
- At the end of the role play, learners in that group could ask others in the class questions: *What was our first question? What did … say? Do you think … is an interesting or boring person?*

Play the game! What's my job?

- Write the following underlined words on the board. Learners make questions with them. Tell them that they will use the questions to try to guess someone's job. Write the questions on the board:
  Do you work inside or outside?
  Do you wear a uniform?
  Do you get up early?
  Do you earn a lot of money?
  Is your job quite dangerous?
  Do you use a computer?
  Do you work in one place?
  Do you have to go to university?
  Do you make things?
  Do you travel?
  Do you have to use any special programs?
  Do you have to go to meetings?
- Learners work in groups of 4–5. Each person chooses a job and writes it on a piece of paper. The other learners in the group have to guess which job the learner has written by asking the questions on the board (and any other questions they can think of).
- The winner is the person whose job remains undiscovered or who has been asked the most questions.

39 In villages and towns

Topics places, sports and leisure

Equipment needed
o Flyers audio 39C.

A You're walking through a village. What can you see?

o Teach/revise 'village' then ask learners to stand up. Say: *You aren't in a classroom now! You're in a village.* Make sure learners understand that they need to use their imaginations.

o Say: *Look behind you. What can you see?* Learners answer.

o Write key words on the board, for example: *house, garden, road, shop, playground, school, cars, wall, sky, birds, grass, pond, stream, seat, windows, people, cat.* Ask further 'What can you see' questions:

   Look left. What can you see?

   Look right. What can you see now?

   Look up! What can you see?

   Look down! What can you see?

   Look in front of you now. What can you see?

   What can you hear?

   Put out your hand. What can you touch?

o Make sure that everyone in the class has told you at least one thing they can see. Continue until learners tire of the task or you have a board full of village vocabulary. Learners sit down again.

   Note: If you have a small class and a large classroom, you could actually ask learners to walk around the room imagining they are walking through the village.

o Ask: *Who saw a post office?* (learners put up their hands) Ask two or three of these learners: *What colour was the outside of the post office? Can you see a post box? How many people are there inside the post office? Is the post office busy or quiet?*

B Read the story. Choose a word from the box. Write the correct word next to numbers 1–5.

Reading & Writing Part 3

o Learners read the story quickly without completing the text. Ask: *Where does Mrs Forest work?* (in a village post office). *What's Mrs Forest like? Is she kind / friendly / tired / lazy / fun? What do you think?*

o Learners listen to what you say about Mrs Forest (see below). If they think it's true, they remain sitting. If they think it's false, they stand up. (Learners sit down between each question.)

   Mrs Forest is a young woman.   (stand up)

   Mrs Forest likes asking questions.   (sit down)

   Mrs Forest's birthday was on a Saturday.   (sit down)

   Mrs Forest's husband is called Robert.   (stand up)

o Learners read out the first paragraph of the story. Stop and start different learners to make this fun and to make sure that everyone is listening. You could clap once to indicate when one learner should stop and the next learner start.

o Learners read the rest of the story and choose words from the box, crossing them out as they use them. They then choose the best name for the story (More and more questions!).

Check answers:
> 1 stamps   2 tent   3 sold   4 huge   5 dinner

o In pairs, learners choose the best name for the story. Check their answers by asking: *Is the best name for the story 'Mrs Forest makes a pizza'?* (no) *How about 'Pat's special birthday present'?* (no) *So, is it 'More and more questions'?* (yes) Learners tick the correct box.

Busy buses and businesspeople

o Ask: *Does Mrs Forest work in a busy shop?* (yes)

o Write on the board: *busy.* Say: *I'm always busy!* (As you speak, remove the final 'y' and write 'i': *busi.*) *But I don't go to business meetings because I'm not a businessman/woman.* Ask learners how to finish the spellings of these three words and write them on the board.

o Tell learners that the words 'businessman/woman' and 'business' all have the word 'busy' in them because we think businessmen and businesswoman are busy people and all these words start with the sound /bɪz/. Say: *My brother Ben's a really busy businessman! Would you like to be busy businessmen and businesswomen one day?*

o Write on the board: *bus.* Point to 'bus' and ask: *Does my brother the businessman catch a /bɪz/or a /bʌs/ into town at the weekend?* (Your brother the businessman catches a bus!)

o Write on the board: *My brother the businessman catches a bus.*

o Ask learners to repeat this slowly and then quickly in pairs. Check that they are using the correct pronunciation.

C ▶ What did Lucy's mum buy in each place? Listen and write a letter in each box.

Listening Part 3

> **Flyers tip**
>
> In Listening Part 3, all eight pictures in the second group will be mentioned in the conversation, but only six of them will be answers. Candidates should not think a picture is an answer just because they hear someone say the word.

o Ask: *What's the difference between a village and a town?*

   A town is … ? (bigger, noisier, busier etc)

   In a town you can see… ? (more cars / people / shops, bigger schools etc.)

o Learners look at the six places. Ask: *Which places can you see?*

   Ask questions: Point to the six places in the pictures. Ask: *Where are they? Can you see places like these in your town/city? What can you see in these places? What can you do in them? What can you buy?*

o Say: *Lucy's mum went to all of these places today and bought some of the things that you can see in the other pictures. Listen to Lucy and her mother talking.* Learners listen and write the letter of the correct shopping item under each place picture. Remind learners that Lucy's mum didn't buy all these things so they won't need to use two of the letters.

o Play the audio. Learners listen twice.

> **Check answers:**
> chemist's – **h**   bus station – **d**   shopping centre – **f**
> sports shop – **b**   clothes shop – **a**

Audioscript

○ Ask different learners: *Is shopping boring or exciting?*

Does your family drive or walk to the shops?

Who do you usually go shopping with?

How often do your parents go shopping?

What's the most interesting kind of shop?

Tell me about something you or your parents bought last week.

Ⓓ Find words in each wheel. What are the three places in town?

○ Learners look at the three word wheels. Ask: *How many wheels does a lorry / bicycle / plane have?*

○ In pairs, learners find words in the wheels and draw circles round them. You might like to only give them two minutes to do this and say: *Put up your hands when you have all the answers.*

○ Ask different pairs for the words they have found.

> **Check answers:**
> stage, actors, seat, lights / suitcases, lifts, waiters, beds / passengers, planes, timetables (or time and tables)

○ Ask learners where they might find these things. (at a theatre, in a hotel, at an airport)

Ask: *Is there a theatre / a hotel / an airport in your town? Have you ever been there?*

○ In pairs or small groups, learners try to write two or three sentences about one of the word wheel places. They should include at least two words from the wheel in each sentence.

Say: *If you can put all the words and the name of the place in one sentence, that's really clever!*

Suggestions:

*The theatre **lights** are very bright.*

*There were two **actors** on the **stage** at the theatre.*

*When we sat in our **seats** in the theatre, someone turned on the **lights** and we saw all the **actors** on the stage.*

*The **beds** in the hotel were really nice!*

*The **waiter** in the hotel brought us our dinner.*

*One of the **waiters** came with us in the hotel **lift** and put our **suitcases** on our **beds**.*

*We went to the airport to catch a **plane**.*

*There was a large **timetable** in the airport.*

*Lots of **passengers** who were waiting for their **planes** were looking at the **timetable** on the screen at the airport.*

○ One learner from each group reads out their sentences to the others in the class.

Ask the learners who are listening: *Are these sentences OK, good or excellent?* (Learners decide how good a sentence is for any reason – *It's really long / clever / funny.*)

Ⓔ What's this? Choose the correct words and write them on the lines. Reading & Writing — Part 1

○ Learners look at the sentences and possible answers. Ask: *How many questions are there?* (10 plus the example). *How many answers are there?* (15). Check that learners know they do not need to use four of these answers.

○ Look at the example together. Tell learners to draw a line through 'a restaurant' and remind them they can only use an answer once.

○ To make the practice as authentic as possible, learners work on their own. They read the definitions and write the answers.

> **Check answers:**
> **1** a factory **2** a bicycle **3** a sledge **4** a concert **5** traffic
> **6** a flashlight **7** an entrance **8** camping **9** goals **10** a journey

Ⓕ Play the game! Guess the describing word.

○ Give each learner a piece of paper with a noun on it (see suggested nouns below).

Suggested nouns:

a jacket, a film, a cake, a holiday, a room, a flower, a ball, a car, a message, a balloon, an alien, an insect, a king, a website, a garden, a trip, a timetable, a cushion, a tune, a spaceship, trainers

○ Learners write an article and either an adjective or another noun in front of their word to describe it. For example, the word is 'mouse' and the learner decides to write *a computer* in front of their word. They now have 'a computer mouse' on their piece of paper. Say: *Don't show your words to anyone!*

○ Divide learners into groups of 4–5. In their groups, learners take turns to answer questions from others in the group as they try to guess the describing words. For example, if Learner A wrote 'a computer mouse':

Learner B: Is it a *big mouse*?	Learner A: *No.*
Learner C: *A plastic mouse*?	Learner A: *No.*
Learner D: Is it a *toy mouse*?	Learner A: *No.*
Learner E: *A grey mouse*?	Learner A: *No.*
Learner E: Is it a *computer mouse*?	Learner A: *Yes.*

○ To round up, write on the board: *a .... businessman!* and ask: *What's the answer?* Learners guess: *a busy businessman!*

93

40   What a strange planet!

Topics animals, body and face, the world around us

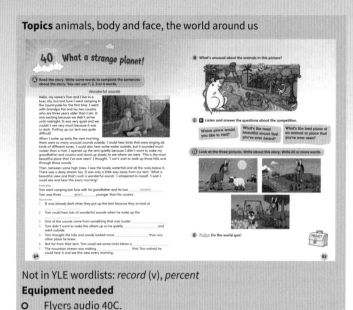

Not in YLE wordlists: *record* (v), *percent*

Equipment needed
- Flyers audio 40C.

A   Read the story. Write some words to complete the sentences about the story. You can use 1, 2, 3 or 4 words.

Reading & Writing **Part 5**

- Point to the picture and ask: *How many people can you see?* (2) *Where are they?* (in the countryside, near a river and waterfall) *Why are they at this place?* Learners suggest why.

- Say: *Let's read the text to find out who these people are and why they are at this place!* Learners read the text. (This is Tom and his Grandpa Pat. They are camping in the countryside. This is a beautiful place, with woods, hills and a waterfall.)

- Learners read the text again and complete sentences 1–7.

> **Check answers:**
> **1** midnight   **2** next morning   **3** than a river
> **4** opened (up) the tent   **5** beautiful   **6** (lovely) waterfall   **7** such a wonderful sound

- Write on the board *Who? What? Where?*

  Learners work in groups. They write three questions about Tom's camping trip. Say: *Your three questions must begin with 'Who', 'What' and 'Where'.*

  Groups write their questions on a piece of paper. For example:
  Who did Tom go camping with?
  What is Tom's grandpa's name?
  Where did they camp?

  Groups then exchange questions and write answers before handing them back. Groups then read the answers and mark them. Say:
  You can give three marks for a really good answer, two marks for a good answer and one mark for an OK answer! Add the three marks together.

  Walk round and monitor to check answers are being marked fairly.

  The group you think wrote the best questions and the group with the most points for their answers win this competition.

B   What's unusual about the animals in this picture?

- Make sure learners' books are closed. Ask: *Which animals have short tails?*

  Suggestions: rabbits, birds, ducks and swans, giraffes, hippos, camels etc.

- Write on the board:

  Animals that:

  have wings -

  swing from trees -

  are big and heavy -

  have really long legs -

  have spots or stripes –

  have very long tails -

- Learners work in pairs or small groups. Point to the six categories on the board and say: *Talk together about animals you can describe like this and then write them in your notebooks.*

  Give learners plenty of time to copy the category list and add their chosen animals. Encourage use of dictionaries if necessary.

- Ask different pairs/groups for their animal answers.

  Suggestions:

  have wings – bee, penguin, duck, bird, parrot, swan, fly, butterfly, bat, chicken,

  swing from trees – monkey

  are big and heavy – donkey, polar bear, elephant, hippo, horse, cow, whale

  have really long legs – giraffe, spider, jellyfish

  have spots or stripes- butterfly, spider, fish, frog, tiger, zebra

  have very long tails – horse, cat, lizard, dinosaur, mouse

- Say: *A mouse is usually grey and usually runs from one place to another place.*

  Talk about monkeys, horses, cows, frogs and kangaroos now. What colour are these animals usually? How do they usually move from one place to another?

- Say: *You're going to see a picture with some very strange animals in it now. Open your books.*

  Learners look at the picture in **B**. Ask: *Which animals can you see here?* (a mouse, a monkey, a horse, a cow, a frog, a kangaroo)

  Ask: *Why is this planet strange?* Learners answer, for example:
  The sky is purple and blue. The clouds are pink. The leaves on the trees aren't green. The animals are bigger or smaller than they are on our planet. Cows and frogs can't fly on our planet!

  Optional extension:

  In pairs or small groups, learners decide what these strange animals might be saying to each other because on this strange planet, animals can speak English! Groups then read out their sentences to others in the class.

  For example:

  The mouse: I've just had a really big breakfast!
  The frog: I love flying above the river!
  The cow: I can fly higher than the frog!
  The kangaroo: Come and play games with me!
  The horse: This banana tastes horrible!
  The frog: This is my new boat. Do you like it?

C ▶ **Listen and answer the questions about the competition.**

o Ask: *Do you like competitions? Have you ever tried to win a competition? Have you ever won a competition?*

o Ask: *Which of these questions did Tom answer?* (*What's the most beautiful sound you've ever heard?*)

o Learners read the three competition questions in **C**.
   Play the audio. Point to the three questions in **C** and ask:
   1 *How many questions do you have to answer?* (one)
   2 *What might you win?* (the chance to film a new TV programme.)

Audioscript

Man: We have three questions for you! Choose one of the questions and write your answer. We will invite the winner of this writing competition to come and help us film our new TV programme. The TV programme is all about strange places on our planet and the strangest animals that live there.

o Ask 2–3 different learners: *Which question would you like to answer?*
   Ask: *Would you like to help film a TV programme? Would you like to film a TV programme about a strange place one day?*

o Tell learners to imagine they are going to make a TV programme about somewhere strange now. Learners work in small groups. They decide where they want to film and what they want to film. Give learners time to discuss this then ask different groups to tell others in the class about their TV programme.

   Suggestions:

   We want to film a programme about the hottest desert in the world. We want to film the animals that live under the ground there.
   We want to film a programme about the highest, largest cave in the world and the bats that live inside it.

   Optional extension:

   In pairs, learners choose another question from **C** and write their own competition text. It doesn't need to be true! They could also illustrate it.
   Display the texts on the classroom wall or pass them round so that learners can read all the texts.

D **Look at the three pictures. Write about this story. Write 20 or more words.**   Reading & Writing Part 7

o For an authentic test practice, tell learners to look at the three pictures and to write the story that they see there. See the suggested stories below.
   If you would prefer to give learners more support, you could follow the process below.

o Point to the donkey in the field and ask: *Which animal is this?* Point to the sheep and the bee and ask the same questions.
   Ask: *What's the weather like? Is the grass in the field long or short? Does the donkey like this grass?*
   Say: *Listen to my questions again. This time, write sentences to talk about picture 1.*

o Point to picture 2 and ask: *Where's the bee going now? Which animal is following the bee? Where are they going?* Learners write one or two sentences to answer these questions.

o Do the same with picture 3 and ask: *Where's the donkey now? What's it eating? What are the children doing? Why? Is the man looking at the donkey? Is the donkey hungry now?*

   Suggested stories

   The donkey is hungry. A bee flies into its field. The donkey goes with the bee into a garden. The donkey eats the nice red flowers and green grass there! Some children say, 'We're happy now. The donkey isn't hungry.' (39 words)

   Dan the donkey is hungry. The grass in his field is very short. His friend, the bee, comes to help Dan. It says, 'Follow me!' Dan and the bee go through the gate into Mr Farm's garden. The flowers and grass taste really good. Two children see the donkey! 'Shall we tell it to stop?' asks the boy. 'No! It's hungry. Poor donkey,' says the girl. (66 words)

E **Do the world quiz!**

o Learners work in pairs or groups of 3–4. Read out the sentences below. In their notebooks, learners write *yes* if the sentence is right or *no* if the sentence is wrong.

o Read the sentences again. After each one, give learners time to agree on an answer for their group.

o Check answers. Give one point for each correct answer.
   Teams could then write two sentences of their own to test other teams.

   ### *yes/no* sentences:

   1 *Some mountains are more than four kilometres high.* (yes)
   2 *In the desert, it's hotter at night than in the day.* (no)
   3 *The moon is nearer the sun than our planet.* (no)
   4 *Jungles are always wetter places than forests.* (yes)
   5 *Some crocodiles can live in the sea and other crocodiles can live in rivers.* (yes)
   6 *A person is colder than a fish.* (no)
   7 *The sound that a snake makes is louder than a lion's.* (no)
   8 *Dolphins and whales can hear each other under the water.* (yes)
   9 *Around 70% of our planet is the water in the oceans and seas.* (yes)
   10 *Crocodiles, eagles, rabbits all build nests.* (yes)

📋 **Wonderful places**

o Learners look online or in atlases to choose an amazing place they'd like to visit in the future.

o They find and print pictures of their chosen place from the internet or cut pictures out of magazines and then glue their pictures onto a large piece of paper. They draw and add a map and then write:
   where they would like to go.
   how they would like to travel there.
   who they would like to go there with.
   what they would like to see there.

o Learners present their project to the rest of the class then add it to their project file. Alternatively, display the projects on the classroom walls if possible.

41 Meet the pirate actors

Topics family, the world around us, clothes

Equipment needed
- Colouring pencils or pens.
- Flyers audio 41B.

(A) Write the correct words on the green lines and the correct names on the pink lines.

- Teach 'costume'. Say: *Actors have to dress up in costumes when they are filming. Costumes are special clothes which actors wear when they must look like someone or something else. They do this in the theatre, on TV or in a film. They might have to look like someone who lived 200 years ago, a monster or a pirate.*
  Ask: *What costume should you dress up in if you want to look like a clown?*
  Suggestions: *a funny hat, big trousers, striped socks, long shoes.*

- Teach 'play'. Say: *In a play you watch actors on a stage in a theatre. This is different from a film. In a film you watch actors on a screen at the cinema.*
  Ask: *Have you ever seen a play? What kind of costumes did the actors wear? Have you ever been in a play? What was your costume like? Have you ever been to a party where people dressed up in funny costumes? What did they wear?*

- Say: *Look at the picture. Is this a clown family, a pirate family or an astronaut family? Look at the flag!* (a pirate family)

- Ask: *Would you like to be a clown? A pirate? An astronaut? Choose one job!* Learners put up their hands to show their choice. Ask one learner to count the number of hands for each choice and say, for example: *Eight of us would like to be pirates.*

- Ask: *Have you been to the cinema this month? What film(s) did you see? Do you like films about pirates? Why? Why not? Would you like to be an actor?*

- Say: *This is William's family. They're actors. We're going to read about the things they do as members of a pirate family in a film.*
  Read out the first sentence. Learners find William in the picture.
  Ask: *What's William wearing?* (a white T-shirt and blue swimming shorts with red stars) *What's he got in his hand?* (a flag) *How does he help on the ship?* (He looks after the flags and tidies the kitchen.)
  Say: *These sentences are about the different people in the pirate family. Find the correct word in the box to complete the sentences and write them on the <u>green lines</u>. If you look carefully, you'll find the people's names too! Write each person's name on the <u>pink lines</u>.*

- In pairs, learners complete sentences 2–6.

> **Check answers:**
> **2** Robert, made **3** Anna, never **4** Sue, costume
> **5** Richard, dangerous **6** light, May

- Ask questions about the text and picture.
  Suggested questions:
  Is the ship next to land or in the middle of the ocean? (probably in the middle of the ocean)
  Whose shoulder is the parrot sitting on? (Anna's)
  Who keeps the family's money? (Richard)
  Who thinks he's a really good actor? (Robert)
  Whose hat has got spots on? (May's)
  Who makes the meals? (Sue)
  Whose left leg is made of wood? (Robert's)
  Whose shorts have got stars on them? (William's)
  Who holds the ship's wheel when it's dark? (May)

- In pairs, learners write one more 'Who?' question and one more 'Whose?' question. They then ask another pair their questions.

- Learners work in pairs and take turns to answer questions. One learner closes their book. The other learner looks at the picture of the pirate family and asks their partner clothes questions.
  For example: *What's William's mother wearing on her head? Is William's sister wearing shoes?* This learner then closes their book and answers the other learner's questions.

(B) ▶ Listen and colour and write. Listening Part 5

- Say: *Look at the picture in B. Can you see the cameraman? He's filming William and Anna. Look! William's in the water! What's he looking at?* (some treasure) *And his sister Anna is watching him! Can you see her? Where is she?* (in the boat)
  Ask: *What is already coloured here?* (the butterfly) *Can you see another butterfly in this picture?* (yes – on the boat) *Which butterfly is already coloured?* (the one that's flying) *How many rocks can you see under the water?* (4)

- Make sure that everyone has a complete set of colouring pencils or pens. Say: *Listen and colour different things and write a word somewhere in the picture.*

- Play the audio twice without stopping.

> **Check answers:**
> **1** Colour stripe on William's shorts – red
> **2** Colour large shell under William – green
> **3** Write 'gold' on treasure box
> **4** Write 'Daisy' on boat under the water
> **5** Colour fish with smaller tail – purple

Audioscript

Man: Can you colour some of the things in this picture now?
Girl: Yes! Can I colour the butterfly? I'd like to colour the one that's flying.
Man: That's a really good idea! Colour it blue, please.
Girl: OK.

Can you see the blue butterfly? This is an example.
Now you listen and colour and write.

1 Girl: What can I colour next?
  Man: How about the stripe? You could colour that.
  Girl: Do you mean the one that I can see on William's shorts?
  Man: Yes. I think red's a good colour for that? What about you?
  Girl: Great! No problem! There!

2 Man: Now, can you see the shell?
  Girl: The one that's between the two big rocks on the right?
  Man: No, the larger one that you can see on the sand under William.
  Girl: Oh, OK. Yes, I can see that one. Shall I colour it?
  Man: Yes, please. You choose the colour this time.
  Girl: Brilliant! I'd like to use green for that. Can I do that?
  Man: If you want! Sure!

3 Man: I'd like you to write something next. Can you do that?
  Girl: I can try. What must I write?
  Man: Write 'gold' on the box that William's looking at.
  Girl: Oh! Because it's full of treasure! All right!

4 Girl: Can I write another word here?
  Man: That's a good idea. Can you see the old boat? The one under the water?
  Girl: Yes. Can I write its name on it?
  Man: I was thinking the same. Write 'Daisy' on it.
  Girl: Like the girl's name? OK.
  Man: Thank you.

5 Man: Now colour the fish.
  Girl: OK. Do you mean the one with the stripes and the big tail?
  Man: The other one actually. It's smaller.
  Girl: Fine. Can I colour it purple? I haven't used that colour yet.
  Man: Yes.
  Girl: Thanks. It looks good now! I'd like to learn to swim under the water like that!

C Let's talk about swimming.

Speaking Part 4

o Say: *Listen! I'm going to say some letters! What do they spell?* Write the letters! *m-n-i-m-i-g-s-w.* Learners write the letters then spell the word (swimming)

o Say: *Let's talk about swimming! Read the questions in C and in pairs, talk about your answers.* Pairs of learners ask and answer the questions.

o Learners ask you the questions and you answer them.

D What was each person doing when the photographer took these photos?

o Say: *William's family have been in lots of films. Cameramen filmed some of these movies in different countries. Photographers take photos of them for magazines.*

o Learners work in A and B pairs. Learner A looks at the three pictures that the film photographer took in **D** on this page. Learner B looks at the three pictures that the photographer took on page 127.

o Using the words from the box, learners ask and answer questions about who is in the photo and what they were doing when the photographer took each picture. For example:
  Learner A: *Who's in the photo?*
  Learner B: *Robert.*
  Learner A: *What was Robert doing when the photographer took the photo?*
  Learner B: *He was eating some special pasta.*

> **Check answers:**
> **Learner A: 1** Richard was hiding behind a pyramid. **2** May was collecting lovely shells. **3** Anna was riding a friendly camel.
> **Learner B: 1** Sue was holding a sweet puppy. **2** Robert was eating some special pasta. **3** William was climbing a rock.

E Think hard! How much can you remember?

o Learners look at the picture in Unit 3 (page 11).
  Ask: *Where are these people?* (in an airport)
  Three people have arrived, but what are the other people going to do next? (leave / get on a plane / fly to another country etc.)
  What has just arrived outside? (a big plane)

o Write on the board: *When the big plane arrived at the airport …*

o Say: *Look at the picture and remember as much as you can. You have one minute and then I will ask you five questions about the picture.* Learners write the numbers 1–5 in their notebooks ready for their answers.

o Allow learners to look at the picture for one minute.

o Read out the questions (see below). Allow learners time to write their answers.
  Say: *When the big plane arrived at the airport …*
  1 *was everyone in the picture sitting down?* (no)
  2 *did the woman under the clock have a drink or a sandwich in her hand?* (a drink)
  3 *was a man or a woman pushing the suitcases?* (a woman)
  4 *was someone crying?* (yes)
  5 *was the man with the beard reading a book or a newspaper?* (a newspaper)

42 Holiday news

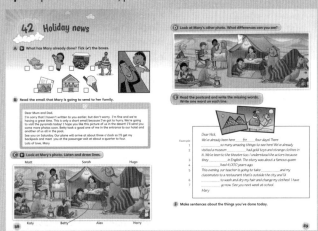

Equipment needed
- Flyers audio 42A, 42C.

A ▶ What has Mary already done? Tick the boxes.

- Ask: *What have you already done today? Have you had breakfast / lunch / dinner? Have you spoken to your friends? Have you phoned anyone yet?* etc.

- Point to the pictures in **A** and say: *Mary is phoning her father to tell him about her school trip.*
  Ask: *Where do you think Mary has gone? To the mountains / the beach / a city / the desert?*
  What has Mary done on holiday? Learners suggest ideas.

- Play the audio. Learners listen twice and tick the things Mary has already done.

  > **Check answers:**
  > Learners should have ticked boxes next to: the camel, the girl with the camera, the ice cream and the museum.

- Ask learners to tell you a sentence about the camel. For example: *Mary has ridden a camel.*
  Note: Point out that we often use the short forms of 'has' and 'have' in sentences like these. Write on the board: *Mary's already ridden a camel.*
  Ask learners to tell you a sentence about tea. (Mary hasn't drunk any tea yet.)

- Learners write three more sentences in their notebooks about what Mary has already done, and two sentences about the things she hasn't done yet. Play the audio again if necessary.

  > **Check answers:**
  > She's already eaten ice cream. She's already visited three museums. She's already taken hundreds of photos.
  > She hasn't sent any postcards yet. She hasn't been shopping / to the shops yet.

  Note: All these verbs are <u>irregular</u>. There is a complete list of the Flyers irregular verbs on pages 142 and 143 of the Student's Book.

Audioscript

Listen and tick the boxes.

Girl: Hello, Dad!
Man: Oh, hello, Mary. Are you enjoying your school holiday?
Girl: Yes. It's great! We're very busy.
Man: What have you done, then?
Girl: Well, you won't believe this, but I've ridden a camel!
Man: You're very brave! That sounds dangerous!
Girl: No, it was fine.
Man: How's the food? Is it good?
Girl: It's OK. But I haven't drunk any tea.
Man: Why not?
Girl: I don't like it. But the ice creams are excellent!
Man: Have you sent Mum and me a postcard?
Girl: Sorry! I haven't written any yet!
Man: And what about photos? Have you taken any?
Girl: Oh yes. I've taken hundreds. Oh, it's so exciting here!
Man: And have you seen lots of interesting things?
Girl: Yes. We've visited three museums.
Man: Wow! And have you spent all your money?
Girl: No. We haven't been to the shops yet. We're going to go shopping tomorrow!
Man: Oh! Right!
Girl: Dad, I have to go now. See you at the airport on Saturday!
Man: OK! Bye!

B Read the email that Mary is going to send to her family.

- Learners read Mary's message. Ask: *Has Mary seen the pyramids yet?* (no) *Has Mary stayed in a hotel yet?* (yes) *Has Mary already swum in a pool?* (yes) *Has Mary already arrived back at the airport?* (no)

- Write the following sentences on the board, one by one.
  Say: *Complete these sentences. Find your answers in Mary's message. Write one, two, three or four words in each sentence.*
  1 *She hasn't emailed .... yet.*
  2 *Mary hasn't visited .... yet. She's going there today.*
  3 *Mary and her friends have already swum ....*
  4 *Mary will see her parents again at about .... on Saturday.*

  > **Check answers:**
  > **1** (her) Mum and Dad / her parents   **2** the pyramids
  > **3** in the (swimming) pool   **4** 3.45/a quarter to four

C ▶ Look at Mary's photo. Listen and draw lines.

Listening **Part 1**

- Say: *Mary's in the desert. Have you ever been to a desert?*
  (If yes) *What did you see/do there?*
  (If no) *Would you like to visit a desert? What would you see/do there?*

- Learners look at the picture. Ask: *What are the people doing/wearing?*

- Learners listen to the audio, look at the example line and then draw five more lines between other names outside the picture and people in the picture.

  > **Check answers:**
  > Lines should be drawn between:
  > **1** *Alex* and boy sitting on blanket with rucksack.
  > **2** *Katy* and girl with pink face drinking tea.
  > **3** *Harry* and boy sitting reading diary.
  > **4** *Hugo* and boy wearing shorts with lots of pockets and putting blanket on camel.
  > **5** *Sarah* and girl looking at map with scarf round head.

Audioscript

D Look at Mary's other photo. What differences can you see?

Speaking Part 1

○ Point to the picture and say: *This is the other photo that Mary sent to her family. It's nearly the same as the first photo in C but some things are different. In pairs, talk about the differences.* Allow learners time to do this.

○ Point to the picture in **C** and say: *I'm going to say things about this picture. You tell me how the picture in D is different.*

Give learners an example first, pointing to each picture in turn. Say: *In this picture, I can see **a map** in the rucksack but here, there are **some oranges** in the rucksack.* Read out the following sentences about the picture in **C**. Learners put up their hands to talk about six more differences.

In this picture:

The girl's wearing a long dress with camels on it. (She's wearing a dress with **butterflies** on it.)

The man's making tea on a fire. (He's making/cooking **pasta**.)

Someone's closed the book on the table. (Someone's **opened** the book.)

The boy who's looking at the map has got a torch in his hand. (He's got a **brush** in his hand.)

There's no flag by the entrance to the tent. (There **is** a flag.)

Only one of the camels is sitting down. (**Both** of them are sitting down.)

Optional extension:

○ Learners work in pairs. Say: *Look at the picture in D again.* Ask: *What can't you see? You decide!*

○ Ask the following questions for learners to think about:

What else is in the tent? What's behind the tent? What's the man cooking? What's under the table? What's in the two rucksacks? What's between the two camels? What's behind the hills that are behind the tent and the children?

○ Learners write ten extra things that they can imagine in this picture. Their sentences should begin with *There's a ...* or *There are ...*

For example:

There's a village behind the hill.

There's a dangerous spider under the table.

There are two torches in the brown rucksack.

There's a baby camel between the two big ones.

There are three more chairs inside the tent.

E Read the postcard and write the missing words.

Reading & Writing Part 6

> **Flyers tip**
>
> In Reading and Writing Part 6, some of the missing words will be grammatical (eg *the, to, me, been*) and others lexical (eg *read, live, toy*). Looking carefully at the words before and after the gap should help candidates choose the right kind of answer.

○ Learners look at the text quickly. Ask: *What kind of text is it?* (a postcard) *Who wrote it?* (Mary) *Who's she writing to?* (Nick)

○ Learners read the text. Ask them:

What places has Mary been to? (a museum, a theatre)

What did she see at the museum? (gold toys, strange clothes)

What language did the actors speak? (English)

Where's the restaurant? (outside the city)

○ Learners read the text and complete the gaps.

> **Check answers:**
>
> **1** are **2** which/that **3** spoke **4** who/that **5** me **6** like **7** to

F Make sentences about the things you've done today.

○ Draw a circle on the board and write *have* inside it. Say: *This verb can mean different things. Sometimes, it means 'to eat'. For example, in the morning, people eat things like cereals, toast* (say things that your class is likely to eat). *They have cereals and bread for breakfast. They have breakfast.* Write: *breakfast, cereals, toast* on the board next to 'have'.

When we eat in the middle of the day, we have ... (lunch) *What do you have for lunch? Chicken? Rice?* Write *lunch* and the foods that learners know for lunch on the board outside the circle with 'have'. *And in the evening, we have ...* (dinner). *When you're not very hungry and it's not time for a meal, what might you have?* (a snack)

○ Say: *'Have' can also mean 'drink'. You can have a cup of coffee or ...* (tea / hot chocolate) *And you can also have a glass of ...* (fruit juice, water, milk, milkshake). Add *coffee* and the other drinks learners suggest to the board.

Say: *We also use the verb 'have' when we wash. We have a* (shower / bath / wash) Add these words to the board under 'have'.

○ Say: *Take your notebooks. At the top of the left hand side of the page, write 'already'. At the top of the right hand side of the page, write 'not yet'.*

Think about the things you've already done today and the things you haven't done yet. Write the things you've done today in the left half of the page under 'already'. Write the things you haven't done (e.g. 'had dinner') under 'not yet'.

Say: *Now, in pairs, try and guess where your partner wrote each thing.* For example: Learner A: *(Alberto), I think you've already had breakfast.* Alberto: *(Yes, that's right.)* Learner A: *But I don't think you've had dinner yet.* Alberto: *(You're right again!)*

43 Have you ever ... ?

Topics time, sports and leisure

Not in YLE wordlists: *New York, skier*

A Write the words to complete the questions.

○ Teach/revise the present perfect tense if necessary.
Look at the first sentence together: *Have you ever **gone** to a **concert?*** Point out that the missing words are shown in the pictures.

○ Learners complete the other questions.
Note: Learners could look at the list of irregular verbs on pages 142–143 of their books to help them with this.

> **Check answers:**
> **2** slept/tent   **3** eaten/chopsticks   **4** won/sports
> **5** flown/London   **6** broken/arm   **7** met/person

○ Learners work in groups of eight. (If you have different numbers, make smaller groups and use fewer questions.) Each learner in the group asks a different question from the list (in **A**). Tell learners to answer the questions with *Yes, I have!* or *No, I've never done that*.

○ Each learner asks the other people in the group his/her question and counts how many people answer *Yes, I have*.

B Make sentences about your group.

> **Flyers tip**
> In Reading and Writing Parts 2, 6 and 7, grammatical structures (meaning and form) are tested so candidates need to know how to use words and expressions like *most people, more than two, none of them, quite a lot of things, a few people*. Make sure learners have plenty of practice in using these kinds of phrases.

○ Teach/revise the difference between the quantifying expressions listed here.

○ Ask four learners who are wearing similar clothes to come to the front. Say a sentence about their clothes. For example: *Look! Everyone is wearing trousers / a uniform / skirts.* To half the class (if several have short hair and some have long hair), say, for example: *Several of you have short hair and some of you have long hair.*
Note: If necessary use pictures of people to explain these words instead.

○ Do the same for the other words (*everyone / most / quite a lot / half of us / only a few / no-one / none of us*). Write some of the sentences on the board.

○ Learners work together in groups of four or six. They check their answers to the questions in **A** to see how many of them have done the things listed there. They then complete the sentences in **B**. When they have finished writing their sentences, ask some learners to read out some of their sentences. For example: *Quite a lot of us have eaten with chopsticks.*

C Read about winter sports. Choose the right words and write them on the lines.

Reading & Writing Part 4

○ Ask: *Stand up if you have tried to ski or snowboard.* Say (as appropriate): *OK! No one / only one of us has tried to ski. Only a few of us / half of us / quite a lot of us / most of us / all of us have tried to ski.* Make sure learners are using weak 'of ' in these expressions (/əv/).

○ Ask: *Is skiing fun? What's it like?* Learners think of four adjectives to describe skiing. Write their answers on the board.
Suggestions: exciting, difficult, dangerous, easy, great, excellent, expensive, fast, hard, wonderful

○ Ask: *What kind of person does winter sports?* Learners think of four more adjectives. Write their answers on the board.
Suggestions: strong, brave, clever, careful, happy, lucky

○ Show learners how to add 'er' to a verb to change its meaning to 'a person who does this'. Write on the board: *teacher, player, singer* underlining the 'er' endings. Say: *A teacher is someone who can teach. A player is someone who plays in a game or sport. A singer is someone who can ... ?* (sing). Say: *We can add '-er' to other verbs too*. Add *climber, painter* and *dancer* to the board. Explain that because the last letter in 'dance' is already an 'e', we just add 'r' to that verb.

○ Write on the board: *design score listen camp ski*
Ask learners to make the words for the people who do these things.
Check answers: *designer, scorer, listener, camper, skier*

100

o   Say: *You are a skier and you are going to go on a skiing holiday. Which warm clothes must you take?*
Suggestions: gloves, hat, scarf, socks, sweater, jacket, trousers
Which things must you take with you?
Suggestions: camera, phone, money, rucksack, toothbrush, soap, towel, book, pen, games, sledge, a pair of skis, a pair of sunglasses.

o   Check again that learners are using weak 'of' (and weak 'a' plus linking /r/) when they say 'a pair of' (ə peə rəv).

o   Say: *Is skiing a new sport or an old sport? Let's read the text and find out!*
Allow learners a few minutes to read through the text without writing the words in the gaps. Ask: *How old are the cave paintings of the skiers?* (more than 5,000 years old)
When did Sondre get his first pair of skis? (about 180 years ago)

o   Learners read the text again and write the missing words.

Check answers:
1 There **2** who **3** these **4** used **5** of **6** When **7** many **8** call **9** them **10** or

D   Look at the three pictures. Write about this story.

o   Ask different learners these questions: *Have you ever been on a skiing holiday? Have you ever skied, snowboarded or skateboarded to school? What's the best way to travel if you live in the mountains in the summer/winter? On horse back? On a big sledge – with dogs' pulling it?*

o   Point to the pictures in D and say: *Look at these pictures. They show a story. Everyone, you're going to write the story! Remember – it's good to give the people names. Write one or two sentences about each picture. Write about what happened. You can write how the people felt and about what they said or thought.*
Learners write the story for the pictures.

Suggested stories

There's lots of snow in Harry's village. Harry's Dad can't open the door and can't drive Harry to school. Harry has an idea. He opens the window, climbs out, puts on his skis and skis to school. (37 words)

It snowed a lot in the night in Harry's village. In the morning, Harry's dad couldn't open the door of their house or drive his car because he couldn't see the road! Harry wanted to go to school. He had an idea. He opened the window and jumped out. Then he put on his ski boots and skis and skied down the hill to school. (65 words)

E   Let's talk about things we've all done!

o   Write on the board:
We've all watched …
We've all eaten …
But none of us has eaten …
We've all felt …
But none of us have felt …
We've all travelled to …
But no-one has travelled to …
This year we've all bought …
But no-one has bought …
Today, we've all learned about …

o   Read out the first sentence beginning: *We've all watched …*
Ask learners to suggest how to continue. For example: *We've all watched (favourite programme) on TV.* Learners work in groups of 5–6. They talk together to find things they have all done or have all never done. For example: *Have you ever eaten octopus / felt really frightened / travelled to China / bought a comic?* They write their sentences in their notebooks.

o   Different groups read their sentences to the rest of the class. For example:
Today, we've all learned about skiing.

44 What has just happened?

Topics friends, leisure, the home

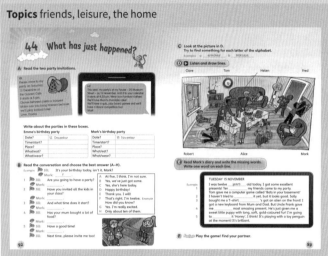

Equipment needed

o Flyers audio 44D.

o Photocopies (one for every 16 learners) of the sentences on page 142, cut up and stuck on card. See F.

A Read the two party invitations. Write about the parties in these boxes.

o Ask learners questions about birthday parties:
Do you and your friends usually have birthday parties?
What do you/people do at birthday parties?
What do you/people like eating at birthday parties?

o Point to the two birthday invitations. Ask:
Who sent them? (Emma and Mark)
How did they send them? (Emma posted them or gave them to her friends and Mark sent emails/texts.)

> **Flyers tip**
>
> In Speaking Part 2, candidates have to form questions from short prompts, for example: *Where/party?, What/wear?* Show learners that the slash shows that other words need to be added in that place. The words either side of the slash should not be changed. So for *Where/party?* candidates could ask **Where's the party?** and for *What/wear?* they could ask **What** must we **wear**?

o Divide the class into two groups, A and B. Learners in group A read Emma's invitation and complete the table for Emma's birthday party. Learners in group B read Mark's email and complete the table for Mark's birthday party. Walk round checking that learners have found the information they need to complete their table.

o Ask learners to form the questions from the prompts: *Date? Time / start? Place? What/eat? What/wear?* Write their questions on the board.

Suggestions:

Date?	*What's the date of the party? / When's the party?*
Time/start?	*What time does the party start?*
Place?	*Where is the party?*
What/eat?	*What can you eat at the party?*
What/wear?	*What must we wear?*

Suggested answers:

Emma's party: It starts at five o'clock. It's at the Concert Café. A pizza or a burger. Trainers.

Mark's party: It starts at four thirty. It's at Mark's house. Chocolate cake! Our funniest clothes.

o Learners work in A and B pairs – one from each group (A and B). Learner A asks questions about Mark's party. Learner B looks at the information in Mark's table and answers them. Learner B asks about Emma's party and learner A looks at the information in Emma's table and answers them.

o Ask: *Which party would you prefer to go to? Why?*

B Read the conversation and choose the best answer (A–H).

o Ask 2–3 learners: *Is it your birthday soon? When's your birthday?*
Say: *Today is Mark's birthday. Happy birthday, Mark!*
Learners read what Jill, Mark's friend, says and, without looking at the options, choose and write their own answers to her questions. They should do this in their notebooks.

o Read Jill's part of the conversation, pausing for different learners to respond with their own answers.

o Learners look at Mark's answers in the box on the right and choose five of them to complete the conversation.

> **Check answers:**
> **1** G **2** H **3** A **4** B **5** E

Optional extension:

o Learners practise the conversation in pairs. Different pairs of learners act out the conversation for the rest of the class.

C Look at the picture in D. Try to find something for each letter of the alphabet.

o Learners look at the picture in **D** and find something beginning with each letter of the alphabet.
They tell you words to write on the board, or they write words in groups or pairs and then tell you.

o **Suggested answers:**

arms, armchair, bandage, book, bookcase, bottle, child, chocolate cake, clock, coat, cushion, door, drink, elbows, envelope, face, girl, glass, glasses, hair, hands, insect, juice, knees, knife, legs, lemonade, mouth, nose, orange juice, people, plate, present, radio, rain, sandwich, sofa, stripes, shoes, socks, sweater, table, trainers, trousers, T-shirt, umbrella, window, wood, yellow jumper

Note: There are no words beginning with q, v, x or z.

D ▶ Listen and draw lines.

o   Learners look at the picture. They listen to the audio and draw lines between the people and the names. Let them listen twice.

> **Check answers:**
> Lines should be drawn between:
> **1** *Mark* and boy playing on tablet in green sweater.
> **2** *Fred* and boy on floor looking for glasses.
> **3** *Alice* and girl in armchair, papers on her knees.
> **4** *Robert* and boy who's arriving with a present.
> **5** *Clare* and child who's fallen over and hurt her elbow.

Audioscript

Listen and look. There is one example.

Man:	It's going to be fun at this party. Come on!
Woman:	But I don't know anyone here …
Man:	You soon will. There's the woman who sent us the invitation. She works at the airport like you do.
Woman:	The one with the glass and bottle in her hands?
Man:	That's right.
Woman:	I've already met her somewhere else. Is her name Helen?
Man:	Yes!

Can you see the line? This is an example. Now you listen and draw lines.

Man:	I teach most of these children! There's Mark. It's his birthday.
Woman:	Do you mean the boy who's playing a game on that new tablet?
Man:	Yes. I think his green sweater is new as well.
Woman:	What's that boy looking for?
Man:	Sorry, which boy?
Woman:	The one on his knees on the floor.
Man:	Ah! I see! You mean Fred. He's looking for his glasses. Perhaps he dropped them.
Woman:	That person's smiling!
Man:	Yes, he is.
Woman:	Not the boy on the sofa. The girl in the armchair.
Man:	Oh, yes. Sorry! That's Alice. She's got the quiz questions for everyone.
Woman:	Great!
Woman:	What time did the party start?
Man:	About half an hour ago, I think. We were only five minutes late. Oh, and here's Robert!
Woman:	Where? That boy? The one who's just taken off his coat?
Man:	Not him. I don't know his name. I mean the one who's just arrived with the present. He's always late for lessons, too!
Woman:	Oh dear!
Man:	What's the matter?
Woman:	Look! Someone's just fallen over!
Man:	That's Clare. I'll go and help her. I think she's hurt her elbow.
Woman:	I'll come with you.
Man:	OK. And then let's dance!

Guess the words in the sentences.

o   Write the name of one of the people in the picture and a line for each missing word on the board. Tell learners that all the sentences contain the word 'just', as in the sentence: *The party has just started.* Write on the board:

Fred has just ....

o   Learners guess the missing words. Each learner/team gets a point for every correct word.

Sentences:
Fred has just dropped his glasses.
Helen has just given a boy a drink.
Clare has just fallen over.
Robert has just arrived.

E Read Mark's diary and write the missing words. Write one word on each line.

o   Point to the diary page. Say: *This is Mark's diary. What do you think he wrote about on 15 November?* (his birthday party)

o   Learners read Mark's diary and write one word on each line.

> **Check answers:**
> **1** of   **2** play   **3** It   **4** the/my   **5** call

Optional extension:
Learners write about their last birthday or a special birthday they have had. They can write about a real or an imagined birthday. They write about the presents they got and about their party.

F Play the game! Find your partner.

o   Form groups of even numbers of learners. Give out photocopies of the sentences on page 142, cut up and stuck on card if possible. Give each learner in the group a card, making sure you give out all the cards.

o   Learners read what is written, stand up and move around. When they meet another learner, they say what is written on their card. If the situation matches the expression, the learners stay together. When all the pairs have found each other, ask them to read out the situation and the expression.

Smaller groups: repeat this, giving out new pairs of cards until learners have made all the sentences.

45 Talking about the time

Topics time, numbers

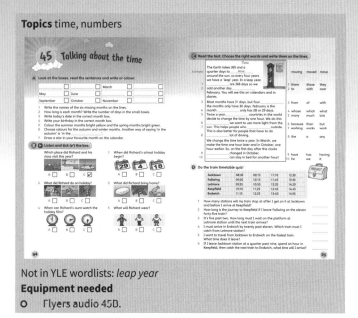

Not in YLE wordlists: *leap year*
Equipment needed
○ Flyers audio 45B.

A Look at the boxes, read the sentences and write or colour.

> **Flyers tip**
> In the Speaking, most questions will be in the present tense, but candidates may have to answer questions about the past and the future. They should be able to answer questions about what they did last week or what they are going to do at the weekend, for example.

○ Point to the months on the calendar page. Ask: *How many months are there in a year?* (12)

○ Write on the board: *Jan   Feb.* Ask: *What are the missing letters?* Write them on the board as: *Jan u ary Feb ru ary*

○ Say: *It's difficult for some people to spell these words because they can't hear some of the letters.* Say: *January, February.* Ask: *What letters <u>don't</u> you hear?* (the 'a' in both words 'Janu<u>a</u>ry', 'Febru<u>a</u>ry', and the first 'r' in 'Feb<u>r</u>uary')

○ Say: *Look at the first sentence under the calendar. Write the missing months.* Learners write: *January, February, April, July, August* and *December* on the lines. Ask: *Which is the first / third / eighth month?* (January, March, August) Check pronunciation of 'January', 'February', 'July' and 'August' again as these are the months that learners usually find most difficult to say and spell.

○ Learners read sentences 2–8 and follow the instructions or add answers.

○ Find out when everyone's birthday is. Ask: *Whose birthday is in January?* Learners who have their birthday in that month put up their hand. Ask one learner to count the hands. Do the same for the other months. Write the numbers of birthdays against each month on the board. Ask: *When are the most/fewest birthdays?*

○ Ask one learner questions:
Teacher: *Which month is your birthday in? What day of that month is it?*
Learner: (*In August. It's on the 22ⁿᵈ.*)
Teacher: *Which is your favourite month?*
Learner: (*June.*)
Teacher: *What do you like doing in (June)?*
Learner: (*I like swimming in June. I like going for bike rides in June.*)

○ In pairs or small groups, learners compare their calendars in this way. They explain why they like one month more than the others and talk about things they do in the spring, summer, autumn and winter months.

B ▶ Listen and tick the box.

Listening **Part 4**

○ Revise time prepositions ('in', 'on' and 'at'):
in   (months) for example: in July
        (seasons) for example: in the autumn
        (years) for example: in 2020
on   (parts of days) for example: on Wednesday morning / evening
at   (specific times) for example: at six o'clock / midnight / the weekend / Christmas

○ Point to the boy in the pictures in 5. Say: *This is Richard. What does he do? Is he a businessman? Is he a doctor?* (no) *Is he a student?* (yes)

○ Play the audio. Learners listen to the example. Ask: *Where does Richard's class usually go with their school?* (to the mountains) *Where did they go this year?* (to an island) *Who's Richard talking to?* (his aunt Helen)

○ Learners listen to the rest of the conversation twice and tick the boxes.

> **Check answers:**
> **1** B **2** A **3** A **4** B **5** C

○ Ask learners if they have visited any interesting places. Ask them further questions, for example: *Where/when did you go? What did you see? What did you do there? Who did you meet there?*
Note: If learners have not been anywhere, ask them to imagine a holiday with their school or family and to invent the answers.

Audioscript

Listen and look. There is one example.
        Which place did Richard and his class visit this year?
Woman: Hello, Richard. Did you have a good holiday with the school?

Boy: Yes, thanks, Aunt Helen. But we didn't go to the mountains this year.

Woman: Oh! Did you go to the beach then?

Boy: No. We stayed on an island this year. It was excellent!
Can you see the tick? Now you listen and tick the box.

1 *When did Richard's school holiday begin?*
Woman: When did your holiday start, Richard?

Boy: In the first week of June. Our teacher wanted to go at the end of April but we couldn't because she was ill.

Woman: Oh dear! Your uncle and I always go on holiday in September.

Boy: Do you?
Woman: Yes.

2 *What did Richard do on holiday?*
Boy: We spent one day in a village where people always live in tents.

Woman: Wow! Did they cook on fires there?

Boy: Yes. We did that too that day. It was fun.

Woman: And was the water warm enough to swim in?

Boy: No. And I wanted to climb the trees and get a coconut, but our teacher said, 'It's too dangerous!'

3 *What did Richard bring home?*

Boy: I brought a present home for you!

Woman: That's kind of you. Let me guess. Is it some sweets?

Boy: I know you like those, but no, it's some soap. They make it from one of the plants on the island. I got some for Mum too.

Woman: Great!

4 *When can Richard's aunt watch the holiday film?*

Boy: Our teacher made a film of the holiday.

Woman: What a good idea!

Boy: We're going to watch it at ten o'clock tomorrow, and other people in the family can watch it after school at a quarter past four. I think it's about 30 minutes long. Will you come Aunt Helen?

Woman: Yes. I'll come on my bike.

5 *What will Richard wear?*

Boy: We aren't going to wear school uniforms when our teacher shows the film.

Woman: Why not?

Boy: Because it was too hot to wear jeans on the island so we all bought some funny shorts. We're going to wear those.

Woman: Will your teacher let you do that?

Boy: Oh yes. She's going to wear some too!

C Read the text. Choose the right words and write them on the lines.

Reading & Writing **Part 4**

○ Ask: *What time is it? What time is it in London? Is it the same time as here?*

○ Write on the board:

   1 What do we call a year which has 366 days?

   2 Why do some countries change the time twice a year?

   3 When do the clocks change?

○ Learners read the text and find the answers.

> **Check answers:**
> **1** a leap year
> **2** to use the light from the sun
> **3** at the end of March and October

○ Learners read the text, find the correct answers 1–10 and write them on the lines.

> **Check answers:**
> **1** there **2** to **3** of **4** which **5** many **6** because **7** work
> **8** a **9** have **10** we

Let's talk about your important times and dates.

○ Ask learners to write down four important dates in their life. They do not write why these dates are important.
For example: *5 December.*
Note: Learners do not need to add 'st', 'nd', 'th' to numbers in dates as this is considered a little old fashioned, but they should understand the convention if they see it in written texts.

○ Learners think about their day. They write down four times when they do things. For example: *8 o'clock.*

○ Write these questions on the board:
Why is your date important?
What do you do at that time?

○ Learners work in pairs. They show their lists to each other and ask and answer questions about one of their four dates and times. Learners then move on to ask another person about another time or date.

Optional extension:

○ Make a year calendar with all the important dates for your class. These could include birthdays, competitions, holidays, sports, etc.

D Do the train timetable quiz!

○ Stand at the front of the class and mime the following situation. You are standing on a platform. Lean out as if to look for a train. Lean back again as you imagine a train travels past really quickly. Look at your watch. Lean forward again as you see the next train. Smile. Watch the train as it arrives. Pick up an imagined suitcase, open a door, step up and sit down.
Ask: *What was I doing? What happened? Where am I now?* Learners make suggestions until someone guesses correctly. (You were waiting for a train. Your train arrived. You are sitting on your train.)

○ Ask: *Do you sometimes go on train journeys?* Ask 2–3 learners where they travelled from/to and how long the journey took.

○ Learners look at the timetable. Familiarise them with timetable formats if necessary. Say: *These four trains all leave Jacktown at different times. When does the earliest one leave?* (8.30) *What time does the latest one leave?* (12.30) Say: *Some train journeys from Jacktown to Endwich are faster than others. Let's find out a bit more about these trains.*

○ Divide learners into groups of 3–4. Say: *Look at the timetable and answer the six questions. The questions get more and more difficult so you need to help each other! When you have all six answers, put up your hands and sit quietly. Are you ready?*
You could blow a whistle to signal the start of the puzzle!
Give learners time to understand the questions, check the timetable and do the maths. Time each group so when all the groups have finished you can say: *Group A took 3 minutes and 45 seconds, Group B took … etc.*
If you would like to make one group the winners, give five points to the group that finishes first, four to the next and so on, then add one point for each correct answer. The group with the highest total number of points are the winners.

> **Check answers:**
> **1** 2 (stations) **2** 1 hour **3** 15 minutes **4** 9.55 **5** 12.30 **6** 13.40

 Railway stations

○ Learners find out about their nearest station and create a fact sheet about it. They find out information such as:
how old the station is
where it is in town
how many platforms are there
how many trains pass through the station each day
when the station is busiest / quietest
what's in the station (eg ticket office / café / waiting room)
the time of the first train / last train
the colour of the trains / how old / new the trains are.

○ If they prefer, learners can write about an imagined train station.

○ Learners illustrate their fact sheets with a photo of a local train, plan or map of the station. Learners add their train fact sheet to their project file. Alternatively, display their fact sheets on the classroom wall if possible.

46 We're all at home today

Topics the home, sports and leisure

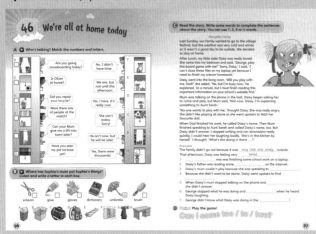

Equipment needed
○ Flyers audio 46A, 46B.
○ Photocopies of the task on page 143, enough for each half of the class, cut up into two parts. See D.

A ▶ Who's talking? Match the numbers and letters.

○ To introduce the topic of this unit, ask learners questions about where they live:
Do you live in a house or a flat / apartment?
Have you always lived in the same house / flat / apartment?
Are you friends with other people who live near to you?
You may like to teach 'neighbours'.

> **Flyers tip**
> For Reading and Writing Part 2, train learners to look at the tense of the auxiliary verb form (*be, have, do*) and modal (*can, will* etc) used by the first speaker as this will sometimes help them choose the correct reply. For example: '*Did you enjoy the party?*' '*Yes, I did!*'

○ Learners look at the picture. Say: *Look at the people in the two buildings.*
Ask: *Who is answering each question?* (the people in the building on the right) Point to the example 1–D. Learners then write the other letters on the right in the correct boxes on the left.

○ Tell learners that the recorded conversations are in a different order and then play the audio. Pause after each conversation if necessary. Learners listen and check their answers.

> **Check answers:**
> **2** C **3** A **4** F **5** B **6** E

○ Learners circle the auxiliary/modal verbs in each matching pair. Ask: *Are they the same in each pair?* (yes, for example: *Have/have, Can/can't, Were/were, Did/didn't, Is/isn't, Are/are*)

Audioscript

Listen and check your answers.

Boy:	Have you seen my pet tortoise yet?
Boy:	Yes, I have. It's really cool.
Girl:	Can your Mum give me a lift into town later?
Girl:	She can't today. Sorry!
Woman:	Were there lots of people at the match?
Woman:	Yes, there were thousands!
Man:	Did you repair your bicycle?
Man:	No, I didn't have time.

Boy:	Is Oliver at home?
Boy:	He isn't now, but he will be later.
Woman:	Are you going snowboarding today?
Woman:	We are, but not until this afternoon.

What might the people on the left say next?

○ Write on the board: *I can help you fix it now if you like!*
Ask: *Which person on the left of the picture might say this?* (the man in flat 4 / on the fourth floor)

○ Do the same with these sentences:
Wow! Who scored the most goals? (the woman on the third floor)
Yes, he is, but he's very slow! (the boy on the first floor)
Come with us if you like! (the woman on the top floor)

○ Ask learners to suggest what the people on the second and fifth floors might say next. **Suggestions: 2** No problem. I'll go on my bike. **5** OK, thanks!

B ▶ Where has Sophia's mum put Sophia's things? Listen and write a letter in each box.   Listening **Part 3**

○ Point to the pictures of the objects in the first row and ask questions:
What are scissors usually made of? (plastic/metal)
What can you glue together with glue? (two pieces of paper/wood)
What's another way of saying two gloves? (a pair of gloves)
Which letter do the first words in a dictionary start with? (A!)
Has someone opened or closed this umbrella? (opened)
What do you brush with a brush? (your hair/clothes)

○ Divide learners into groups of 3–4. Say: *I'm going to ask you some more questions now. Put your hands up quickly if you know the answer.* Ask the following questions. Groups answer. Check the pronunciation of 'dictionary' /dɪkʃəneri/.

Which might you need in cold weather?	(the gloves)
Which is spotted?	(the umbrella)
Which helps you learn spellings?	(the dictionary)
Which might I use to cut my hair?	(the scissors)
Which might you use in front of a mirror?	(the brush)
Which haven't I spoken about yet?	(the glue)

○ Point to the woman on the sixth floor in the picture in **A**. Say: *This woman's daughter is called Sophia.* Say: *Sophia's family have just moved flats. Sophia needs some things but she doesn't know where they are.*

○ Play the first part of the audio. Ask: *Where's Sophia's umbrella?* (in the hall next to the coat)
Which picture shows this? (**G**) Point out the letter **G** in the box under the umbrella.

○ Play the rest of the audio twice. Learners write letters in the boxes under the objects.

> **Check answers:**
> scissors – **D**, glue – **C**, brush – **F**, dictionary – **B**, gloves – **A**

○ Ask learners if they heard the words 'desk' and 'shelf'. (Yes – the scissors were in Sophia's desk in their old flat and the shelf is under the bathroom cupboard.)

Audioscript

Listen and look. There is one example. Where has Sophia's mum put Sophia's things?

Girl:	Mum, I've written the things I will need for school tomorrow on a piece of paper.
Woman:	Let me see, Sophia.
Girl:	The first thing I need is my umbrella.

Woman: No problem. I brought that in with me from the car and put it in the hall. It's next to Dad's coat.
Girl: Thanks, Mum.

Can you see the letter G? Now you listen and write a letter in each box.

Woman: What's the word that you've written here? Is it 'scissors'?
Girl: Yes, that's right.
Woman: Well, they were in the desk in our old flat so I put them with some other things in your rucksack, Sophia.
Girl: All right. I'll go and look in the pockets.
Woman: In a minute. Not now.
Girl: OK.
Woman: And why do you need glue tomorrow? Have you broken something?
Girl: No, Mum. It's for my art class. We're making models.
Woman: Oh! That sounds interesting! Now, where have I put that? Oh, I remember…
Girl: You didn't throw it in the bin, did you? It wasn't empty.
Woman No, I didn't. I put it in the bag that you take to the sports centre.
Girl: Great! Thanks.
Woman: And you've written 'brush' here too. Have you looked for that in the bathroom?
Girl: Yes, but I couldn't see it anywhere.
Woman: That's because it's in the cupboard. The one on the wall.
Girl: So it's inside that, not on the shelf?
Woman No. You'll have to open the doors.
Woman: Which dictionary do you need for school tomorrow?
Girl: My English one.
Woman: I put it in a big square box. You'll find it under the stairs. It's full of books. Please…
Girl: (cutting in) Don't worry, Mum. I'll open it carefully.
Woman: OK.
Woman: But you won't find your gloves, Sophia.
Girl: Why not?
Woman: Because Billy the kitten found them and started playing with them! I had to put them in the bin! But we can go and buy some new ones on Saturday.
Girl: That's OK. Where IS Silly Billy?
Woman: Asleep on your favourite cushion!

C **Read the story. Write some words to complete the sentences about the story. You can use 1, 2, 3 or 4 words.**

Reading & Writing **Part 5**

○ Point to the picture of the girl. Say: *This is Daisy. Sometimes Daisy is naughty. What do you think Daisy likes doing? I'm going to ask you some questions. Answer with: 'Yes, she does!' or 'No, she doesn't!'*
Does Daisy like brushing her hair? (No, she doesn't!)
Does she enjoy making lots of noise? (Yes, she does.)
Does she enjoy tidying her bedroom? (No, she doesn't!)
Does she love going on dangerous adventures? (Yes, she does.)
Does she like drawing pretty pictures? (No, she doesn't!)
Does she like hiding other people's things? (Yes, she does!)
Does she enjoy washing her face? (No, she doesn't!)
Does she love eating sweets and chocolate? (Yes, she does!)

○ Write on the board: *Did Daisy want to:*
play outside / do some homework / play a game?
Learners find the answer in the text. (She wanted to play a [board] game.)

○ Learners look at the example sentences and then complete sentences 1–7. Remind learners they can write 1–4 word answers.

Check answers:
1 George/Daisy's brother   **2** (important) information
3 Aunt Sarah   **4** her favourite doll   **5** called Daisy's / her name
6 ran downstairs (really quickly)   **7** the kitchen (by herself)

○ Ask: *Does the story tell us what Daisy was doing in the kitchen?* (no) Ask learners to suggest what she might be doing. Write their suggestions on the board. (See below for some suggestions to share with learners.)
Suggestions:
1 She was taking everything out of the cupboards and was putting it on the floor / the tops of the cupboards / the chairs.
2 She was making a chocolate cake / hot chocolate / sandwiches for her doll. Bits of cake / chocolate were all over the table/ floor.
3 She was drawing on the walls, the cupboard doors and the floor.
4 She was carrying her backpack and climbing out of the window with her doll.

○ In pairs or small groups, learners choose the end of the story and write it. They could also draw a picture to show the ending. They can then read and act out the endings to their stories.

D **Play the game!**

Can I come too / to / two?

○ Write on the board: *Can I come too / to / two?* Point to the three options and ask: Which is the right word in this sentence? (too). Point to the three words in turn asking: *How do we say this word?* Learners answer. Say: *So all these words look different but they all sound the same.* (yes)

○ Say: *We're going to work with some other words that look different but sound the same.*

○ Divide the class into two groups. Give group A the top half of the photocopiable on page 143 and group B, the bottom half.

○ In pairs within their groups, learners look at the spelling options in each sentence and draw a circle around the correct spelling.

○ When they have finished, learners in group A get up and find a partner to work with in group B. In pairs, learners check their spelling answers and discuss any differences of opinion! They then find matching conversation turns (similar to the work they did in A in this unit).

○ Seven pairs each read out one of the mini conversations. Check that they fully understand that the spelling options are pronounced exactly the same way.

Check answers:
Is that Ann over there? No, she's standing by the bus stop. Look!

I've got to find some more flour. Why? Do you want to make two cakes?

What are you going to buy in town, Ben? I don't know yet. Perhaps some gloves.

I can't spell 'alphabet', Aunt Jill. Help! Don't worry. I'll write it on your board.

Bill rode all the way up the hill on his bike. Did he? Right to the top?

There's a sports car outside, Dad. Is it ours? No, Uncle Tom's, but we can go for a ride in it. Come on!

Did you hear the news about our favourite band? No, but I read about it online.

Optional extension:

○ Advanced learners: In pairs or small groups, learners try to write a line of conversation that contains both homophones.
Suggestions:
I'm going to school by bus today. Bye!
Put some flour in that bowl – the one with the blue flower on it.
I'm so bored with writing long words on this board.
We read a story called 'The Red Balloon' yesterday.
That's not our house. We have to walk another half an hour to get to ours.
He rode all the way to Longfield Road.

47   I will or perhaps I won't

Topics work, family and friends

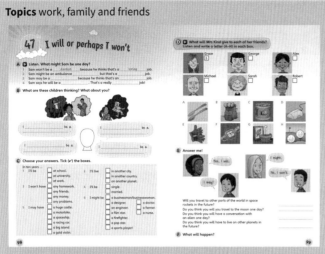

Not in YLE wordlists: *China, music, charts*

Equipment needed

○ Flyers audio 47A, 47D.
○ Colouring pens or pencils.

Ⓐ ▶ Listen. What might Sam be one day?

○ Say: *It's difficult to choose a job. What do you want to be?* Write some of the learners' suggestions on the board.

Ask: *What don't you want to be?* Write some of their suggestions on the board. Ask learners why they don't want to have these jobs.

Note: Jobs in YLE wordlist are: actor, artist, astronaut, businessman/woman, clown, cook, dentist, designer, driver, engineer, farmer, film star, firefighter, journalist, manager, mechanic, nurse, painter, photographer, pilot, police officer, pop star, singer, teacher, tennis player, waiter. You may like to extend this list with compound nouns such as: train driver, maths teacher, hockey player, sports star, etc.

○ Tell learners they are going to hear Sam talking about different jobs. Play the audio.

Ask: *How many jobs did you hear about?* (5)

Which jobs were they? (dentist, engineer, ambulance driver, journalist, teacher) Add these jobs to the board if they aren't already there.

Audioscript

Father:	What do you want to be, Sam? A dentist?
Sam:	No, I don't want to be a dentist. I'm sure about that! I won't be a dentist. I think that's a boring job!
Father:	An engineer?
Sam:	Hmm, no! I might be an ambulance driver, but that's a difficult job.
Father:	A journalist?
Sam:	I may be a journalist because that's an interesting job.
Father:	Or a teacher?
Sam:	Wow, yes! That's a great job!

○ Ask questions. Learners answer with *Yes!, Perhaps!* or *No!*

Does Sam want to be a journalist? (Perhaps!)

Does Sam want to be a dentist? (No!)

Does Sam want to be a teacher? (Yes!)

Does Sam want to be an ambulance driver? (Perhaps!)

○ Ask: *What did Sam say about each job? Listen!* Play the audio a second time. (*dentist – boring job, ambulance driver – difficult job, journalist – interesting job, teacher – great job*)

Ask learners to spell 'boring', 'difficult', 'interesting' and 'great'. Write the words on the board.

○ Learners complete the sentences about Sam.

> **Check answers:**
> **2** driver / difficult **3** journalist / interesting **4** teacher / great

Ⓑ What are these children thinking? What about you?

○ Learners look at the pictures of the two children and their thought bubbles. The class chooses a name for each child.

Ask: *Which jobs can you see?* (singer, doctor, astronaut)

What are (boy's name) and (girl's name) thinking?

Suggested answers: I might be a singer or I might be a doctor. I'll be an astronaut.

○ Learners show their own job preferences/predictions by completing the picture of their own face and writing *will, may, might, won't* and *singer, doctor, astronaut* in their own speech bubbles.

Note: learners will need to add one more job of their choice to complete the four sentences (see Unit 17 for more job ideas if necessary).

Note: There used to be a subtle difference between 'may have done' and 'might have done' (see dictionaries for current/past situation explanations) but this difference in usage has generally disappeared in spoken English.

At this level, learners should use 'may' or 'might' interchangeably both meaning 'perhaps'/'will', for example: *I may/might live on the moon.* Perhaps *I* will *live on the moon!*

Ⓒ Choose your answers. Tick the boxes.

○ Ask: *How old will you be in ten years? What will your lives be like? You will be older but will you be happier? Cleverer? Will you live in this country or in another country?*

○ Learners look at questions 1–6 and tick the boxes to show their own predictions. In pairs, they ask and answer the questions and then discuss any differences in their answers.

Optional extension:

To practise using 'will' and 'won't', learners answer your questions (see below) by calling out together: *Yes, you will!* or *No, you won't!*

Suggested questions:

Will I be an astronaut one day?

Will I grow wings and learn to fly like a bird one day?

Will I write a book like 'Fun for Flyers' one day?

Will I have ten grandchildren one day?

Ⓓ ▶ What will Mrs Kind give to each of her friends? Listen and write a letter (A–H) in each box.   Listening Part **3**

> **Flyers tip**
> In Listening Part 3, candidates will hear all the matching answers from one person – usually a grown-up. The other person, who is usually a child, says very little. When you play the audio, identify the difference in these two roles. This will help candidates to focus on the turns in which they will hear the answers.

- In pairs, learners look at Mrs Kind's friends and the presents, and predict which present Mrs Kind will give each one. They make a list in their notebooks. For example: *She will give Robert the watch.*
- Play the example. Ask: *Who is the backpack for?* (Grace) *Will Grace like her new backpack?* (Yes!)
- Learners listen to the rest of the audio.

> **Check answers:**
> Robert – **E**, Alex – **G**, George – **H**, Michael – **C**, Sarah – **A**

- Play the audio again. Ask the following questions:
  Who will like their present? (Grace, Alex, Michael)
  Who may like their present? (Sarah)
  Who might like their present? (Robert, George)
  Which country did the tea come from? (China)
  If learners don't know where China is, show them where it is online or in an atlas.

Audioscript

Listen and look. There is one example.
Helen's mum, Mrs Kind, wants to give each of her friends a present.
Which present is for each friend?

Mrs Kind:	I like giving presents, Helen. It's such a nice thing to do! But I have to decide which present to give each of my friends.
Helen:	But it isn't their birthdays.
Mrs Kind:	I know it isn't, but I still like giving presents!
Helen:	Well what are you going to give Grace?
Mrs Kind:	Let me think … she loves travelling so this new backpack, I think. She can carry all her things in it on long journeys.

Can you see the letter B? Now you listen and write a letter in each box.

Helen:	Who else are you giving a present to?
Mrs Kind:	Do you remember Robert, the mechanic? He gave us lots of help last month when we were worried about our car.
Helen:	Yes, I remember.
Mrs Kind:	Well, he'll like these gloves … Yes, I'll give him these. They'll be good for carrying all those heavy engine parts.
Mrs Kind:	And this is for Alex. She'll like this a lot.
Helen:	What is it? I can't see.
Mrs Kind:	It's a box of very expensive tea. She likes having things that you can't buy in this country. I bought this online. I got these spoons at the same time but I'll give those to someone else. They came from China!
Helen:	Amazing!
Mrs Kind:	And now a present for George … Actually, he might like these golf balls – or shall I give him this computer mouse?
Helen:	He won't want that, Mum! Your first idea is better. Give him those instead.
Mrs Kind:	You're right. He's improving a lot because he plays every weekend now.
Mrs Kind:	And this is for Michael.
Helen:	Who's he?
Mrs Kind:	Oh, he's an old friend. I want to give him this wonderful honey because he's such a busy man – he's always working on his computer – and it'll be really good for him. He'll like the taste of it too!
Helen:	So he'll like that more than a new watch, Mum?
Mrs Kind:	Yes, I'm sure he will.
Mrs Kind:	And last of all … Here's something for Sarah!
Helen:	Oh! The silver spoons.
Mrs Kind	Yes. She's buying things to put in her new kitchen and I'm sure she'll really love these.
Helen:	Can't I have them?
Mrs Kind:	No. You won't ever use them.
Helen:	Oh! OK (disappointed).

E Answer me!

- Learners look at the four questions and the four possible answers. They write their own answers to each question on the lines. Check answers by asking different learners to answer the questions.
- Write the four answers on the board: *Yes, I will. I may! I might. No, I won't!* Ask learners to stand in a circle. (Large classes: divide the class into smaller groups of 8–10 learners.)
- Ask the first learner on your right the first question (see the list below). This learner answers the question with one of the answers from the board. They then turn to the person on their right and ask the same question. Continue in this way till everyone has asked and answered. Then do the same with the rest of the questions.
  Suggested questions:
  1 Will you help me answer some questions now?
  2 Will you text me tomorrow?
  3 Will you play on the computer later?
  4 Will you go to bed before 11 o'clock tonight?
  5 Will you make a cake for me next weekend?

F What will happen?

- Divide the class into groups of 3–4. Say: *You are going to guess, then write down, what will happen next month.*
- Write on the board:
  … will win the football / soccer / basketball championship/cup.
  I might travel to …
  We'll learn about …
  Someone will give me a wonderful …
  … will be number one in the online music charts.
- Learners copy and complete the sentences on a piece of paper and write their names.
- Ask: *Who thinks that* (the name of a strong football team in your learners' country) *will win the league?* Learners put up their hands. Count the number of hands. *Who doesn't agree?* Learners who chose a different team say which team they think will win. Again, count the number of hands. On a piece of paper, one learner writes the different teams and the number of learners who think that team will win. Do the same with the other sports that are popular in your learners' country and with the names of the songs that learners wrote.
- Keep learners' predictions or put them on the wall. The next week, tell them to check the online music charts and see which song was number one. After a few weeks or at the end of the school year, check to see which group guessed the most predictions correctly.

48 Doing different things

Topics family and friends, work, sports and leisure

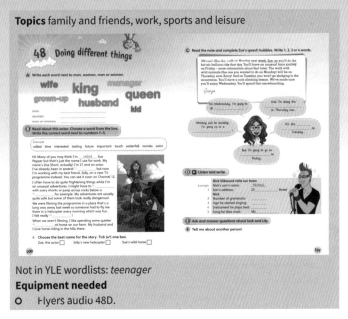

Not in YLE wordlists: *teenager*

Equipment needed

o Flyers audio 48D.

Ⓐ Write each word next to *man, woman, man or woman.*

o Learners look at the seven words. In pairs, they decide where to put each word and then write the words on the lines.

Write on the board: kids = boys and girls AND son and daughter. Explain that kids and children can mean both of these things – for example: a boy and a girl and a parent can talk about their children, for example: my son and my daughter/my sons. You could also explain that especially in America, people sometimes use the word *kids* to mean 'children'.

> **Check answers:**
> man: king, husband
> woman: wife, queen
> man or woman: grown-up, manager, kid

o Learners turn to page 127 of their Student's Book and read and complete the sentences.

> **Check answers:**
> **1** aunt   **2** cousins   **3** grown-up   **4** parents   **5** grandparents
> **6** wife   **7** husband   **8** granddaughter   **9** grandson
> **10** classmates

Note: If you would like to revise all the family and friends words, in pairs, learners could list them all in alphabetical or word length order. Alternatively, learners could work in small groups, each drawing individual people then making a collage to form a large family group of about twenty people. They could then label each person with arrows and invented choice of names/relationship, for example: Uncle Albert, my grandfather, Jose, cousin Alexandra, my business partner, Serpil etc. Groups could then present their fun family collages to the rest of the class.

Ⓑ Read about this actor. Choose a word from the box. Write the correct word next to numbers 1–5.

Reading & Writing Part **3**

o Learners look at the picture of the woman. Ask: *How old do you think this woman is? Guess! What's her job? Guess!* Learners read the first part of the text quickly to see if they guessed correctly. (21, an actor)

o Learners read the text. Ask: *What's Zoe doing now?* (working on / making a new TV programme)
How is she travelling to work now? (by/in a helicopter)

o Look at the example with learners. Ask: *Why does this woman have two names?* (Her name is really Zoe Short, but her acting name is Sue Pepper.)

o Learners read the text again, choose words from the box and write them on the lines.

> **Check answers:**
> **1** movies   **2** swim   **3** waterfall   **4** important   **5** time

o Learners choose the best name for the text. (*Zoe, the actor*)

o See Speaking Part 2 tip in **E**.

o Write on the board, leaving space for answers:

How old	?
What/job	?
Hobby	?
How / go to work	?
Who / work with	?

o Complete the table on the board with learners' answers about Zoe (*21, actor, horse-riding, helicopter, Jolly*).

o Point to the board and say: *Use these words to make five questions.* Learners write the five questions in their notebooks. Walk round and help if necessary. See suggested questions.

o Read out each question in the order below, pausing to ask different learners to answer using the words on the board. This will help prepare learners for the test practice in **E**.
Say: *I don't know anything about Zoe, but you do. So I'm going to ask you some questions.*
What's Zoe's job? (She's an actor)
How does she go to work? (by helicopter)
Who is Zoe working with? (Jolly)
What's her hobby? (She likes horse-riding)
How old is she? (She's 21)

Ⓒ Read the note and complete Zoe's speech bubbles. Write 1, 2, 3 or 4 words.

o Say: *George is Zoe's manager. Look at George's note to Zoe. Learners read the note.* Ask: *What's George telling Zoe about?* (Zoe's TV work next week)

o Learners read the note and in pairs decide which information they need to write in each speech bubble.

> **Check answers:**
> Wednesday – snowboarding   Thursday – walk with wild animals
> Tuesday – rock climbing lesson   Monday – hot air balloon
> Friday – an unusual train journey

o Say: *I'll have a rock climbing lesson. I'll enjoy Wednesday. We'll spend that snowboarding.*
Write on the board: *I'll   we'll*
Point out that 'I'll' looks a bit like 'ill' and 'we'll' looks a bit like 'well' but stress the difference in their pronunciation: 'I'll' /aɪ jəl/ and 'we'll' /wiː jəl/ which is exactly the same pronunciation as 'wheel'.

If learners understand what a syllable is, also point out that 'ill' and 'well' only have one syllable but *I'll* and *we'll* have two. Practise: 'you'll' /juː wəl/. You might also include 'he'll', 'she'll', 'it'll' and 'they'll' in this practice by asking learners to say what they think they and others will do later today. For example: *I'll go home on the bus. You'll drive your car. He'll walk home. She'll do her homework. It'll rain. We'll watch TV. They'll go to bed at eleven thirty.*

Optional extension:

o   If your group is confident enough, in small groups they could take information from the note and the corresponding speech bubble and write a three turn conversation to role play in class. Plan the first conversation together asking learners to help you as you write it up on the board. For example:

George: *We can't film the walk on Monday next week, Zoe, so you'll do the hot air balloon ride that day!*

Zoe: *OK, George! So Monday will be exciting! I'm going up in a hot air balloon that day! My husband wants to come too!*

George: *That will be fun then!*

o   In groups of 3–4, learners write the other four conversations. Two learners from each group role play one of the conversations. Check the pronunciation of any ''ll' forms.

Stronger classes:

o   In groups of 3–4, learners plan their own exciting filming jobs for the week. One pair from each group then role plays a conversation between an actor and a secretary or cameraman using language practised above.

 Listen and write.

D   Listening Part **2**

o   Learners look at the box. Ask: *Who's visiting the town?* (Nick Silkwood)

o   Learners listen to the first part of the conversation. Ask: *What is Nick Silkwood's job? Is he a journalist?* (No, he's a singer)

o   Learners look at the form and the example and then guess what the answers might be.

Suggestions:

1 a street name, **2** and **3** numbers, **4** a musical instrument, **5** a word that's missing from the name of a song.

o   Learners listen to the conversation twice and write a word or a number on each line.

Check answers:
1 Kingly   **2** 5/five   **3** 11/eleven   **4** drums   **5** winter

Audioscript

Listen and look. There is one example.
Girl: Excuse me! Aren't you Nick Silkwood, the singer?
Man: Yes, that's right.
Girl: I'm surprised! I didn't know you were here in our town.
Man: My son lives here. I've come to visit him.
Girl: That's nice! What's his name?
Man: It's Michael. He works at the concert hall.
Girl: Oh! Can I ask you some questions about your family and your job for our school magazine?
Man: Yes, of course.
Can you see the answer? Now you listen and write.

Girl: Where does your son live?
Man: At number 23, Kingly Street.
Girl: Do you spell that K-I-N-G-L-double E?
Man: No. K-I-N-G-L-Y.
Girl: Oh, OK. I don't know it. Sorry. Have you got any other children, Nick?
Man: Yes. I've got a daughter. She's married. I've got five grandsons, too!
Girl: Wow! And when did you start singing?
Man: When I was quite young. I was 11, actually. I had a really great music teacher at school.

Girl: That's lucky! I've seen you on television. You play the guitar very well.
Man: Thanks, but I play the drums best. I enjoy them the most too.
Girl: I didn't know that! One last question, if you don't mind.
Man: That's fine.
Girl: What's your favourite song?
Man: Let's think … I know – it's called 'My winter'.
Girl: I don't know that one, but is that your favourite time of year too?
Man: Yes! I love skiing!
Girl: Me too! Thank you very much for answering my questions.
Man: That's OK!

Optional extension:

o   Learners write a short article about Nick Silkwood's visit.

Suggestion:

Nick Silkwood is visiting our town. He's a famous singer. Nick's son lives here. Nick has a daughter and five grandsons too.

Nick started singing when he was a child. His music teacher helped him a lot. Nick plays the guitar but he prefers the drums. His favourite song is called 'My winter'.

E   Ask and answer questions about Jack and Lily.

Speaking Part **2**

Note: Learners have practiced this task in **C**.

o   Say: *Now you're going to ask or answer questions about two people. They're called … ?* (Jack and Lily) *Jack and Lily have just started their first jobs.* Ask three learners: *How old are they? Guess!* Write the three learners' names and their guesses on the board.

o   Divide class into A and B pairs. A learners look at their set of questions and answers on page 126. B learners look at their set of questions and answers on page 128.

o   Say to B learners: *You don't know anything about Jack's first job, but your A partners do. Ask them questions about it.* Say to A learners: *Look at the answers about Jack's first job. Find the right answer to each question.* Learners work in pairs, asking and answering the questions.

o   Say to A learners: *You don't know anything about Lily's first job, but your B partners do. Ask them questions about it.* Say to B learners: *Look at the answers about Lily's first job. Find the right answer to each question.* Learners work in pairs as before.

o   Ask questions in open class about Jack and Lily and their jobs to check understanding. For example: *How old's Jack? How does Lily go to work? What's Jack's hobby? Who does Lily work with?*

F   Tell me about another person!

Note: In Speaking Part 4, candidates might be asked to talk about a person they know. It is a chance for them to show off their vocabulary and expressions.

o   Write on the board: *Tell me about your favourite actor or singer.*

Ask learners to tell you what kind of information they could give about this person. For example: What he/she looks like. (*He's tall and thin. / She's pretty and has long black hair and green eyes.*)

His/her family. (*She's married and has five children. / He's single.*)

Where he/she comes from. (*He's American. / She's French.*)

Why you like him/her. (*He's really kind. / She's very funny.*)

o   Having practised talking about an actor or singer, ask 3–4 different learners to tell you about their best friend.

Suggestion:

His name's Mario. He's 11. I like him because he's funny.

49 Busy families

Topics family and friends, the home, weather

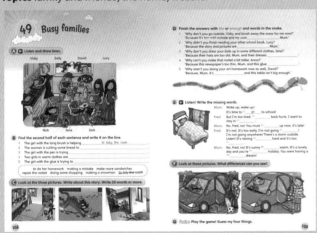

Equipment needed
- Flyers audio 49A, 49E.

A ▶ Listen and draw lines.

- Point to the line between the name 'Jane' below the picture and the girl playing with the dolls. Play the example on the audio. Ask: *What do we hear about Jane?* (She's on the floor / playing with her dolls.)
- Play the rest of the audio twice. Learners listen and draw lines between the names and the people in the picture.

> **Check answers:**
> Lines should be drawn between:
> **1** *David* and boy eating sandwiches.
> **2** *Sally* and girl with purple scarf making snowman.
> **3** *Lucy* and girl with hat doing homework.
> **4** *Jack* and boy cutting newspaper.
> **5** *Vicky* and girl cleaning floor.

Audioscript

Listen and look. There is one example.
Man: Who are all these people in your picture?
Girl: Hi, Mr Boots. It's my mum, my brothers and sisters and my cousins. We were all really busy that day!
Man: I can see that! Is that one of your sisters? The girl on the floor?
Girl: Yes, that's Jane. She's playing with her dolls.
Man: They're wearing pretty dresses.
Girl: Mmmm. She likes dressing them up in funny costumes too, sometimes.
Can you see the line? This is an example.
Now you listen and draw lines.

Girl: My brother David is always hungry!
Man: Which boy is he? The one with curly black hair?
Girl: That's right, and the sandwiches.
Man: Did he make those?
Girl: He likes cooking, but no, Mum made them for him.

Girl: Do you know my cousin, Sally?
Man: No. Which one's she in your picture?
Girl: She's the girl who's outside. She's making a snowman!
Man: The girl with long blonde hair?
Girl: No. The other one. She's got a purple scarf round her neck.
Girl: Poor Lucy had quite a lot of homework that afternoon.
Man: Doesn't she enjoy writing?
Girl: She prefers reading, playing chess or making things. Look! She's wearing her favourite hat!

Man: Why?
Girl: She says it's her lucky hat! I don't know how she can study in our kitchen. It's always so noisy there!
Man: Why's that boy cutting up that newspaper? Was he doing some English homework?
Girl: Art, actually. That's Jack. He was helping my other sister to make her model of a spaceship. He's really good at that. He wants to be a designer or engineer one day.
Man: Well, it looks quite difficult …
Girl: It was. They couldn't make the rocket tall enough.
Girl: Our house is usually quite untidy but my oldest sister doesn't mind that.
Man: Doesn't she? Which girl is she?
Girl: The one who's cleaning the floor. She's really nice. She's never unkind to anyone.
Man: That's good. I see she's got a brush in her hand.
Girl: Yes. That's right. Her name's Vicky. I think I'll go and tidy my room up now. See you later, Mr Boots.
Man: OK!

How much can you remember?

- Learners look at the picture in **A** for one minute. Say: *Try to remember everything you can see.* Learners then close their books. Read out the following questions. Learners write one-word answers in their notebooks.
  1. *How many knives were there in the picture?* (2)
  2. *How many people had curly hair?* (3)
  3. *Where was the butter?* (on the plate/cupboard, near the bread/woman)
  4. *Where were the sandwiches?* (on the plate/table, in a red box on the cupboard)
  5. *How many dolls were there on the floor?* (5)
- Learners work in teams of 3–4. Each team writes five more questions about the picture. One team closes their books. Teams take turns to ask or answer the questions. The team with the most correct answers wins.

B Find the second half of each sentence and write it on the line.

- Read out the first sentence. Ask: *Which girl in the picture in A is the sentence about?* (Learners point to the girl with the long brush.) *What's she using it for?* (to tidy the room)
- Learners read 2–5, find the correct second half of each sentence in the box and write it on the line.

> **Check answers:**
> **2** make more sandwiches.　**3** to do her homework.
> **4** making a snowman.　**5** repair the rocket.

- Write on the board: make　do
  Say: *Look at the word box in B. Find the words 'make', 'making' and 'do', 'doing' and draw lines under them.* Learners then tell you which words follow each verb. Write them on the board under 'make' or 'do':

make	do
a mistake	her homework
more sandwiches	some shopping
a snowman	

- Teach/revise: (adding to the lists) *make a bed, make a meal, do a test, do a sport, do a job, do a school subject.*
- Divide learners into A and B pairs. A learners turn to page 126 and B learners turn to page 128. They each cross out the wrong 'make' or 'do' word to complete their own set of five questions. Learners then work in A and B pairs, asking and answering the questions.

C Look at the three pictures. Write about this story. Write 20 or more words.

o For an authentic test practice, learners look at the three pictures and write the story. See the suggested stories below.

   To give learners more support, you could do the following:

o Say: *Books closed! Listen! I'm going to tell you a short story!*
   Mum, Tom, Zoe, and Sue are cleaning the kitchen. A mouse and a cat come into the kitchen. Now the kitchen is dirty again.

   Say the sentences twice, asking questions after each sentence. Say: *Mum, Tom, Zoe, and Sue are cleaning the kitchen. What do you think mum is cleaning? How old are Tom, Zoe, and Sue? What are they cleaning?* Learners say what they think.

o Do the same with the next part: Say: *A mouse and a cat come into the kitchen. Do they come in together? Are they friends? Now the kitchen is dirty again. What's dirty? The cupboards? The floor? The walls or windows?* Learners talk about their answers in pairs.

o Learners open their books and look at the pictures on page 102. They compare their 'stories' with the story in the pictures there.

o Explain that the three sentences tell the story, but they don't tell us what the four people were cleaning, how the mouse and cat came into the kitchen or how the kitchen got dirty. These things make the story more interesting. Learners write the story.

Suggested stories:

Mum, Tom, Zoe, and Sue are cleaning the kitchen. A mouse and a cat come into the kitchen. Now the kitchen is dirty again. (23 words)

Tom, Zoe, and Sue are helping their mother clean the kitchen. A mouse comes into the kitchen. The cat sees it and runs after it. They run out into the garden again. Mum is standing on a chair because she's afraid of mice. The floor is dirty again. The children are laughing. (51 words)

D Finish the answers with *too* or *enough* and words in the snake.

o Revise the use of 'too' + adjective and 'not' + adjective + 'enough'. Check that learners understand that 'too' goes <u>before</u> an adjective and that 'enough' goes <u>after</u> 'not' + adjective. Show how we can talk about the same problem by using 'too' and 'not enough' with opposite adjectives, for example 'hot / cold'.
   Say: *Why isn't it snowing today? Because the weather's **too hot**. Because the weather **isn't cold enough**.*

o Ask: *Why can't you climb the highest mountain in the world this afternoon? Because … ?* Write answers on the board.
   Suggestions: *it's too far away / difficult / dangerous, we're too young / weak / frightened, it's not near / easy / safe enough, we aren't old / strong / brave enough*

o Learners look at the sentences in D. Say: *Look at the people's names. Who are they?* (the mother and children in A)
   Say: *Look at the first two lines again. How many people are talking?* (two) Say: *Mum is asking a … ?* (question) *and Vicky is … ?* (answering). Explain: the children are using the words 'too' and 'not enough' because they're talking about problems.

o Learners draw circles around each adjective. Say: *You can use some of these words in your answers.*

o Look at the first question and answer together. Ask: *How can we use <u>not enough</u> to finish Vicky's answer?* (isn't warm enough). Accept other answers using words from the snake if they make sense. Learners complete Vicky's answer.

o In pairs, learners choose ways to complete other children's answers using 'too' or 'not enough' and appropriate adjectives. They then choose the one they like most to write on the dotted lines.

Suggested answers:

2	too small/boring	aren't big / interesting / funny enough
3	are too dirty/small	aren't pretty / new / nice enough
4	is too old/dry	isn't strong / good / thick enough
5	too noisy / difficult / boring	not quiet / easy / interesting enough

E ▶ Listen! Write the missing words.

o Learners close their books. Write these questions on the board: *Where's Fred? Why doesn't he want to get up?*

o Play the audio. Learners listen and answer the questions.
   Where's Fred? (in bed) *Why doesn't he want to get up?* (He's tired, his back hurts, there's a storm, it's raining and cold.)

o Ask learners: *Is Fred awake or is he sleeping?* (He's sleeping.)

o Learners open their books and write the words in the story.

o Play the audio again to check answers.

> **Check answers:**
> 2 My 3 bed 4 get 5 anywhere 6 too 7 cold 8 and
> 9 on 10 bad

Audioscript

Listen, then write the missing words.
Woman:	Wake up, wake up! It's time to go to school!
Boy:	But I'm too tired. My back hurts. I want to stay in bed.
Woman:	No, Fred, no! You must get up now, it's late!
Boy:	It's not. It's too early. I'm not going out! I'm not going anywhere! There's a storm outside. Listen! It's raining too hard and it's too cold.
Woman:	No, Fred, no! It's sunny and warm! It's a lovely day and you're on holiday. You were having a bad dream!

F Look at these pictures. What differences can you see?

o Point to the boy in the two pictures. Ask: *Who's this?* (Fred)
   Say: *These two pictures are nearly the same, but some things are different. In pairs, talk about the differences that you can see.*

o Point to the picture on the left. Say: *This is my picture.* Point to the picture on the right. Say: *This is your picture. I'm going to say sentences about my picture. You tell me how your picture is different.*
   Begin with an example. Say: *In my picture, the boy's got a scarf round his neck, but in your picture, he's got a … ?* (**towel** round his neck)
   Read out these sentences, one by one. Learners put up their hands to say a sentence about the differences in the second picture.
   The boy has opened the door of the red car. (… the **green** car.)
   The boy's wearing a grey school uniform. (He's wearing **beach clothes / shorts and a T-shirt**.)
   The car driver is a man. (The driver is a **woman**.)
   The boy's putting a rucksack in the back of the car. (He's putting **a beach bag** in the car.)
   I can see a storm. (I can see a **rainbow**.)
   A football has fallen out of the car. (An **umbrella** has fallen out.)

G Play the game! Guess my four things.

o Divide the class into two or more teams. Say an adjective, for example: *round*. Explain you have four round things on your list (*plate, ball, zero, snowball*). Learners guess the words on the list. Every time a learner says a word that is on the list, write the word on the board and give that learner's team a point.

o After a few turns, give different adjectives and four other things.

Suggestions:

striped:	scarf, towel, umbrella, T-shirt
square:	table, picture, room, box
metal:	ring, scissors, knife, key
loud/noisy:	traffic, music, storm, rocket
heavy:	rucksack, chair, rock, dictionary
pretty:	sweater, picture, girl, flower
special:	cake, day, person, present
wild:	bird, horse, bear, elephant
popular:	programme, game, person, story
huge:	elephant, skyscraper, whale, ocean
delicious:	milkshake, sauce, meal, cookies
deep:	cave, ocean, waterfall, hole
furry:	teddy bear, kitten, rabbit, dog

50 On TV

Topics work, places

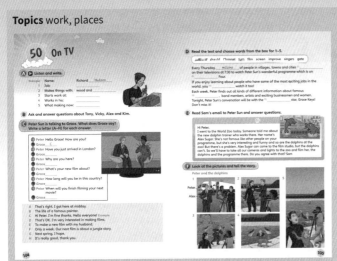

Not in YLE wordlists: (*dolphin*) *trainer, studio, fold* (v), *sculptor, carpenter*

Equipment needed

○ Flyers audio 50A.

○ Photocopies (one per group of four learners) of page 144, cut into four cards. See **B**.

○ Sheets of paper (one for each learner or pair of learners). See 'Play the game!'

A  Listen and write.   Listening Part 2

> **Flyers tip**
>
> In Listening Part 2, candidates often have to listen and write a name which is spelled out. Many candidates find this difficult so it is important to continue to practise spelling names in class. (In this Part 2, learners hear the man's surname spelled out in the example.)

○ Say: *Look at the man in this picture.* Point to the lines in **A** and ask:
What's this man's first name? (Richard)
What's his surname? (Hudson)

○ Point to the word 'job' in 1 and ask: *What do you think this man does? What's his job? Is he a doctor?* (no) *A teacher?* (perhaps)
Learners suggest jobs.
Suggestions: an artist, sculptor, carpenter

○ Point to 2 and say: *This man works with wood and he also uses something different. What could that be?* Learners make suggestions. (glass, metal, silver, gold, wool)

○ Point to the words in 3–5. In pairs, learners think of possible answers.
Suggestions:
3 (a time) 8 o'clock/8.30 etc
4 (a place) kitchen / living room / garage etc
5 (an object) a box/picture etc

○ Say: *Listen to a journalist talking to Richard. Write Richard's answers.*
Play the audio twice.
Ask: *Did any of you guess the answers?*

> **Check answers:**
> **1** (an) artist **2** metal **3** 9.30 (am) / half past nine **4** basement
> **5** (a) lamp

Audioscript

Listen and look. There is one example.

Woman: Good morning. I'm a journalist and I'm making a programme for television. Can I ask you some questions, please?

Man: Yes, of course.

Woman: Thank you. First, what's your name?

Man: Richard Hudson.

Woman: Is that H-U-D-S-O-N?

Man: That's correct.

Can you see the answer? Now you listen and write.

Woman: What do you do, Mr Hudson? What's your job?

Man: I'm an artist.

Woman: Oh, I see. You paint pictures.

Man: No. I don't paint. I make things.

Woman: Do you? What kind of things do you make?

Man: Lots of different kinds of things. I work with wood and also with metal.

Woman: That sounds interesting. And difficult too! And do you start work early?

Man: Not very early. I go for a run at eight o'clock. Then I have a shower and start working after breakfast at about half past nine.

Woman: Oh! And where do you work? In a factory?

Man: No, I do all my work in my basement. I like working there because it's nice and quiet.

Woman: I understand. And what are you making now?

Man: I've just started making a lamp. It's going to be one of the most beautiful things that I've ever made, I think.

Woman: How clever! Well, I'd like to thank you for answering my questions, Mr Hudson.

Man: That's OK!

B Ask and answer questions about Tony, Vicky, Alex and Kim.

○ Learners work in groups of four. Give each learner in each group a different card from page 144 .
Say: *You're going to ask and answer questions about four different people and their jobs. Look at the words in the first column. Which questions do you need to ask to find out the answers?*
Write their suggestions on the board if necessary:

Name?	*What's his/her name?*
Job?	*What's his/her job? / What does he/she do?*
Starts work at?	*What time does he/she start work?*
Works for?	*Who does he/she work for?*
What/doing now?	*What's he/she doing now?*

○ In pairs, learners ask and answer questions about the people on their cards. They change pairs twice so that they have talked to all the people in their group.

○ Tell learners to put their cards on the table, face down. Say: *Let's see how much you remember! I'm going to ask you some questions about these people. What were their first names?* (Tony, Vicky, Alex, Kim) Write these names on the board.

○ Ask the following questions. One person in each group is the secretary and writes the group's answers on a piece of paper or in their notebook.

Questions:

What's Mr Sugar's first name? (Alex)

Who starts work the earliest? (Vicky)

Who works with animals? (Tony and Alex)

Who is good at a sport? (Kim)

Who starts work the latest? (Tony)

Who's talking on the telephone now? (Kim)

Groups give their written answers to another group who check them. Ask the questions again. Groups get a point for each correct answer. The winning group is the one with the most points.

C Peter Sun is talking to Grace. What does Grace say? Write a letter (A–H) for each answer.
Reading & Writing Part 2

○ Point to the half-conversation and explain:

This is part of the conversation Peter Sun had with Grace Keys. You can read Peter's questions here.

Learners read Peter's questions.

○ Point to the answers in the box and say: *These are Grace's answers to Peter's questions.*

○ Learners complete the conversation by writing the correct letters (A–H) on the lines.

Check answers:
1 A   2 E   3 B   4 F   5 G

D Read the text and choose words from the box for 1–5.

○ Write these questions on the board, or read them out, one at a time.

1   *When can you see Peter Sun on TV?*

2   *What kind of people can you see on the programme?*

3   *Who will be on the programme tonight?*

Learners read the text and find the answers to these questions. (**1** on Thursdays, **2** band members, artists, famous businessmen and women, **3** Grace Keys)

○ Learners complete the text with words from the box.

Check answers:
1 turn   2 Channel   3 should   4 singers   5 film

E Read Sam's email to Peter Sun and answer questions.

○ Say: *Peter Sun has a team of journalists who find interesting people to go on his programme. Sam is one of the journalists. He's sent Peter an email.*

○ Learners read Sam's email. While they are doing that, write the following sentences on the board for learners to complete.

1   *Sam went to see Alex Sugar at .... today.*

2   *Alex looks after .... there.*

3   *Sam thinks Alex and her animals are funny and .... too!*

4   *Sam says they'll have to .... the interview at the zoo.*

5   *Sam's team from the programme must take ....*

Check answers:
1 the (World) Zoo   2 the dolphins   3 interesting
4 film   5 the/their cameras and lights

F Look at the pictures and tell the story.
Speaking Part 3

○ Point to the five pictures and say: *These pictures tell a story. It's called 'Peter and the dolphins'. Just look at the pictures first.*

Give learners time to look at the pictures before reading out the first part of the story:

Peter Sun and Sam the cameraman are arriving at the zoo. Peter is meeting Alex. He's going to talk to her about the dolphins. Sam will film their conversation.

○ In pairs, learners look at the other pictures and tell the story.

○ Two pairs join together to form groups of four learners. They compare their stories.

Suggested story:

Picture 2

Peter Sun is by the pool now. He's talking to Alex. There's a monkey on Alex's shoulder.

Picture 3

The monkey is jumping on to Peter's shoulder. Peter's very surprised. Sam is filming the monkey.

Picture 4

Peter's fallen into the water. He's between two dolphins in the pool. The monkey is watching Peter!

Picture 5

Peter, Alex and the monkey are all laughing. Sam's film will be really funny.

Play the game! Actor meets actor.

○ Give out sheets of paper (one to each learner or pair of learners). Say: *I'm going to ask you some questions. Write your answers on the paper.*

○ Say: *Write the name of a famous actor (a man or a boy) at the top of the page.* They should then fold down the page so that the actor's name is no longer visible. (Demonstrate this with a piece of paper.) The pieces of paper are passed on to the next learner or pair of learners.

○ Say: *Now, write the name of another famous actor (a woman or a girl). Fold the paper so that you can't see that name.* They pass on their sheets.

○ Continue this process, with learners writing the answers to these questions:

Where did they meet?

What was he wearing?

What was she wearing?

What did he say to her?

What did she say to him?

○ When these things have been written, the learners unfold the pieces of paper and read the stories, then practise reading them out. The best ones can be acted out to the rest of the class, with learners using the actors' voices and gestures.

Topics school, sports and leisure, time

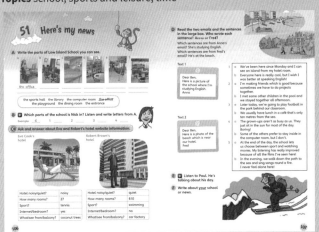

Not in YLE wordlists: *secretary*

Equipment needed
- Flyers audio 51B, 51E.
- (Optional) Postcards of your area or photos of your school. See F.

Ⓐ Write the parts of Low Island School you can see.

- Ask: *Which parts of your school do you like best? Why?*

  Point to pictures **a–f** and say: *These are pictures of different parts of Low Island School.*

  Point to the woman in picture **a** and say: *This is Mrs Day, the school secretary. She works in the office at the school.* Point to the words 'the office' on the line under picture **a** and in the wordbox.

- Learners look at pictures **b–f** and choose and write words from the box on the line under each picture.

  > **Check answers:**
  > **b** the computer room   **c** the sports hall   **d** the library
  > **e** the playground   **f** the dining room

- Ask learners: *Do you have places like this in your school? Which of these places would you like to be in now? Why?*

- Ask: *Can you see the entrance to Low Island School here?* (no) Ask these questions. Learners think of their answers but don't say anything. *What do you think the entrance is like? Are there steps in front of it? Is there one big door or a double door? What colour is the door? What's the door made of?* Ask the questions again, stopping after each one to give learners time to talk about their answers in pairs or small groups.

Ⓑ ▶ Which parts of the school is Nick in? Listen and write letters from A.

- Point to the picture of the boy and say: *This is Nick. He goes to Low Island School. Let's listen to him. He's speaking to someone. Where is Nick?* Play the example.

- Say: *Nick's in the … ?* (school library) *How do we know?* (He has to be quiet, he wants to take a book home, he gives the woman his card. He has to bring the book back on Thursday.)

- Say: *Listen to Nick again. He's talking to other people in different parts of the school now. Where is Nick talking each time?* Learners listen to the other conversations and write the letters from the pictures in **A** on the lines.

  > **Check answers:**
  > **1** a (the office)   **2** f (the dining room)
  > **3** b (the computer room)   **4** c (the sports hall)

- Write these questions on the board. Learners listen again and write their answers.
  1. *What does Nick want to tell his parents?* (he's not going home for lunch)
  2. *What's Nick going to have for lunch?* (chicken, fries, a green salad and a pear)
  3. *What's the name of the museum?* (the North Museum)
  4. *What's on the floor of the sports hall?* (white lines)

Audioscript

Listen and look. There is one example.

Woman: Sshh! Be quiet, Nick. You mustn't talk in here.
Boy: Sorry, Miss Key. Can I take this book home with me? Here's my card. When do I have to bring it back?
Woman: Next Thursday.

Can you see the letter 'd'? This is an example. Now you listen and write letters.

1 Boy: Good morning, Mrs Day. Can I phone home? I forgot to tell my parents something. I want to have lunch at school today so I'm not going home in the break at midday.
Woman: OK, Nick. I'll tell the kitchen manager. Here's the phone.

2 Woman: What can I give you for lunch today, Nick?
Boy: I'll have chicken and fries with a green salad. And I might have some fruit. Can I take a pear from this bowl?
Woman: Of course you can.

3 Man: Now listen everyone, Nick's going to tell us about the website he's just looked at.
Boy: The North Museum's home page has lots of paintings on it. It's very quick and easy to use and looks great on screen. And you can also play games! The address is www.northmuseum.org.

4 Boy: What are we going to do today, Mr Park? Basketball?
Man: No, badminton.
Boy: I've never played that before. Where are we going to play – outside?
Man: No, inside. Over there.
Boy: Oh! Those white lines on the floor are for badminton. Of course!

C Ask and answer about Eva and Robert's hotel website information.

Speaking Part 2

Flyers tip

In Speaking Part 2, candidates need to ask questions as well as answer them. Practise using the present simple to form questions about different people or situations. Questions are often about people, numbers, places and activities.

○ Point to the woman and the man in front of the two hotels. Say: *Eva and Robert are both looking on the internet at hotel websites.*

Ask: *Whose hotel has more floors?* (Robert's) *Which hotel do you think is nearer the beach?* (Eva's)

Learners work in A and B pairs. Learner A looks at the information that Eva is reading on her hotel's website. Learner B looks at the information that Robert is reading on his hotel's website. They should cover their partner's information with a piece of paper.

○ Ask questions about the hotels in a different order to the order of the information in the table. Learners put up their hands to answer.

What can you see from Robert's balcony? (a car factory)

Is Eva's hotel noisy or quiet? (noisy)

How many rooms are there in Robert's hotel? (610)

What sport can Eva do at her hotel? (tennis)

Whose hotel has internet in the bedrooms? (Eva's)

○ Learner B asks Learner A the five questions about Eva's hotel. Then Learner A asks Learner B five questions about Robert's hotel.

○ Ask: *Which hotel do you like more – Eva's or Robert's? Why?*

D Read the two texts and the sentences in the large box. Who wrote each sentence? Anna or Fred?

○ Point to two texts (1 and 2) and ask: *What's Anna writing about?* (her school) *What's Fred writing about?* (his holiday) *Who are Anna and Fred writing to?* (Ben)

○ Read out sentence 1a in the large box 1: *We've been here since Monday and I can see an island from my hotel room.* Ask: *Is this sentence about studying English* (text 1) *or about a beach holiday* (text 2)? (about a beach holiday [text 2])

○ Divide the class into two groups: A and B. Learners in group A copy the start of Anna's text into their notebooks. Learners in group B do the same with Fred's text.

○ Learners read the other a and b sentences and choose and write sentences in their notebooks to complete each text.

Check answers:

Text 1: 1b 2a 3a 4b 5a

Text 2: 1a 2b 3b 4a 5b

○ Read out these sentences. If the information in a sentence is correct, learners shout '*Goal!*' If the information is not correct, they say '*Actually, no!*'

Anna could choose to watch films in the evenings. (Goal!)

The café is only 100 metres from the beach. (Actually, no!)

The park is opposite Anna's school. (Actually, no!)

Fred danced round the fire by the sea. (Actually, no!)

Anna liked staying inside and doing homework. (Actually, no!)

Fred met some other children when he was swimming. (Goal!)

E ▶ Listen to Paul. He's talking about his day.

○ Say: *Listen to Paul talking about his day. How does Paul go to school?* Play the audio.

Answer: He gets the ski lift up and down the mountain or skis down the mountain in the winter.

○ Write on the board:

two kilometres   warm clothes   15   Jane
geography and maths   a ski teacher / ski team for his country
over his shoulder

Explain: *Paul uses these words to talk about his day. Listen again and tell me how he uses them.*

Answers:

2 kilometres – Paul lives two kilometres up a mountain / two kilometres from school.

warm clothes – He has to put on warm clothes because the weather is always cold there.

15 – There are 15 students in his class.

Jane – She sits next to Paul. She comes to school on a dog sledge.

geography and maths – Paul likes these subjects.

a ski teacher or ski team for his country – Paul would like to do these things in the future.

over his shoulder – Paul carries his skis over his shoulder in winter when he goes home on the ski lift.

Audioscript

Listen to Paul talking about his day.

Hello! My name's Paul. I'm going to tell you about my school day.

Well, my house is about two kilometres away from my school. But I live at the top of a mountain!

I wake up at seven o'clock and I always have to put on warm clothes because it's cold up here. In winter, I always have a hot breakfast because it can be very, very cold outside!

There are no bus stops near my house, so I use the ski lift to go down the mountain to my school in the village, but when there's snow, I put on my skis and ski down the mountain to school. I love going to school that way!

There are 15 students in my class and I'm not the only person who comes down the mountain to school. Jane, the girl who sits next to me in class, comes on a dog sledge with her brother and sister!

My favourite lesson is geography and I also like maths. I'm good at sport too. I'd like to be a ski teacher or to be part of my country's ski team one day.

School finishes at quarter past four. Sometimes after school I go to a friend's house in the village. In winter, I have to carry my skis over my shoulder! Then I take the ski lift up the mountain to go back to my house.

F Write about your school or news.

○ Learners write a letter, a postcard, a text or an email about their school or they write news about things they are doing or have done recently.

If they write about their school, you could send their postcards, letters, emails and photos to another class (at the same school or to another class in another country).

If your school or class has a blog, they could also write a short blog about their news.

52   What a lot of questions!

Topics the world around us, sports and leisure

Not in YLE wordlists: *a swarm*

Equipment needed

- Flyers audio 52B, 52E.
- Colouring pencils or pens. See E.

A Complete each question with words from the box.

- Write on the board: *Wh*

  Note: If learners find the pronunciation of /w/ difficult, tell them to make their lips round and hard. As /w/ is sounded, lips then open and relax back into their neutral position.

  Say: *In pairs, write as many different question words as possible that begin with these two letters. You have 90 seconds!*

- Pairs say how many question words they have written. Ask the pair with the highest number of question words to read out their list. Make sure they pronounce the /w/ sound correctly.

  Note: The seven question words that start with 'wh' in the YLE wordlist are: what, when, where, which, who, whose, why.

  Revise meanings by asking a few questions using present, past and future forms:

  Which day of the week do you like most?

  Who do you look like in your family?

  Where would you like to live in the future?

  What kind of food did you like eating most when you were little?

  Whose pencil are you using?

  When will you be 12? (or another age if more appropriate to group)

  Why do people visit your country? What do they come to see?

- Say: *Spell the question word 'who'!* (w-h-o) Ask: *Which other question word has the same three letters as 'who'?* (how)

  Ask: *How do you come to school? How do you spell 'school'?*

- Write on the board: *How often   How long*

  Say: *We have English classes three days a week: on Mondays, Wednesdays and Fridays.**

  Ask: *Which question am I answering: How often or How long?* (How often)

  Say: *I came into this classroom at 9 o'clock.* It's 9.15* now. I've been here for 15* minutes.*

  Ask: *Which question am I answering: How often or How long?* (How long)

  * Adapt as appropriate.

- Learners open their books and look at the first question in **A**. Ask: *Why can't the answer be 'What'?* (we use 'Who' for a person and 'What' for a thing. A friend is a person.)

- Learners complete questions 2–9. They use each question word or phrase in the box once only.

> **Check answers:**
> **2** How often   **3** How long   **4** How many   **5** Which
> **6** Have you ever   **7** What kind   **8** Whose   **9** How

B ▶ Listen. Which questions from A does Holly's mum answer?

- Say: *You're going to hear part of a conversation between a girl called Holly and her mother. Listen to two of Holly's mother's answers.*

- Ask: *Which question asked about the past?* (How many times have you been on a theatre stage?) *Where and when did Holly's mum do her acting?* (at school)

  Say: *The second question asked about … ?* (how often Holly's mum goes online). *When does she go online?* (in the afternoon) *Where is she when she goes online?* (at home, on her computer)

- Learners work in pairs (or small groups). They think of two more questions that begin with 'How many times' and 'How often'. They also think of two short answers to their questions, for example '100 times', 'every summer'.

- Pairs work with another pair and ask their 'How many times' and 'How often' questions and compare answers.

  They could have fun with this as answers might not fit with the context, for example:

  Q (pair 1): *How many times have you washed your face this year?*

  A (pair 2): *Only once.*

  Q (pair 1): *How often do you go to the moon?*

  A (Pair 2): *Every Monday.*

Audioscript

Listen. Which questions from A does Holly's mum answer?

Girl: Mum. Have you read the questions in this magazine? Can I ask you them?

Woman: OK, Holly.

Girl: Right. How many times have you been on a theatre stage?

Woman: Wow! I don't know! I was in the school theatre group for five years. We did lots of acting, so I've been on stage hundreds of times, I guess!

Girl: Really! You never told me that!

Next … how often do you go online?

Woman: Every day! But I only use the internet when you or your brother aren't on my computer! I try to answer my emails in the afternoon.

Girl: Before we get home from school?

Woman: That's right.

C Write your own answers, then ask a friend.

o Explain: *When you answer a question that begins with 'Where' and 'When', you can usually talk about when you do or did something and where you do or did it. Read questions 1–9 in A and write your answers, giving information about when and where.*

Note: Learners should only write the key words from their answer.

o Learners work in pairs. They write their partner's name on the line at the top of the second column in **A**, ask them the questions, then write one or two important words from their answers.

o Ask 3–4 confident learners to come to the front of the class. Other learners ask each of them one or two of these questions. The group at the front tell the class their own and their partner's answers.

D Read the story. Write some words to complete the sentences about the story. You can use 1, 2, 3 or 4 words.

Reading & Writing Part 5

o Learners read the story, taking it in turns to read out sentences to the class. Teach/revise vocabulary if necessary.

o Say: *Listen and find four words for things beginning with 'C' in the first two paragraphs of the text.*

  1 *People who are this know more than other people.*
  2 *And this? People like to win this!*
  3 *Who are these people? These are people who are not grown-ups yet.*
  4 *What's this? There are lots of different cities in this place.*

Check answers:
1 cleverest **2** clouds **3** competition **4** children **5** country

o Learners look at the examples then complete questions 1–7 with 1, 2, 3 or 4 words.

Flyers tip
In Reading and Writing Part 5, all the answers are in the text. For example, in this task, question 1 could be completed with 'computers' or 'his computer', but those words do not appear in the story. The text says that Harry 'often searched the internet' so the answer can only be '(often searched) the internet' or 'the internet'.

Check answers:
1 (often searched) the internet   **2** (TV) programme/competition
3 cleverest children   **4** Mr Silver   **5** (important) information
6 (all) his answers   **7** birthday

o Learners close their books. Ask three more questions. Tell them the answers all begin with the letter T.
  When will Harry be on the TV programme? ([on] Tuesday)
  Where does Harry have to go for the TV programme? (Television House)
  How will Harry and his parents go there? ([by] taxi)

E ▶ Listen and colour.

o Learners look at the picture in **D**. Make sure they have a full set of colouring pencils or pens.

o Say: *You are going to hear two of Harry's friends talking about the competition. You have to colour four things in the picture while you listen.*

Flyers tip
In Listening Part 5, candidates should just mark each item with the right colour, check their choice of colour and object during the second listening and finish colouring it at the end of the audio. They do not lose marks or get extra marks for colouring something badly or well.

o Learners listen to the audio and colour the items. Pause the audio to give them time to colour.

Check answers:
boy's sweater – red, man's scarf – yellow, girl's hair – brown, prize computer – green.

o In pairs, learners tell each other to colour two more items in the picture. Ask different learners to hold up their pictures and explain what they have coloured. For example: *In my picture, the rocket is blue and the man's jacket and trousers are purple.*

Audioscript

Listen and colour.
Girl: Did you see that competition on the television last night? Harry Doors was in it!
Boy: Harry Doors? The boy at our school? Was he?
Girl: Yes. He looked great! He had a red sweater on and he answered lots of questions. He's so clever. He knows how far it is to the moon!
Boy: Well, I don't! Who asked all the questions?
Girl: An old man with a funny yellow scarf on. I remember another question. It was: 'How many letters are there in each of the words "alphabet" and "moustache"?' Harry put his hand up so quickly! But a girl got the next question right. She had long brown hair.
Boy: What was the question?
Girl: What's 30 times 15?
Boy: Hmmm … 450!
Girl: Yes! I want to find Harry and ask him about the competition.
Boy: Did he win it?
Girl: Yes.
Boy: What did he win?
Girl: A computer that he can use at home. It was green! Harry wants to be an astronaut one day! He told the man on the programme.
Boy: Wow!

Guess my question!

o Draw five lines on the board. Add an apostrophe between the first two lines and a question mark at the end. Say: *Each of these lines is a word. How many words are there?* (5) Point to the question mark and ask: *What kind of sentence has this at the end?* (a question)
.... ' ....?

o Point to the first line on the board and ask: *Can you guess the first word of the question? It's a question word and it has five letters and we use it when we are asking about a place.* (Where) Write *Where* on the first line on the board.

o Point to the apostrophe (') between 'Where' and the second line on the board.
Ask: *When do we write this in English – when we add letters or when we take letters away?* (When we take them away)

o Say: *Mr Silver asked Harry this question. Can anyone remember the whole question?* If they cannot remember the question, they can find it in Harry's story text. (Where's the River Thames?) Ask: *What was Harry's answer to this question?* (in London) You may like to show learners a map so they can see where the River Thames starts then flows east under many bridges in London and then out to the North Sea.

o Each learner writes a question about a famous place / person / holiday and draws lines for each word in their notebook. In pairs or groups of three, learners guess their partner's question then they answer it.

53 Finding your way

Topics places and directions

Equipment needed

o   Flyers audio 53B.

(A) Look at the map and read about Castletown. Find each place.

o   Point to the map. Tell learners to find these places on it and say where they are:

the River Cross (*It goes under the bridge and round the castle.*)

the castle (*It's near the river.*)

the bridge (*It's on River Road, near the castle.*)

the library (*It's in Station Road.*)

the supermarket (*It's on High Street, between the newspaper shop and the shoe shop.*)

the railway station (*It's on the corner of Station Road and High Street.*)

o   In pairs, learners read sentences 1–8 and write the places on the roofs of the buildings. To check answers, ask different pairs to hold up a book and show others in the class where each answer goes.

o   Ask questions about the places:

   1   *Which place has a car park?* (the station) Point to the car park behind the supermarket and ask: *And which other place in Castletown has a car park?* (Pat's /the supermarket)
   2   *If you don't live in Castletown, where can you stay?* (at the Station Hotel)
   3   *What can you see outside the chemist's?* (a green cross)
   4   *Which shop is near to the place where you can catch the town centre bus?* (the bookshop)
   5   *Where can you go to use the internet and have something to eat or drink too?* (the Internet Café)
   6   *The Station Hotel is on the corner of two streets. Which ones?* (Station Road and High Street)
   7   *Which place has a path outside it that goes down to the river?* (the restaurant)

o   In pairs, learners talk about where the different places are in the picture. For example: *The post office is opposite Pat's supermarket, between the fruit shop and the restaurant.*

o   Say: *At the moment, you're not in this classroom! You're in Castletown! You're in one of the places in town. What can you see? What can you buy? In pairs, tell your classmate what you can do, see and buy at your place. Your classmate has to listen and guess where you are.*

(B) ▶ Listen and tick the box.

Listening Part **4**

> **Flyers tip**
>
> In Listening Part 4, candidates should read each question and look at each set of picture answers carefully before they hear the conversation. The questions are all about the same topic and the conversation has the same two speakers throughout.

o   Say: *Harry and his family live in the country, but today he and his mother have travelled to Castletown. You are going to hear Harry and his mother talking together about their trip.*

o   Play the audio twice. Learners listen and put a tick in the correct box for questions 1–5.

> **Check answers:**
> **1** A   **2** C   **3** B   **4** A   **5** B

o   Ask: *Who gave all the answers? Harry or his mother?* (Harry) *Which different places did Harry go to?* (the sports shop, the library, the castle, the train station, a restaurant)

Audioscript

Listen and look. There is one example.
What does Harry need?

Woman: So Harry … I like walking round Castletown, don't you? What do we need to get for you here, today? I've forgotten!
Boy: Only a Castletown football shirt, Mum. Nothing else.
Woman: Oh, yes! What about some new shorts, too?
Boy: My old ones are still fine.
Woman: And you don't need any new sports shoes yet, so that's good.

Can you see the tick? Now you listen and tick the box.

1   *What is opposite the library now?*
Boy: How far is the library from here? I'd like to go there, too.
Woman: Not far. It was opposite this railway station, wasn't it, but it isn't here now.
Boy: Where is it then?
Woman: It's in a new building opposite the chemist's – the one I like – so it'll only take us another five minutes to get there.
Boy: Oh … OK. So we just have to go past the post office and then turn left?
Woman: That's right! Well done!

2   *Which way will Harry and his mother go to the castle?*
Woman: And after lunch, we can walk round the castle again. We can go down that road where all those nice houses are.
Boy: Last time, we went through the park and saw a volleyball competition.
Woman: I remember. But that other road to the castle is always so busy. All the town traffic uses that.
Boy: Yes, that's no fun. I don't want to go that way.

3   *Which train will Harry and his mother take home?*
Boy: Which train will we go home on today? Not the one that leaves at five thirty? It's so slow.
Woman: No. That one's too early.
Boy: Well, the next one's at ten to six. I know the timetable for all our trains now!
Woman: Yes, we'll catch that one. It arrives home at eight o'clock.

4   *What will Harry have to eat?*
Boy: I'm getting hungry. I might have chicken with a salad for my lunch.
Woman: Why don't you have something different this time? I'm going to have some of the wonderful fish soup that they make in the restaurant by the river.
Boy: I don't want a salad if we go there. Can I have some pasta? You get lots and lots on a really big plate in that place!
Woman: Ha ha! Good idea! Of course you can!

5 *What has Harry lost?*

Woman: What's the matter, Harry? You look worried. Have you lost your money?

Boy: No, I haven't lost that, but my train ticket isn't in my pocket. Did I drop it?

Woman: You gave it back to me, remember? But what about your camera? You were holding that too, weren't you?

Boy: Oh no! I think I left it at the station!

o Write on the board: *information   station   competition*

Ask: *Did Harry or his Mum say any of these words? Can you remember?* (They said 'station' and 'competition' but not 'information').

o Underline 'tion' in each word. In pairs, learners say the three words out loud to each other and try to hear the sound these letters make. Ask: *Does anyone know?* Check that learners recognise the sound as /ʃən/.

o Say: *Did you see the inforMAtion about the compeTItion in the STAtion?*

o Learners repeat the sentence in a chain. Make sure learners put the main stress on the syllable before /ʃən/ in each word.

Asking the way and where things are.

o Write on the board and revise: *Turn left/right. Go straight on. Walk across / Cross the road/bridge. Walk past.*

Say: *Stand up!* Learners walk around the classroom, following your directions. Say: *Go straight on. Turn left. Walk past the door. Turn right. Turn right again. Walk back to your chair and sit down. Thank you.*

o Tell learners to look at the sentences about Castletown in **A** and to tell you words they find for saying where things are. Add their suggestions to the board:

across, next to, opposite, behind, between, near, on the corner of

o Say: *Listen and say which place I've chosen. Start at the bottom of River Road. Go up River Road and turn right onto High Street. Go past Pat's supermarket and the shoe shop. Cross South Street. The place is on the corner of South Street and High Street.* (the bank)

o In pairs, learners choose two places on the map in **A**. They write sentences to say how to get from one to another, but they should not name the two places.

o Pairs work in groups of four and take turns to listen to directions and try to guess the places at the beginning and end of each journey.

Advanced classes:

o Pairs decide where they are now on the map but keep that secret. They then choose their destination and work out how to give directions from one place to the other. Learners then role play asking for and giving directions to the rest of the class. For example:

Learner A: *Excuse me! I need some information! Can you tell me the way to the station?*

Learner B: *Yes, of course. Walk across the bridge. Turn left and walk straight on. Go past Station Road. The entrance to the station is on your left!*

Learner A: *Thanks!*

Others in the class work out where the two people are now. (outside the castle in River Road)

C Choose the correct words and write them on the lines.

Reading & Writing **Part 1**

o Learners look at the sentences and possible answers. Ask: *How many questions are there?* (10 plus the example). *How many answers are there?* (15).

o Look at the example together. Tell learners to draw a line through 'months' outside the box and remind them they can only use an answer once.

o To make the practice as authentic as possible, learners work on their own. They read the definitions and write the answers.

> **Check answers:**
> **1** the news **2** buildings **3** autumn **4** a path **5** minutes
> **6** a bridge **7** cartoons **8** a channel **9** a calendar **10** a city

o Ask: *Which were the four wrong answers?* (websites, midnight, a festival, the internet). Build definitions on the board for each of these. Write the first two or three words only for each definition then different learners suggest a following word for you to add to the definition. For example for 'midnight', on the board write: *This is the*

Learner A:	middle	Learner B:	of
Learner C:	the	Learner D:	night
Learner E:	when	Learner F:	you
Learner G:	can	Learner H:	see
Learner I:	the	Learner J:	moon.

D Ask and answer questions.

Speaking **Part 4**

o Write the name of a shop (or place for example: a cinema, a square, the station) in the area where your class live that most learners will know. Ask different learners questions. (Adapt questions for other parts of town.)

Where is this shop?
Is it big or small?
What kind of things does it sell?
Is it fun to go there or is it a boring place?
How often do you go there?

After learners have answered the questions, ask them to tell you the questions you asked them. Write the questions on the board.

o Say: *You are going to ask and answer questions about places and shops that you know.* Learners work in A and B pairs. Learner A asks Learner B the questions on page 123 of their book. Learner B answers.

o Learner B asks Learner A the questions on page 125 of their book. Learner A answers.

Note: Remind learners that the questions on the board will help them talk about the last question in each group of questions. (Tell me about ...)

E Be actors in a shop or town!

o Learners work in pairs and prepare to role play a situation. They choose either to be in a shop or in a restaurant choosing what to eat.

o Learners write a similar conversation to the ones they heard in the audio in **B**. Encourage learners to be creative. Say: *Try to make your conversations funny!*

For example:

Learner A: *Waiter! Waiter! I'm really hungry!*

Learner B: *What would you like to eat?*

Learner A: *I'd like some pasta, a chicken, lots of chips, a big plate of salad and some chocolate ice cream please.*

Learner B: *Anything else?*

Learner A: *Yes! Your biggest pizza and three glasses of milk.*

Learner B: *You ARE hungry!*

o In pairs, learners act out their conversations in front of the class.

> **Travel book**
>
> o Learners choose their favourite place in town (a museum, a park, a new shop, an important square, etc.) and create an information page to go in a travel book. It could be real or imagined.
>
> o Learners draw a map to show visitors how to get to it and take a photo of it (or find a picture of their place on the internet.)
>
> o Learners then write a short article about the place saying why people who come to the town on holiday should visit it.
>
> o They add their travel book page to their project file. Alternatively, display the pages on the wall of your classroom if possible.

54 Let's have some fun!

Topics sports and leisure, places

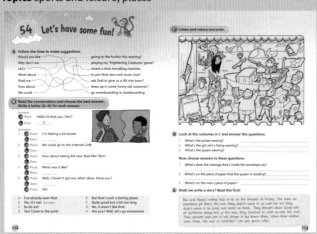

Equipment needed

○ Sets of seven 'suggestion starters' (one set per 3–4 learners).
One of the following suggestion starters is written on each strip:
Would you like? Why don't we? Shall we? Let's … We could … What about? How about? See A.

○ Flyers audio 54C.

○ Colouring pencils or pens.

○ Photocopies (one for each pair of learners) of the dialogue and story on page 145. See E.

(A) Follow the lines to make suggestions.

○ Ask learners what fun things they want to do today.
Say: *Let's …* . Learners complete the sentence with their own ideas. Write five or six of their suggestions on the board. For example:
Let's … play on the computers, play volleyball, watch something on the DVD player, go for a swim at the pool, play games, run round the playground.

○ Learners look at the joined sentence halves in **A**. In pairs, they decide why the lines are three different colours.
Answer: They show three different forms of verbs following suggestions. Write up the six sentences on the board and focus on the differences between them:

Would you like?	+ main verb (with 'to')
Why don't we? Shall we? Let's …	+ main verb (without 'to')
We could …	
What about? How about?	+ main verb ('-ing' form)

Note: 'Let's' … and 'We could'… do not need question marks.

○ Learners look again at the seven activities in **A**.
Write on the board:
Would you like to put your foot on that piece of wood. Or we could cook some good cookies!
Say: *Can you see two words that sound exactly the same but look different?* (would, wood) Underline the 'ou' and 'oo' in these words.
Ask: *How many other words here have got the same /ʊ/ sound that we can hear in these two words?* Learners work in pairs and answer. Based on spellings, they might suggest: *you, foot, wood, could, cook, good, cookies*

If they do this, say: *There are seven other words with this /ʊ/ sound in them, but one of your answers is wrong and there's another word that you haven't found yet: 'you' is wrong. You should look at put!* 'Put' has the same /ʊ/ sound. In pairs, learners practise saying the sentence correctly.

○ Divide learners into groups of 3–4. Give each group a set of seven suggestion starters. They put these upside down on a table so they can't see the different structures. Write on the board: *go   have   play*

○ Point to 'go'. Ask: *What word can we put after go? Think of a place you'd like to go to or a sport you'd like to do.* Learners suggest: *to the beach, swimming etc.*

○ Learners take turns to pick up a suggestion starter and use it to make different suggestions to the group using 'go', 'have' or 'play', or verbs of their own choosing, for example: *How about going to the beach? Let's dance! Would you like to play tennis? We could have a party! Shall we call Fred? Why don't we watch TV? What about going for a walk in the rain?* When groups have used all seven suggestion starters, they choose the suggestion they like best and report that one to the class. The class then decides which suggestion they like the best. Make the final suggestion to the class. The class says: *Yes! Good idea! OK!* as appropriate.

(B) Read the conversation and choose the best answer. Write a letter (A–H) for each answer.
Reading & Writing Part 2

Flyers tip
In Reading and Writing Part 2, there will be either a grammatical link, or a vocabulary link (or both) between the sentence and its correct option. Remind learners to silently read the whole conversation after they've chosen their answers to make sure it makes sense.

○ Learners read Paul's side of the conversation. Ask: *Who's he talking to?* (Dan)
What's Paul talking about? (different places to go to / things to do)

○ Look at the example together. Learners cross out the example answer in the options box. In pairs, they choose Dan's best answer in 1–5, and write the letter on the line.

Check answers:
1 H **2** E **3** A **4** F **5** D

Point out that **C** and **G** were not used. In pairs, learners think of a sentence to come before **C**, and a question to come before **G**.
Suggestions: I like going to the park best. Did it look like this?

(C) ▶ Listen and colour and write.
Listening Part 5

○ Ask questions about the theatre and acting:
Have you ever been to a theatre?
Would you like to be an actor?
What kind of job is this – hard / easy / fun / boring?
Are most actors very rich / poor / clever / pretty?
Who's your favourite actor?
Tell me about your favourite actor.

- Learners look at the picture of the actors on the stage. In pairs, they find six things that begin with 'w' (wings, water, window, woman, whales, writing) and six things that begin with 'b' (boat, boy, butterfly, book, bag, board).
- Make sure that learners have yellow, blue and red colouring pencils or pens amongst other colours. Learners guess three things that they might have to colour and write them in their notebook to check later. For example: the woman's bag, the girl's dress, the flag on the boat.
- Play the audio. Learners listen, colour and write. They show their pictures to their partners.

> **Check answers:**
> 1 Colour whale with smaller tail – blue
> 2 Colour boot of girl wearing striped top – red
> 3 Write 'Julia' on the boat - either on the roof or on the side.
> 4 Colour light above actors – yellow
> 5 Write 'water' on board

Audioscript

Listen and look at the picture. There is one example.

Girl: Are all these people actors?

Man: No. Some of them are, but these people all work at the theatre.

Girl: Well, it's a funny picture. Shall I colour a few things here? Can I colour the girl's spotted wings?

Man: Yes, please. Make them green.

Girl: OK. I think she's a butterfly!

Can you see the girl's green wings? This is an example.

Now you listen and colour and write.

1 Girl: How about colouring one of the whales?

Man: Erm, all right. Colour the one with the smaller tail.

Girl: OK. Why don't I use blue for that?

Man: Yes! Good idea!

Girl: Great! I'll do that now.

2 Girl: There's a girl by the flag. What about colouring her striped T-shirt next?

Man: Sorry! We don't need to colour that, but you can colour her boot. You can only see one of her feet!

Girl: Oh yes! Shall I use red for that?

Man: Yes, please. She's brilliant at acting, that woman…

Girl: Oh!

3 Man: Let's write something on the ship next. Write its name. What shall we call it?

Girl: Let's call it 'Julia'? That's my favourite girl's name but it's a good name for a boat too, I think.

Man: Yes, it is. Great! Thank you.

Girl: There!

4 Man: And now some more colouring … Colour the light, please.

Girl: Do you mean the one that the man's holding?

Man: No, I mean the one that's above the actors. Colour that one yellow.

Girl: All right. It's not going to fall down, is it?

Man: No!

5 Girl: Shall I write something on that board next? There, under 'This afternoon'?

Man: Yes. Write the word 'water' before the word 'dance'. Can you do that?

Girl: Yes. Is that the missing word?

Man: Yes, it is. It's a kind of swimming dance.

Girl: Oh! That sounds funny! … Right! I've finished now.

Man: Excellent! Thanks!

D Look at the costumes in C and answer the questions.

- Say: *The people in this theatre are wearing some fantastic costumes!* Point to the girl who's carrying the envelope and walking up the stage steps and ask: *What's this girl wearing?* (A dancing dress and shoes and a shell in her hair) *Is she going to dance do you think?*
- Point to the pirate, the girl who's flying and the queen and then to the questions in **D** and say: *Now, write about the clothes that these three people are wearing. Remember, you can write about what the clothes are made of too!*
  Ask different learners to tell you about each person's clothes.
  Suggestions:
  The pirate is wearing a spotted scarf, a striped T-shirt, a short wool skirt and pirate boots.
  The girl who's flying is wearing a butterfly costume and her wings are spotted and green.
  The queen is wearing a long dress. She has a shell bracelet and necklace and a gold crown.
- Say: *Now, you're going to answer more questions. But the answers to the questions aren't in this picture! The answers are in your head! Point to the chair and ask: Who sits in this chair? One of the people in the picture? Why do you think that?* Different learners answer. Accept any reasonable answer. (**Suggestions:** *It's the man's chair. He's the manager. / It's the queen's chair. She's the most important actor.*)
  In pairs, learners read the three questions and think about, then write, their answers.
- Ask different pairs to read out their answers to the different questions. You could give a prize for the most creative answers!

E Shall we write a story? Read this first!

- Learners read the short story. Ask them these questions:
  1 *Which person in the theatre picture is Bill and Mary's mother?*
  2 *Bill and Mary are brother and sister. How old are they?*
  3 *Why do you think the children weren't at school that day?*
  4 *What do you think they found in the different boxes?*
  5 *Why do you think their mother was very surprised when she came home from the theatre?*

  Note: There are no right or wrong answers. The questions are to encourage learners to use their imagination.
- Give out photocopies (one for each pair of learners) of the dialogue and story on page 145. Learners write letters for Mary's answers.

> **Check answers:**
> E, D, A, C, B

- Learners write Bill and Mary's dialogue to complete the story.

  Optional extension:
  Learners work in pairs. They choose five words to delete from the story text in **E** and underline them. Pairs then work in groups of four (pairs A and B). Pair B closes their books. Pair A takes turns to read sentences from the story text, stopping at the five missing words. Pair B tries to remember the five words. When they have finished, pair A then closes their books and has to try to remember pair B's five missing words.

55 If I feel bored

Topics family and friends, health

Equipment needed

○ Flyers audio 55C.

○ Photocopies (one half for each learner / pair of learners) of the definitions on page 146 . See G.

A Draw lines between the two halves of the sentences.

○ Read out the first half of sentence 1: *When I need to talk about something.* Ask: *Which is the second part of this sentence?* (**b** I phone my best friend.) Learners draw a line between **1** and **b**.

○ Ask: *Do you talk to your best friend when you're unhappy? Do you talk to your best friend when you're happy, too? Who else helps you when you need to talk about something?*

○ Learners read sentences 2–5 and draw lines to their correct endings.

> **Check answers:**
> 2 c 3 a 4 e 5 d

Ask: *What was the last thing you drank? What did you drink for breakfast this morning? Do you agree that most medicines taste terrible? Do you know any medicines that taste good?*

B Finish these sentences about yourself.

○ Read out the first sentence: *When I'm tired, I close my eyes and try to sleep for a few minutes.*
Ask: *What do you do if you're tired but are not in a place where you can sleep?*
Suggestions: Stand up and move around. Have a drink of water / coffee / tea. Wash my face. Go outside.

○ Learners read and finish sentences 2–7.

○ Learners compare how they have completed the sentences in pairs or groups of 3–4.

○ Ask one learner in each group to tell the rest of the class why their group laugh and what they do if they are bored. For example:
We laugh when we watch funny films on TV.
If we are bored, we play computer games.

C ▶ Listen and say which picture. Then listen and say how picture 3 is different.

○ Ask:
Do you prefer to be inside or outside?
What things do you like doing in your free time?

○ Ask questions about the two pictures in **C**.
How many people are there in each picture? (2)
Are they the same people in each picture? (yes)
In picture 1, are they inside or outside? (outside)
Where are the people in picture 3? (inside / in the living room)
Note: The pictures are numbered 1 and 3 because they are the first and third pictures in the story in this unit (see below).

○ Play the audio. Learners listen and say which picture is being described. Pause the audio after each sentence and ask learners to answer.

Audioscript

Listen and say which picture.

1 The man's sitting under a blanket, on a sofa.
2 The girl's skipping in a park.
3 The man looks ill.
4 The girl's happy because she's having fun.
5 The man's tired because he's run a long way.
6 The girl's unhappy because she can't go out.

> **Check answers:**
> **1** picture 3 **2** picture 1 **3** picture 3 **4** picture 1 **5** picture 1
> **6** picture 3

> **Flyers tip**
> In Speaking Parts 1 and 3 (describing differences and story telling) adjectives like *tired, happy, unhappy, excited, bored, frightened, worried* may help to describe people in the pictures and make the stories more interesting.

○ Say: *I'm going to say sentences about picture 1. You tell me how picture 3 is different.*
Read out these sentences:
1 *In picture 1, the man looks very hot.* (He looks very **cold**.)
2 *In picture 1, the girl's skipping.* (She's sitting on the **sofa**.)
3 *In picture 1, the girl looks really happy.* (She looks **sad** and **worried**.)
4 *In picture 1, the man's running.* (He's **sitting down**.)

○ In pairs, learners talk about the differences between the pictures. One learner says sentences about picture 1 and the other learner says sentences about picture 3.

D. Read the story. Choose a word from the box. Write the correct word next to numbers 1–5.

o Say: *This is a story about Alice and her dad – the girl and the man in the pictures in C.*

Write these questions on the board. Learners read the story and look for the answers.

When do Alice and her dad go running? (early in the morning)

How far do they sometimes go? (5 kilometres)

Which day will they not go running this week? (Tuesday)

o Learners read the story again and choose words from the box to write on the lines next to 1–5.

Check answers:
1 race **2** faster **3** fell **4** blanket **5** worry

o Learners choose the best name for the story. (Be careful, Dad!) Ask: *Why are the other sentences wrong?* (It was Alice's <u>dad</u>, not Alice who probably got a cold after he fell in the water. Alice skips but the story doesn't say she's won a skipping competition.

E. Complete the sentences about getting ready.

o Point to the man and girl in picture 1 in **C** and say: *Choose a surname for Alice's father.* Learners write his surname on the line next to 1.

o Say: *We're going to complete these sentences about the things Alice and her dad did before they went to the park on Monday.* Read out these questions (and the numbers). Learners complete the other gaps in the text by answering the questions. Encourage them to add information such as colours.

2 *What was the man wearing? A … ?*

3 *What was the man wearing? Some … ?*

4 *Where were his trainers? In … ?*

5 *What did Alice comb? Her … ?*

6 *What was Alice wearing? A … ? And some … ?*

Suggested answers:

2 grey T-shirt

3 black and grey shorts

4 the cupboard / his sport bag

5 hair

6 yellow T-shirt and green and yellow shorts

F. Tell the story.

Note: In Speaking Part 3, the story can be told mostly in the present continuous but in this practice, the story is told mostly in the past simple.

o Say: *The pictures in C are the first and third pictures in the story about Alice and her dad. The pictures in F are pictures 2 and 4.*

o Read out the first paragraph of the story in **D**.

Learners work in pairs. They discuss what is happening in picture 2, the next part of the story. Ask different learners to say sentences about this picture to tell the story.

If you like, tell learners to cover the story text in **D** so they can't see it. Alternatively, let learners find the words they need to tell the story in that text.

Suggested story: *Suddenly, a big dog ran past Alice's dad* (Learners could use the man's name). *Her dad fell into the water and got very wet. Alice was very surprised.*

o Learners tell the next part of the story which they can see in picture 3 in **C**.

Suggestion: *(Man's name) and Alice went home. Alice's dad felt very cold. Alice found a blanket for him. Alice's dad sat down on the sofa.*

o Learners look at picture 4 in **E** and decide how the story ends.

Suggestion: *Alices mother came home. She made some warm soup for them all. Alice's father felt better after that. Alice told her mother the story about the dog, her father and the water in the park. They all laughed.*

o Ask: *Has something like this ever happened to you or someone you know? Or have you seen this kind of thing on TV or in a film? In pairs, tell each other your stories!*

Note: Learners could also draw pictures for their stories.

o To practise Reading & Writing Part 7, learners could write the story for the pictures.

G. Play the game! Which word?

o Divide the class into two teams, A and B.

o Give learners (or pairs of learners) in team A the sentences at the top half of page 146, and learners in team B the sentences at the bottom half.

o Learners in each team read the sentences and write an answer from the word box on each line.

o Write team A and team B's answers on the board. Learners from team A write one word that they think will be in the sentences that describe team B's answers. Learners in team B write words they think will be in the sentences that describe team A's answers.

o Form pairs of learners – one learner from group A and one learner from group B. (With an odd number of learners, put two learners from A with one from B or vice versa.)

o Learner A reads out a definition to B. Learner B has to say which word is being described. If Learner B correctly matches the answer to its definition, they receive a point. Learner B receives another point if their guessed word is in the definition. (They should show it to Learner A.) Learner B then reads out a definition. Learner A matches it with its answer and shows Learner B their guessed definition word.

o The winner is the learner/pair with the most points.

o Write Learner A's first sentence on the board: *People laugh when they see this person with his nose and feet and clothes.*
Ask: *Which words are missing from this sentence?* (round, red, funny, big. strange.) Point out that we can understand this sentence without these words, but it isn't as interesting or precise!
Learners circle words like 'round', 'funny', 'strange' in the other sentences.

56 Fun and games

Topics family and friends, sports and leisure

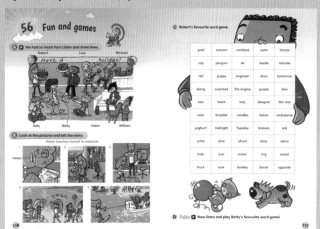

Not in YLE wordlists: *help* (n), *rules* (n), *point* (n)

Equipment needed

o   Flyers audio 56A and 56D.
o   Colouring pencils or pens.

A ▶ We had so much fun! Listen and draw lines.

Listening Part 1

o   Ask: *When was the last time you went to a party? What was the party for? How many people were there? What did you do there? Was it inside or outside? Was it fun or boring?*

o   Ask questions about the picture in **A**: *How many people are at the party?* (9) *What are they doing?* (dancing, laughing, playing the guitar, playing a game)

o   Learners look at the line between Betty and the girl in the spotted dress. Say: *Choose three other people in the picture and guess what each of their names might be! Choose from the seven names above and below the picture.*

o   Play the audio. Learners listen and draw lines from five of the names to five of the people in the picture.

> **Flyers tip**
> In Listening Part 1, the line between the name outside and the person inside the picture should be clear. One of the names will not be needed. In this task, learners see the name Lucy above the picture, but Lucy is not one of the answers.

> **Check answers:**
> Lines should be drawn between:
> 1 *Michael* and boy holding CDs and dancing.
> 2 *Helen* and girl wearing pink shorts, with cake.
> 3 *William* and boy carrying chair, wearing green sweater.
> 4 *Robert* and boy carrying burgers, with book in pocket.
> 5 *Katy* and girl with funny hat and shoes, sitting on floor.

o   Ask: *Did any of you guess the right names for these people?*
    Say: *Choose a word to write in the space on the party banner (for example: amazing, cool, fantastic, fun, great, excellent, exciting, lovely, wonderful).*

o   Point to the picture in **A** and say: *I found three things starting with the letter 'b'. Can you guess my three things?* Learners say words for things in the picture starting with the letter 'b'.
    Suggested three things: *boots, burgers, balloons*

o   When they have said all your three things, say: *There are a few things beginning with the letter 'c' in this picture. How many can you find? In pairs, make a list of 'c' words!* Learners write words in pairs. Give them two minutes, then say: *Stop! Who found two words? Three words? Four words?* Ask different pairs to say their words.
    Suggestions: (in YLE wordlists) *cake, CD, chair, children, chocolate, clothes, crayon, crown, cushion* (not in YLE wordlists) *candle, carpet*

    Optional extension

o   Say: *There were some words on the listening that started with the letter 'c' too! Can you remember any of the words? You could play the audio again.* Learners shout 'Stop!' when they hear a word that starts with 'c'.

    Words from the audio
    CDs, cooking, cake, chocolate, chair, carrying, clever, can, clothes

Audioscript

Listen and look. There is one example.
Girl: I went to a great party last Saturday! It was for the end of school.
Man: And the start of the holidays! Good idea! What did you do there? Did you play games?
Girl: Yes. Look, here's a picture. Betty likes playing word games most of all. She's the girl who's giving everyone the pieces of paper.
Man: Do you mean the girl in the spotted dress?
Girl: Yes.
Can you see the line? This is an example.
Now you listen and draw lines.

Man: Who's that boy? The one who's dancing.
Girl: The boy who's holding all the CDs?
Man: Yes.
Girl: His name's Michael.
Man: Does he enjoy playing word games?
Girl: Yes, but he likes playing his guitar more!

Girl: And there's Helen in the pink shorts. She helped with the cooking. She made that cake!
Man: Wow! What's inside it?
Girl: Chocolate. It tasted great. I ate too much of it!
Man: I love eating cake too.

Man: And what about that boy? What's his name?
Girl: Do you mean the boy on the sofa?
Man: No, the boy with the green sweater on. He's carrying a chair – can you see?
Girl: Oh yes. That's William. He's always helping people. He's very kind!

Man: Who's that? The person who's carrying that big plate of burgers.
Girl: That's Robert. He won the word game later! He's very clever.
Man: Is he?
Girl: Yes, but I think he had some help. Can you see that little red book in his pocket?
Man: Yes …
Girl: I think it's a dictionary!

Girl: My best friend is here too. We never stop laughing.
Man: Is that Lucy?
Girl: No, it's Katy. She's the one in the funny hat and shoes who's sitting on the floor. She likes wearing clothes that no one else wears.
Man: Why?
Girl: Oh … I don't know. She just likes having fun.

B Look at the pictures and tell the story. Speaking Part

○ Ask: *Have you ever tried water-skiing? Would you like to try it?*
Do you think waterskiing is a fun / dangerous / exciting / scary sport?
Do you think it's an easy or difficult sport to learn?

○ Point to the girl in the pictures in **B** and say: *We saw this girl in the picture of the end-of-school party in A. What's her name?* (Helen)

○ Say: *These pictures show a story. It's called 'Helen teaches herself to waterski.' Look at picture 1. Listen to the first part of the story*
Read Part 1 of the script.
Ask: *Where's the party going to be?* (at the beach) *What are they going to do at the party?* (swim and waterski) *Can Helen waterski?* (no)

> **Flyers tip**
> Talking about what people are feeling, thinking or saying makes stories more interesting. If candidates talk about these things when they tell the story in Speaking Part 3, they will probably do well.

○ Learners work in pairs. Say: *Look at the other four pictures now. To tell the story, answer these questions about each picture: Where is Helen now? What's she's doing? What's she thinking?* Learners talk together and answer the questions.
Read out the rest of the script.
One
Helen's reading a message. It's about a swimming and waterskiing party at the beach. Helen's worried. She's thinking 'I can't waterski!'
Two
Helen's in the library now. She's looking at lots of books. The books have got pictures of people who are waterskiing in them. She's thinking 'I can ski on snow, so perhaps I could ski on water.'
Three
Helen's at home now. She's watching a video on her dad's computer about waterskiing. She's learning to waterski on the blue mat. She's thinking 'This isn't so difficult!'
Four
Helen's arriving at the beach party now. All her friends are there. She's thinking 'It's a wonderful sunny day.'
Five
Helen's water-skiing behind the boat. She's going really fast and she's feeling really happy. She's thinking 'I'm good at this!'
Learners listen and compare their stories.

○ In pairs, learners tell the story again. You could also tell the story as a class, with each learner / pair of learners adding the next sentence in the story.

○ Write on the board: *worried, pleased, interested, excited, brave, clever*. Point to the words and say: *We can use these words in Helen's story. Can you make sentences about the pictures in B with these words?* In pairs, learners say or write sentences with the words. Give them time to do this, then ask different pairs to say a sentence.

Suggestions
Helen's worried about going water-skiing.
Helen's very interested in water-skiing. She goes to the library and looks at lots of books.
Helen feels really excited when she gets to the beach.
Helen is very brave and clever. She can water-ski really well. She's really pleased!

C Robert's favourite word game.

○ Point to the boy holding the page of words in **C**.
Say: *This boy is in the picture in A too. Can you remember his name?* (Robert) *And remember, he loves word games! He thinks they're lots of fun! You are going to play one of Robert's favourite word games.*
In pairs or small groups, learners make sentences in their notebooks using as many words from **C** as possible.
Explain: *Here are the rules.*
You get points for using the words in C in sentences. For example, if you write: I can swim, 'swim' is in 'C' so you get 1 point.
If you write: We found a silver necklace in a taxi on Tuesday, you've used four words, so you get four points.

Careful! You can only use each word once. Draw circles round the words you've used. You have five minutes!

○ Pairs or groups then change notebooks, add up the points and write a total mark. (You can collect the sentences in and give them a final mark yourself later if necessary.)

○ The winner is the pair or group with the most points.

D ▶ Now listen and play Betty's favourite word game!

○ Write on the board: *screen keyboard mouse*.
Say: *These words are all for parts of …* (a computer). Cross out the word 'screen'. Ask: *Which word have I crossed out?* (screen) Ask a learner to come to the board. Say: *Cross out the word keyboard, please*. Do the same with 'mouse'.

○ Learners look at the words in **C** again.
Say: *You're going to listen to Betty. She's in the picture in A too. Can you find Betty there?* (She's the girl in the spotted dress.)
Listen to Betty and cross out words. Play the audio, pausing and repeating as necessary.

Audioscript

> *Listen and play Betty's favourite word game.*
> Hi! I'm Betty and this is my favourite word game. I love it. Are you ready? Look at all the words on the page quickly. I'll give you half a minute to do this. OK? Right, now listen to me carefully!
> First – cross out five colours.
> Now, find five animals and cross those out too.
> Great! Now cross out five things that people wear.
> Ready? Cross out five things that people drive next.
> Cross out five time words. Can you see them?
> Cross out five words that say how you feel.
> And cross out five jobs.
> Cross out five fun things that people do.
> Last of all! Cross out five words that help say where something is.
> How many words are left?
> Have some fun with those! And with all the other words in this book too. Bye!

> **Check answers:**
> Lines should be drawn through:
> **colours** – gold, black, silver, red, purple
> **animals** – penguin, beetle, puppy, zebra, donkey
> **things we wear** – necklace, cap, bracelet, trainers, ring
> **vehicles** – tractor, fire engine, taxi, ambulance, truck
> **time** – Tuesday, midnight, autumn, tomorrow, minutes
> **feelings** – surprised, lazy, sick, afraid, sore
> **jobs** – engineer, designer, film star, artist, waiter
> **fun activities** – swim, ski, draw, hide, dance
> **location** – along, near, below, over, opposite
> Five words are left – *kiwi, noodles, yoghurt, olive, cereal* and they are all foods.

○ Each learner chooses a word from a square in **C**. They write down how many letters their word has on a piece of paper. In pairs, they show the number of letters to their partner (for example: 5). Their partner tries to guess their word with as few questions as possible: For example: *Is it 'red'?* (no) *Is it 'zebra'?* (no) *Is it 'olive'?* (yes)

○ Play more games with the learners' words, for example, say:
Guess the words from letters that are said in alphabetical order.
For example: e-i-l-o-v (olive)
Think of and write another word with the same number of letters and the same first letter. (For example: often, onion, other.)

○ Ask learners what their favourite party game is, and if possible, allow them to play it or bring in your own word games to celebrate the end of the book.

1   Hello again

In small groups, learners create a rainbow story by choosing their own words to complete the following text.

Rainbow Story

.... and his sister .... walk to school each morning. They don't go by .... because their school is near their home.

Last .... morning, they got very wet in the rain. Their .... was wet, their .... were wet and their .... were wet.

But then the rain stopped and the sun came out. 'Look!' said .... and pointed at the sky. 'That's the .... rainbow in the world! 'Wow' said .... 'It's amazing! Look at all the colours! I can see ...., ..., ... and ....! Quick! Have you got your phone? Take a picture of it!' .... took the photo and showed it to .... when they got to school.

......................'s photo was so .... the art teacher put it on the school website. After that, every time one of ....'s class mates turned on the class computer to look at the website, they saw ....'s .... rainbow on the screen!

9   In my classroom

✂

A Learner A

There's a .... in our class. His name is Charlie. I knew him before he came here because he goes to my chess club. Charlie and I both like music. We have music every Monday afternoon. It's a really interesting lesson because we .... different instruments and .... Sometimes our teacher brings us instruments to look at. I like trying to .... Charlie and I are learning to play the violin. We have to .... a lot because we want to play in .... or a music festival one day!
Or perhaps in a band!

B Learner B

There's a new student in our class. His name is Charlie. I knew him before he came here because he goes to my .... Charlie and I both like music. We have music every .... It's a really interesting lesson because we learn about different instruments and tunes. Sometimes .... brings us instruments to look at. I like trying to play them. Charlie and I are learning to play .... We have to practise a lot because we want to play in a concert or .... one day! Or perhaps in ....

5   About animals

1a A lot of people are afraid of this creature.	**1b** This is a lot of people's favourite animal.
2a People think they're friendly and clever.	**2b** People think they're dangerous but they're wrong – some of them are very beautiful and they don't hurt people.
3a They live in groups of up to 12 in warm seas in many parts of the world.	**3b** They live in trees or caves and have very strong wings.
4a They sleep during the day and fly at night to find their food.	**4b** They can swim and sleep at the same time and some of them sleep with one eye open.
5a They usually eat fish.	**5b** Some of them eat fruit and others like insects.
6a When you visit a zoo you can often see these animals in swimming pools.	**6b** They have big ears and these help them fly at night.
7a They swim very fast, jump and play with balls. Many people go to watch them playing.	**7b** A lot of people think these animals can't see but they're wrong – they can!

6   My things

Animal Quiz

Read the questions and circle or write the correct answers.

1   Why do African elephants have big ears?
   a so they can hear better
   b because they help them live in hot countries
   c to fly

2   What is the largest animal in the world?
   a the African elephant
   b the blue whale
   c the giraffe

3   How long have creatures lived on Earth?
   a for four million years
   b for four thousand years
   c for four billion years

4   Whales and dolphins are big fish.   Yes ☐   No ☐

5   Can you spell  ?

6   And 🦋 ?

7   Can some animals live at the bottom of the ocean?   Yes ☐   No ☐

8   Can horses stand up and sleep at the same time?   Yes ☐   No ☐

9   How many legs does an insect have?
   a 6
   b 8
   c 4

10   When did dinosaurs become extinct?
   a 10 million years ago
   b 20 thousand years ago
   c 65 million years ago

7   Moving and speaking

Write words to complete the sentences about the story. Use 1, 2, 3 or 4 words.

1   The dog on David's farm is called ....

2   It was .... in the morning when William asked the children to come with him and look for the sheep.

3   David's dad needed to find .... because they weren't in the west field.

4   William, the children and Pirate went up the hill in a ....

5   William told the dog to .... the sheep.

6   After Pirate jumped out of the tractor, he went ....

7   That evening, Pirate was tired but he enjoyed eating his ....

8   School subjects

(A) Write your answers to these questions, then talk to your partner.

1   What different subjects do you study?

....

2   What's your best subject?

....

3   Which subjects are the easiest?

....

4   What would you like to learn more about?

....

5   How often do you use the internet for homework?

....

6   Do you have any apps that help you with homework?

....

7   What would you like to be in the future? A designer?

....

(B) Michael is talking to his dad's friend, Mr Spring. What does Michael say?
Read the conversation and choose the best answer.
Write a letter (A–H) for each answer. You do not need to use all the letters. There is one example.

Example   **Mr Spring:**   Hello, Michael.

Michael: ......B......

1   **Mr Spring:**   I see you're in your school uniform.

Michael: ....

2   Do you like school?

Michael: ....

3   What's your best subject?

Michael: ....

4   What job do you want to do in the future?

Michael: ....

5   Which university do you want to go to?

Michael: ....

A	Yes, we have to wear this jacket and trousers.
B	Hello, Mr Spring.
C	I'm not sure. I'd like to study in another city, I think.
D	I'd like to design cars or motorbikes.
E	I love it, actually!
F	I had Science this morning.
G	I'm good at Maths. It's very interesting.
H	Yes, me too.

13   What horrible weather!

My story is called

....

and this story is by ....

12   A journey into space

Mercury	
What colour does it look?	grey
What/temperature?	427º max, −173º min
Rings or no rings?	No
How long / take / go round / sun?	88 days
How many moons?	0

Mars	
What colour does it look?	red
What/temperature?	−87 to −5º
Rings or no rings?	No
How long / take / go round / sun?	687 days
How many moons?	2

Venus	
What colour does it look?	yellow and white
What/temperature?	462º
Rings or no rings?	No
How long / take / go round / sun?	225 days
How many moons?	0

Jupiter	
What colour does it look?	Light brown, orange and yellow stripes
What/temperature?	−148º
Rings or no rings?	Yes
How long / take / go round / sun?	4,331 days
How many moons?	63 named moons

Saturn	
What colour does it look?	yellow and gold
What/temperature?	−178º
Rings or no rings?	Yes
How long / take / go round / sun?	10,759 days
How many moons?	52 named moons

Neptune	
What colour does it look?	bright blue (like Uranus)
What/temperature?	−214º
Rings or no rings?	Yes
How long / take / go round / sun?	60,190 days
How many moons?	13 known moons

12   A journey into space

Mercury	
What colour does it look?	
What/temperature?	
Rings or no rings?	
How long / take / go round / sun?	
How many moons?	

Mars	
What colour does it look?	
What/temperature?	
Rings or no rings?	
How long / take / go round / sun?	
How many moons?	

Venus	
What colour does it look?	
What/temperature?	
Rings or no rings?	
How long / take / go round / sun?	
How many moons?	

Jupiter	
What colour does it look?	
What/temperature?	
Rings or no rings?	
How long / take / go round / sun?	
How many moons?	

Saturn	
What colour does it look?	
What/temperature?	
Rings or no rings?	
How long / take / go round / sun?	
How many moons?	

Neptune	
What colour does it look?	
What/temperature?	
Rings or no rings?	
How long / take / go round / sun?	
How many moons?	

20 Calling and sending

answer	your phone →	**begin**	to your friends	**connect**
an address	**find**	a conversation	**chat**	to wifi
get	a conversation	**end**	your cousin	**email**
a text	**go**	online	**hear**	your phone
make	a mistake	**make**	a phone number	**join**
a video	**pick up**	emails	**lose**	a group
open	a program	**read**	your messages	**search**
your friends	**speak to**	photos	**send**	the internet
take	the internet	**turn on**	a prize	**write**
pictures	**turn off**	your camera	**win**	a text

22 Important numbers

All the children are in the same class at school. If today is Friday, 17th February, can you write which date each of them has their birthday?

1   David's birthday was only yesterday.

2   Paul's birthday was three weeks ago.

3   Harry can't remember what presents he got for his last birthday because it was 11 months ago!

4   Jim's birthday was two days after Paul's.

5   Anna's birthday was last Sunday.

6   Two children in the class always have a birthday party together because their birthdays are on the same day. For their last birthday, they went to the cinema with some friends. That was six months ago.

7   Katy hasn't had her birthday party yet – it's tomorrow!

Anna	....
Kim	....
David	....
Katy	....
Paul	....
Emma	....
Harry	....
Jim	....

23 World, weather, work

My funny day at work

Arrive →	at work	**borrow**	a word	**dress up**
your hair	**brush**	a laptop	**cross out**	in a costume
build	a model	**clean**	your teeth	**email**
in the lift	**go up**	a competition	**enter**	a website
hurt	your knee	**invent**	a machine	**laugh at**
some money	**spend**	for information	**meet**	a cartoon
thank	someone	**search**	a film star	**open**
the news	**tidy**	a computer file	**save**	a computer program
watch	your desk	**turn off**	down the stairs	**post**
a bus	**wait for**	the lights	**run**	a birthday card

24   Leaving and arriving

A funny trip!

travelled with	
to	
by	
on	!

30   Summer sports and winter sports

This story is called ....!

....

31   Here and there

It started raining	but I had an umbrella so I didn't get wet.
and I didn't have an umbrella so I got wet.	I was hungry and thirsty
and I found a great café with delicious food.	but I didn't have any money to buy any food.
I wrote a letter	but I didn't have a stamp.
and I put it inside an envelope.	I went to a college in London
and I learnt a lot of English.	but I didn't have time to see the city.
I'm a very good chess player	and I always win.
but my brother plays better than me.	There's a new swimming club at our school
and I'd like to join.	but I can't be a member until next month.

37   Exciting days!

Emma has an exciting job. She's a firefighter	at the fire station, which
is a big red and grey square building just outside the city. Every day she gets	up at 6 o'clock and rides her motorbike
to the fire station. When she arrives	there, she collects her blue and yellow uniform. Next,
she tests everything on the red and grey fire engine. When someone telephones	the fire station because there is a fire, Emma and the other firefighters jump into the fire engine. They drive very
quickly through the streets to the fire. Sometimes they help with	other problems, for example when someone forgets or loses
their keys or when	a cat is on a house roof and can't come down!

1   *What was the name of:*
   a *the police officer?*
   b *the firefighter?*
   c *the boy who visited the fire station?*
   d *his teacher?*

2   *What colour:*
   a *is the firefighter's uniform?*
   b *are the police officer's trousers?*
   c *is the fire station?*
   d *is the fire engine?*

3   *Find four different kinds of buildings that are in the texts about the police officer, the firefighter or the visit to the fire station.*

4   *How:*
   a *does David travel round the city?*
   b *does Emma get to work?*
   c *do the firefighters travel when they're working?*
   d *did Jim get to the fire station?*

44 What has just happened?

You've just won a competition.	I'm so happy! Isn't it great news!
You've just missed the last bus.	Oh no! Now I'll have to walk home.
It's just started raining.	Oh no! I forgot my umbrella again.
Your friend has just washed all the dirty plates.	Thank you so much. You're so kind.
You've just eaten two strawberry pies and a plate of pancakes with chocolate sauce.	Nothing else for me. I can't eat anything else.
You've just stood on someone's foot.	I'm so sorry. Did I hurt you?
Someone has just turned off all the lights.	Help! I can't see anything.
The shops have just closed.	Oh no! I forgot to buy some cereal and yoghurt.

46   We're all at home today

Is that Ann over their/there?

I've got to find some more flour/flower.

What are you going to buy/by in town, Ben?

I can't spell 'alphabet', Aren't/Aunt Jill. Help!

Bill road/rode all the way up the hill on his bike.

There's a sports car outside, Dad. Is it ours/hours?

Did you here/hear the news about our favourite band?

Did he? Right/Write to the top?

No, but I read/red about it online.

No, Uncle Tom's, but we can go for/four a ride in it. Come on!

I don't no/know yet. Perhaps some gloves.

Why? Do you want to make two/too cakes?

No, she's standing by/bye the bus stop. Look!

Don't worry. I'll write it on your bored/board.

50 On TV

Name?	Tony Brave	Name?	Vicky Page
Job?	horse rider	Job?	train driver
Starts work at?	7.30 pm	Starts work at?	5 am
Works for?	Rainbow Circus	Works for?	Future Trains
What/doing now?	cleaning the horses	What/doing now?	riding her motorbike
Name?	Alex Sugar	Name?	Kim Cook
Job?	animal doctor	Job?	golf player
Starts work at?	9.45 am	Starts work at?	8.15 am
Works for?	the World Zoo	Works for?	First Golf Shops
What/doing now?	swimming with the dolphins	What/doing now?	phoning her bank

54   Let's have some fun!

What does Mary say to Bill? Read the conversation and choose the best answer.
Write a letter (A–E) for each answer.

Bill:	I'm so bored and there's only you to play with. Shall we visit Grandma?	
1 **Mary:**	....	
Bill:	I know! Why don't we listen to some music? This band is great!	
2 **Mary:**	....	
Bill:	Well, we could watch a movie then!	
3 **Mary:**	....	
Bill:	I've got a good idea!	
4 **Mary:**	....	
Bill:	Let's go up into the roof and look in those big boxes.	
5 **Mary:**	....	
Bill:	I'll show you!	

A	But we saw two films yesterday!
B	How can we get up there?
C	What's that?
D	But we've heard all their CDs hundreds of times.
E	No. Look! It's raining.

Look what we've found!

Bill and Mary's mother had to be at the theatre on Friday. She does an important job there. Bill and Mary didn't want to go with her but they didn't want to be alone and bored at home.

Bill said,...

Mary answered,...

Then Bill said,...

Mary looked at their CDs and said,...

Bill got up, picked up a DVD and said,..

Mary answered,...

Bill thought for a minute and then said,..

Mary looked up at Bill and asked,...

Bill smiled and said,..

Mary jumped up and said,...

They couldn't believe it when they found their old .... and their old .... too!

When their mother came home from work, she looked very surprised!

55   If I feel bored

Learner A   **Write the words on the lines.**

| the address   crocodiles   a clown   treasure   scarves   a lift |

1   People laugh when they see this person with his round, red nose, funny big feet and strange clothes.   ....

2   If you live in a really tall building with a lot of floors, it is good to have one of these.   ....

3   It's important to write this on the envelope before you post a letter.   ....

4   If pirates or other people are lucky, they might find this at the bottom of the sea, or under the ground.   ....

5   People wear these round their necks when it's cold and they want to feel warm.   ....

6   In some places in the world, you have to be careful if you go for a swim because these dangerous animals might be in the water.   ....

✂ -

55   If I feel bored

Learner B   **Write the words on the lines.**

| shelves   a journalist   soap   a tent   an umbrella   sugar |

1   If you go camping without one of these, you may be cold.   ....

2   If you have one of these when you are out walking and it rains, you won't get wet.   ....

3   People often have these in their living rooms and bedrooms to put special things like books or photos on.   ....

4   People often use a spoon to put this in their cup of coffee or tea to make it sweeter.   ....

5   This person writes stories for a newspaper when unusual things happen.   ....

6   This smells nice when you mix it with water to wash your hands.   ....

Listening

Part 1
5 questions

▶ **Listen and draw lines. There is one example.**

Peter   Frank   Sarah   David

Helen   Betty   Robert

Listening

Part 2

▶ **Listen and write. There is one example.**

End of term party

Example	Day:	Friday
1	Time it starts:	....
2	Place:	.... Café
3	Where:	opposite the ....
4	Bring:	....
5	Name of film for Alex:	....

Listening

Part 3
5 questions

▶ **What did each person buy at the supermarket? Listen and write a letter in each box. There is one example.**

Anna Lime ☐A☐

Mrs Lime ☐

Mr Lime ☐

Grandfather Lime ☐

May Lime ☐

Michael Lime ☐

A

B

C

D

E

F

G

H

Practice test

Listening

Part 4
5 questions

▶ **Listen and tick (✔) the box. There is one example.**

Where did Oliver go on holiday this time?

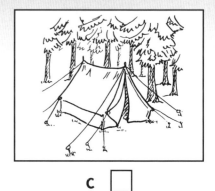

A ☐　　　　B ✔　　　　C ☐

1　What did Oliver eat in the car?

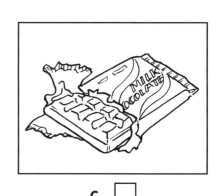

A ☐　　　　B ☐　　　　C ☐

2　What did Oliver buy on holiday?

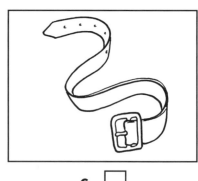

A ☐　　　　B ☐　　　　C ☐

Listening

Part 4

3 What did Oliver see at the cinema?

A ☐

B ☐

C ☐

4 What did Oliver like best?

A ☐

B ☐

C ☐

5 What will Oliver do on his next holiday?

A ☐

B ☐

C ☐

Listening

Part 5

5 questions

▶ Listen and colour and write. There is one example.

Audioscript

Hello. This is the Flyers Practice test Listening.

Part 1

Listen and look. There is one example.

Woman: This looks like a great party, Jane.
Girl: Yes. Everyone has dressed up in different clothes.
Woman: I'm looking for a boy called Peter. Which one's he?
Girl: He's dancing over there.
Woman: Oh yes! What a funny nose and what big shoes he's wearing!

Can you see the line? This is an example. Now you listen and draw lines.

Woman: Who's the boy with the drink in his hand?
Girl: By the bat poster? That's David.
Woman: He looks quite scary in those strange clothes!
Girl: Yes, he does but don't worry! He's really friendly!

Girl: And look! There's Sarah! She's my best friend.
Woman: Which one's she?
Girl She's the girl with the ball.
Woman: Oh! You mean the one in the trainers?
Girl: Yes. We're always laughing together.

Girl Can you see Helen? She's over there. Look!
Woman: The girl in the nurse's costume?
Girl: No, the girl who's jumping up and down.
Woman: Oh! I see the one you mean. Those bat wings are amazing aren't they?
Girl Yes, they are!

Woman: And who's that boy? The one who's shouting?
Girl: That's Robert! His clothes look quite dirty!
Woman: Is he trying to look like a car mechanic?
Girl Yes, I think so.

Girl: One of the girls brought lots of music with her.
Woman: The girl in the police officer's uniform?
Girl No, I mean Betty. She hasn't taken off her coat yet. Can you see her?
Woman: Yes. What do you think she's carrying in that bag?
Girl: All the CDs I think!
Woman: Of course! Well, I can see that everyone's having lots of fun!
Girl: Yes, they are.

Now listen to Part 1 again. That is the end of Part 1.

Part 2

Listen and look. There is one example.

Boy: Hi, Mrs Parker. Is Jack there, please?
Woman: No, Alex, he's not. He's at the adventure park, sorry!
Boy: Well, I'm phoning to invite him to our end of term party. I'll be ten that day, too!
Woman: Fantastic! Tell me all about it and I'll give him the message. When is it?
Boy: Next Friday.
Woman: OK. Just a minute. I'll write that down.

Can you see the answer? Now you listen and write.

Woman: What time should Jack arrive?
Boy: The party will begin at half past five and finish at half past eight.
Woman: Right. And is the party at your school?

Boy: No. We're going to have the party at the Pizza Café. Our teacher says it's really big inside and the food's delicious!
Woman: That sounds good! I've never been there. What does the building look like?
Boy: It's got a red roof and a green door.
Woman: And where is it?
Boy: It's opposite the café in Green Street.
Woman: Oh, I know. OK. And should Jack bring some money with him?
Boy: He doesn't need to do that but please ask him to bring his camera. We want to put some photos on our class website!
Woman: Good idea! And Alex what would you like for your birthday present?
Boy: Oh, I'd love a film called Escapers! It's a spaceship adventure.
Woman: Wow! Can you spell that?
Boy: Sure! E-S-C-A-P-E-R-S.
Woman: All right! I'll make sure we get that for you!
Boy: Thanks a lot!

Now listen to Part 2 again. That is the end of Part 2.

Part 3

Listen and look.

There is one example.

What did each person in Mr Lime's family buy at the new supermarket? Listen and write letters.

Woman: Excuse me. I work here at the supermarket. Would you mind telling me what you've bought here today?
Man: No, that's fine.
Woman: Thanks. Can you tell me your name?
Man: It's Mr Lime. I'll tell you about Anna, first. She's my daughter.
Woman: OK.
Man: She bought some great gloves. She'll use those a lot this winter.

Can you see the letter A? Now you listen and write a letter in each box.

Man: May, my older daughter, came with us today as well.
Woman: Did she buy something, too?
Man: Yes. She chose a new necklace.
Woman: That's nice.
Man: She can't wear it at school, but she'll wear it when she goes out with her friends.

Woman: What else did your family buy here today?
Man: Michael, my son, has a bicycle but it isn't big enough for him now. He never stops eating biscuits!
Woman: Me too!
Man: Well, we found him a new one and he thinks it's really cool!

Woman: And who's that older man?
Man: We call him Grandfather Lime. He didn't want to buy anything today ...
Woman: Oh! He just likes to visit the store then?
Man: That's right. But then someone gave him your newest coffee to try.
Woman: It's good, isn't it?
Man: Yes. He bought some to take home.

Man:	And my wife, Mrs Lime, came here to buy some vegetables, but she thought they were quite expensive.
Woman:	I'm sorry she thought that.
Man:	It's OK. But she did find some cookies that she tried before and really liked …
Woman:	Was that all she bought, then?
Man:	Yes.
Woman:	And what about you, Mr Lime? Did you buy anything?
Man:	Well, I don't need an umbrella but I was looking at those when I saw the torches. I decided to get one of those instead.
Woman:	I always keep one in my car.
Man:	I'll do the same. I'm pleased I got it.
Woman:	Good. Well, thank you and I hope your family enjoys all their new things.

Now listen to Part 3 again. That is the end of Part 3.

Part 4

Listen and look. There is one example.

Where did Oliver go on holiday this time?

Woman:	Hello, Oliver. Have you just come back from camping in the forest?
Boy:	No, Mrs Kite. We didn't do that this year. We stayed by a lake where there were more things to do.
Woman:	Was there an island in the middle of it?
Boy:	No, there wasn't, but it was fun there.

Can you see the tick? Now you listen and tick the box.

1 *What did Oliver eat in the car?*

Boy:	The journey in the car there was really long. We drove past a great burger place but Dad didn't stop!
Woman:	You were hungry, then?
Boy:	Yes! But I found some chocolate in my backpack and I ate some of that. And when we arrived, Mum made us all a salad.
Woman:	That sounds nice.

2 *What did Oliver buy on holiday?*

Woman:	Is that belt new? Did you buy it when you were away?
Boy:	No. Mum got it for me from the new shopping centre.
Woman:	Did you bring anything back with you, then?
Boy:	I found a little chess game that I can carry in my pocket.
Woman:	Did you get that then?
Boy:	Yes. I wanted some little silver spoons too. I collect those but they were too expensive.

3 *What did Oliver see at the movie theatre?*

Boy:	We went to the movie theatre one day but there were no more tickets for 'Treasure Island' so we couldn't see that.
Woman:	Oh dear!
Boy:	We saw a movie about a new rock music band, instead. There was another one about a boy whose father was a police officer, but that was on too late.
Woman:	Oh!

4 *What did Oliver like best?*

Woman:	So, Oliver, what was the best thing about your holiday?
Boy:	We visited a hotel one day and had dinner there which was nice but I enjoyed making some new friends most.
Woman:	Did you all go sailing together?
Boy:	We couldn't. It wasn't windy enough!

5 *What will Oliver do on his next holiday?*

Boy:	I'm going to go away again tomorrow! I'm going to learn to ski with my school.
Woman:	Brilliant! I'd like to try mountain climbing one day.
Boy:	Really? That's so frightening! Dad wants me to have some golf lessons!
Woman:	Does he?
Boy:	Yes, but I'm not interested in that sport at the moment.

Now listen to Part 4 again. That is the end of Part 4.

Part 5

Listen and colour and write. There is one example.

Man:	I'd like you to colour some of this picture now.
Girl:	All right. Is this a music festival?
Man:	Yes. But the people are still getting it ready.
Girl:	OK. Shall I colour the steps first?
Man:	Yes. Make them grey, please.

Can you see the grey steps? This is an example. Now you listen and colour and write.

1

Girl:	What shall I colour next?
Man:	Can you see the lights above the stage?
Girl:	Sure! There are two of them.
Man:	That's right. Colour the one that's under the moon shape.
Girl:	OK. Yellow? I've got that colour here.
Man:	Fine.

2

Man:	Can you write something for me now, please?
Girl:	Yes! I enjoy writing. It's fun.
Man:	Excellent! Write BURGERS on the board. The one between the two flags.
Girl:	OK! That's easy. I love eating those! Do they sell them there?
Man:	Yes. They do.

3

Girl:	Can I colour something else now?
Man:	Of course! Colour the trainers?
Girl:	The ones that the boy is wearing?
Man:	Yes. Let's make those red. No, wait. Let's use another colour.
Girl:	How about blue?
Man:	That's a better idea! Thank you.

4

Man:	Are you ready to write something else again now?
Girl:	Yes. What and where?
Man:	Let's finish the name of the band. The girl's writing it on the poster that she's making. She's already written the word 'The'.
Girl:	Yes, I can see that. How about calling the band The Rocks, then? That's a good name!
Man:	I prefer The Players. Can you write that word instead?
Girl:	All right. If you want. No problem.

5

Man:	Now, I'd like you to colour the largest drum.
Girl:	OK. Can I colour it purple?
Man:	Yes. That's my favourite colour.
Girl:	I think it's an amazing colour too! There!
Man:	Fantastic. Thanks a lot! This festival looks more fun now.
Girl:	Yes, it does.
Man:	Well done!

Now listen to Part 5 again.

That is the end of the Listening Part of the practice test.

Practice test

Reading and Writing

Part 1

10 questions

Look and read. Choose the correct words and write them on the lines.
There is one example.

an entrance   an astronaut   a university

funfair

butter

	This is a person who looks after your teeth. Make sure you visit them every six months.	*a dentist*
1	This is made of milk. It's usually yellow and you need a knife to put it on your bread.	....
2	These are rooms where people write on computers, talk on telephones and have business meetings.	....
3	Use this to eat soup or to add sugar to a hot drink.	....
4	You must walk through this to get inside a building like a theatre or museum.	....
5	This person carries food on plates to people who have come to eat in a restaurant.	....
6	Some people like eating this in sandwiches. It's made by bees and it's very sweet.	....
7	People work in these places and might use machines to make things like cars.	....
8	Only a few people can do this job and they might travel to the moon or to another planet.	....
9	Older students study here after they finish school and before they get their first job.	....
10	People have these when they haven't got enough time to sit and eat a large meal.	....

a waiter

offices

pop star

snacks

a spoon

honey

salt

a firefighter   a dentist   factories

Reading and Writing

Part 2
5 questions

Bill is talking to his doctor. What does Bill say?

Read the conversation and choose the best answer. Write a letter (A–H) for each answer. You do not need to use all the letters. There is one example.

Example

Doctor: Good morning. I'm sorry you had to wait, Bill.

Bill: ....D.......

1 **Doctor:** So, how can I help? What's the matter with you today?

Bill: ....

2 **Doctor:** Right! How long have you had this problem?

Bill: ....

3 **Doctor:** Did you do any sport on the day that the problem started?

Bill: ....

4 **Doctor:** Show me where it hurts the most.

Bill: ....

5 **Doctor:** Well, keep warm and don't do any more sport until next week!

Bill: ....

Doctor: And if it's not OK by next Wednesday, come back and see me again.

A I won't play in the football match, tomorrow then!

B It's my back. It's really sore.

C Right in the middle, but it's not as bad as it was.

D That's all right, Doctor White. I was reading one of your magazines.   **Example**

E Not with any of my classmates, actually.

F Since our morning break at school on Wednesday.

G But I'm getting much better at playing chess.

H No, but I played basketball with my friends the evening before.

 Practice test

Reading and Writing

Part 3

6 questions

Read the story. Choose a word from the box. Write the correct word next to numbers 1–5. There is one example.

Example
fetch   arrived   shower   surprise   terrible   photographer
spend   borrowed   cereal   excited

Yesterday, my mother came into my bedroom and said, 'Wake up Robert. We've got to go to the post office.' 'Why?' I asked. 'To post a letter?'

'No,' Mum answered. 'We need to go and ....*fetch*............... something. Uncle Richard has sent you a present.'

My uncle is a **(1)**...................................... and travels all around the world. He has lots of adventures! I love seeing his pictures and hearing about the people and places he's visited, so I felt really **(2)**.......................................

I got dressed and ran into the kitchen to have my bowl of **(3)**....................................... Mum was pleased that I got ready so quickly. We left the house , cycled into town, and soon **(4)**...................................... at the post office where there was a box with my name on it. I opened it and inside was an amazing new camera!

What a fantastic **(5)**.......................................!' I said. 'I can take much better pictures with this than I can with my phone. Brilliant!'

(6) What's the best name for this story? Tick one box.

My uncle comes to visit us   ☐

My uncle's pictures   ☐

A present from my uncle   ☐

Reading and Writing

Part 4

10 questions

Read the text. Choose the right words and write them on the lines.

Flags

		has	have	having
Example	People ......*have*...... used flags for over 4,000 years.			

The first flags were not like the flags we know today because
1 they were made .... metal or wood.

2 .... country has a different flag and flies it on important days.

3 Some flags are only one colour ...., on most flags, you see two, three or more colours. Some have stars, crosses or stripes on them, too.

You often see flags on famous buildings or at popular sports
4 meetings. There's a flag above the building..................... the Queen lives in London.

5 When she's .... home, the flag is up.

6 When she's .... there, someone takes it down.

In car races, sometimes someone waves a flag to show the
7 racing car drivers they need to drive .... slowly.

8 And the driver .... finishes the race first will see the winner's black and white flag.

9 People often take flags with .... to football matches.

10 Each time a player .... a goal, some people will shout 'Hurray' and wave their flags above their heads!

1	to	for	of
2	Both	Several	Each
3	but	because	so
4	where	which	whose
5	at	in	by
6	no	no-one	not
7	more	many	much
8	which	whose	who
9	you	us	them
10	scoring	scores	score

Reading and Writing

Part 5

7 questions

Look at the picture and read the story. Write some words to complete the sentences about the story. You can use 1, 2, 3 or 4 words.

An exciting trip

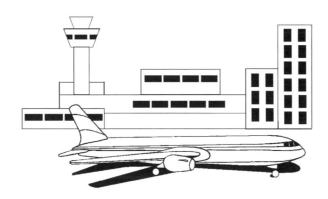

Last September, George and his family went by taxi to the airport. They had tickets to fly to another city to visit George's aunt at her new flat. While they waited for their plane, George's parents had a cup of coffee, and his sister, Holly, went to buy a magazine about pop stars to read on the journey. George just wanted to sit and watch all the planes fly up and disappear into the clouds.

Soon, their plane was ready and after everyone found their seats, the man who looked after the passengers came to speak to George and Holly. 'My name's Tom,' he said. 'Here are some fun puzzles and quizzes for you to do.' George was much more interested in the video about travelling by air!

After a few minutes, Tom came back and said, 'Your father told me you want to be a pilot one day. Would you like to meet our two pilots before we leave?' 'Cool! Yes, please!' George answered, and followed Tom to the front of the plane.

The pilots let George see the different screens and maps and answered all his questions. Then George had to go back to his seat. He loved his adventure so much and now, he can't wait to learn everything he can about being a pilot.

Reading and Writing

Part 5

7 questions

Examples

George's family went to the airport last .... *September* ....

They travelled .... *to the airport* .... in a taxi.

Questions

1 George's family were going to fly to the city where .... lived.

2 Holly wanted to read about .... on the journey so she bought a magazine.

3 George just sat and watched .... that were going up into the sky.

4 After they found their seats, a man called Tom gave George and Holly some .... to look at.

5 Tom took George to speak to ....

6 George had to go back to his seat after asking lots of questions and looking at all the ....

7 George enjoyed .... a lot and wants to learn as much as he can about being a pilot.

Reading and Writing

Part 6

5 questions

Read the diary and write the missing words. Write one word on each line.

Example	I visited ....my........... grandpa today. He's great!
1	Grandpa can't hear very well. Every time I see him I have .... speak more loudly!
2	This afternoon, he told me about when he worked on a farm and learned to .... a tractor around the fields. The farm had more
3	.... 50 fields!
4	He has .... me lots of other stories about looking after all the different kinds of animals and the work on the farm in spring, summer, autumn and winter. His stories are always amazing and I love spending
5	time .... him.

Reading and Writing

Part 7

Look at the three pictures. Write about this story. Write 20 or more words.

....

....

....

....

Answer key

Listening

Part 1
Lines should be drawn between:

David and boy dressed as pirate holding drink

Sarah and girl kicking ball

Helen and girl dressed as bat

Robert and boy with dirty face

Betty and girl in doorway wearing coat

Part 2
1 5.30 **2** (The) Pizza (Café) **3** café in Green Street
4 camera **5** Escapers

Part 3
Mr Lime – H   Mrs Lime – D   Grandfather Lime – B
May Lime C   Michael Lime – F

Part 4
1 C **2** B **3** B **4** A **5** C

Part 5
1 Colour the light under the moon - yellow
2 Write 'Burgers' on the sign between the flags
3 Colour the boy's trainers - blue
4 Write 'Players' on the girl's poster
5 Colour the largest drum - purple

Reading and Writing

Part 1 (10 marks)
1	butter	**6**	honey
2	offices	**7**	factories
3	a spoon	**8**	an astronaut
4	an entrance	**9**	a university
5	a waiter	**10**	snacks

Part 2 (5 marks)
1 B **2** F **3** H **4** C **5** A

Part 3 (6 marks)
1	photographer	**4**	arrived
2	excited	**5**	surprise
3	cereal		

The best name for the story is 'A present from my uncle'.

Part 4 (10 marks)
1	of	**6**	not
2	Each	**7**	more
3	but	**8**	who
4	where	**9**	them
5	at	**10**	scores

Part 5 (7 marks)
1	George's/his aunt	**5**	two pilots
2	pop stars	**6**	(different) screens and maps
3	(all) the planes	**7**	his adventure
4	(fun) puzzles and quizzes		

Part 6 (5 marks)
1	to	**4**	told/wrote/read
2	drive	**5**	with/around
3	than		

Part 7
Sample answers:

Peter and Mary want to cross the river but they can't. An elephant comes to help them. They ride on the elephant's back across the river. A bird carries their bags.

31 words

Peter and Mary want to cross the river but the bridge has broken. They are carrying two big bags and they are worried. But an elephant helps them. They ride across the river on its back. An eagle helps the children too. It carries their big bags across the water.

50 words

Speaking

Examiner's script

To do:	To say:	Response: (Variations in form possible)	Back-up:
Usher brings child in.			
	Hello, *, my name's Janet/Ms Brown. What's your name?	Hello.	
	What's your surname?	Lopez.	**What's your family name?**
	How old are you?	11	**Are you 10?**
	*Use the child's name throughout the test.		
1 Find the difference Show candidate both pictures. Give candidate his/her picture then describe things without pointing.	**Now, here are two pictures. My picture is nearly the same as yours, but some things are different.** **For example, there are three eggs in my picture, but in your picture, there are two. OK?** **I'm going to say something about my picture. You tell me how your picture is different.**		1 Point at relevant difference(s). 2 Repeat statement 3 Ask back-up question.
	In my picture, it's raining.	In my picture, it's foggy.	**Is it raining?**
	In my picture, the cage is in front of the window.	In my picture, the cage is next to a plant.	**Is there a cage in front of the window?**
	In my picture, the boy's bowl is empty.	In my picture, the boy's bowl is full.	**Is the bowl full?**
	In my picture, the girl's opening the cupboard door.	In my picture, the girl's opening the fridge door.	**Is the girl opening the cupboard door?**
	In my picture, the table is square.	In my picture, the table is round.	**Is the table square?**
	In my picture, there are five messages on the board.	In my picture, there are four messages on the board.	**How many messages are there on the board?**

Speaking
Examiner's script

To do:	To say:	Response: (Variations in form possible)	Back-up:
2 Information exchange Briefly show candidate both cards. Then give candidate his/her card.	**Sam and Mary live in the same street. I don't know anything about Sam's house, but you do. So I'm going to ask you some questions.**		
Point to the houses on candidate's card.	**How many floors are there in Sam's house?**	**(it's got) 1 (floor)**	Point at the information if necessary.
Ask the questions.	**Where does Sam watch TV?**	**(in the) kitchen**	
	How old is Sam's house?	**(it's) 20 years old**	
	What colour is the hall?	**(it's) purple**	
	Is Sam's house noisy or quiet?	**(it's) quiet**	
Point to the questions about Mary's house on candidate's card.	**Now, you don't know anything about Mary's house, so you ask me some questions.**		
Respond using information on examiner's card.	**It's noisy.**	**Is Mary's house noisy or quiet?**	Point at information cues if necessary.
	It's orange.	**What colour is the hall?**	
	It's got three floors.	**How many floors are there?**	
	It's five years old.	**How old is Mary's house?**	
	In the dining room.	**Where does Mary watch TV?**	

Speaking

Examiner's script

To do:	To say:	Response: (Variations in form possible)	Back-up:
3 Tell the story	These pictures tell a story. It's called 'A surprise for Bill'. Just look at the pictures first. Bill's in the living room. He's looking outside at his friends. They're making a snowman. Bill's feeling unhappy because he wants to go outside. Now you tell the story.	 Bill's talking to his mother. Bill can't go outside. Bill's hurt his arm. Bill's watching TV. Bill's opening the door. His friends are coming to see him. Bill's friends have made a snowman. The snowman has hurt his arm, too. Bill's laughing now.	1 Point at the pictures. 2 Ask questions about the pictures. Who is Bill talking to? Can Bill go outside? What has Bill hurt? What's Bill doing? What's Bill doing? Who's coming to see him? What have Bill's friends made? Has the snowman hurt his arm too? Is Bill laughing?
4 Personal questions Put the pictures away and turn to the candidate.	Now let's talk about your school. How do you go to school? What's your favourite lesson? What's your English teacher's name? What sports do you play at school? Tell me about what you do after school.	 (I go) by car Maths Mr Brown Football and basketball. I watch TV. I do my homework. I have dinner with my parents.	 Do you go to school by car? Do you like Maths? Is your English teacher's name Mr Brown? Do you play football? Basketball? Do you watch TV? Do you do your homework? Do you have dinner with your parents?
	OK, thank you, *. Goodbye.	Goodbye.	

Speaking

Find the difference

Candidate's copy

Examiner's copy

Practice test

Speaking
Information exchange

Candidate's copy

Sam's house

Noisy/quiet	quiet
Colour/hall	purple
Number of floors	1
How old	20 years
Where/watch TV	kitchen

Mary's house

Noisy/quiet	?
Colour/hall	?
Number of floors	?
How old	?
Where/watch TV	?

Examiner's copy

Sam's house

Noisy/quiet	?
Colour/hall	?
Number of floors	?
How old	?
Where/watch TV	?

Mary's house

Noisy/quiet	noisy
Colour/hall	orange
Number of floors	3
How old	5 years
Where/watch TV	dining room

Practice test

Speaking

Tell the story

A surprise for Bill

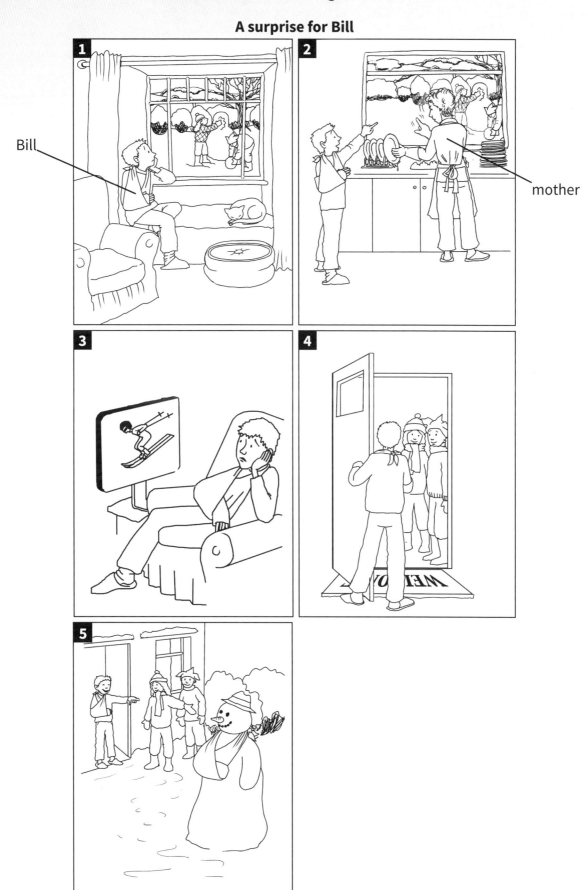

The authors and publishers would like to thank the ELT professionals who commented on the material at different stages of its development.

The authors are grateful to: Niki Donnelly of Cambridge University Press.

Anne Robinson would like to give special thanks to Adam Evans and her parents Margaret and Jim and to many, many teachers and students who have inspired her along the way. Special thanks to Cristina and Victoria for their help, patience and enthusiasm. And in memory of her brother Dave.

Karen Saxby would like to give special thanks to everyone she has worked with at Cambridge Assessment since the birth of YLE! She would particularly like to mention Frances, Felicity and Ann Kelly. She would also like to acknowledge the enthusiasm of all the teachers she has met through her work in this field. And lastly, Karen would like to say a big thank you to her sons, Tom and William, for bringing constant FUN and creative thinking to her life and work.

Freelance editorial services by Katrina Gormley

Design and typeset by Wild Apple Design.

Cover design by Chris Saunders (Astound).

The authors and publishers acknowledge the following sources of copyright material and are grateful for the permissions granted. While every effort has been made, it has not always been possible to identify the sources of all the material used, or to trace all copyright holders. If any omissions are brought to our notice, we will be happy to include the appropriate acknowledgements on reprinting and in the next update to the digital edition, as applicable.

The authors and publishers are grateful to the following illustrators:

T = Top, B = Below, L = Left, R = Right, C = Centre, B/G = Background

The authors and publishers are grateful to the following illustrators:

R and C Burrows @Beehive p172; Bridget Dowty (Graham-Cameron Illustration) pp. 132, 145, 159, 160, 161, 167, 168; Andy Elkerton (Sylvie Poggio Artists Agency) pp. 129, 131; Pip Sampson pp. 166, 178; Melanie Sharp (Sylvie Poggio Artists Agency) pp. 130, 133, 139, 157, 158, 171, 172; Lisa Smith pp. 137, 162; Jo Taylor p. 169; Sarah Wimperis (Graham-Cameron Illustration) pp. 177, 179